THE GAY EMPEROR IS NAKED:

A Critique of Homosexuality

Reverend James R. Hill, MA, M.Div.

The Gay Emperor Is Naked:

A Critique of Homosexuality

Reverend James R. Hill, MA, M.Div.

Copyright © 2014 by James R. Hill

ISBN 978-1-61529-143-4

Vista Books LTD.
1672 Main Street E109
Ramona, CA 92065

December 13, 2013

The Gay Emperor Is Naked: A Critique of Homosexuality by Pastor James Hill is in my opinion one of the finest works available today on the issues faced by those in the process of deciding the truth of the claims made by the LGBT community.

Every aspect of the areas of discussion we face on these issues are addressed in a manner that seems to put to rest the validity of the Gay Theology arguments and its' proponents.

As co-founder of one of the oldest organizations that work in the area of helping those that wish change in gender issues and growth in self-esteem, I feel that this book is in the category of an "absolutely must read".

Dr. Douglas E. McIntyre
Director, Freedom Alternative
Co-founder of Homosexuals Anonymous Fellowship Services

January 10, 2014

In many ways, and for many reasons, I wish this book did not need to be written, or even that I could, in clear conscience, simply limp along with the cultural trends regarding this incendiary topic. However, I can't...not because I have a guilty conscience, but because I love grace and truth, the foundation stones of who Jesus is as the Father's expressed image.

Grace says that God loves all, and understands more than we might care to admit; the struggles of life that difficult hands many have been dealt, the injustices of the world system in which we live. I love grace, which is for all women and men, of all races, creeds, colors; for gay and straight. God loves us all, has, in his mercy and grace, provided for all a path of living that leads to life, health, fulfillment, and purpose.

Of course, by grace we are placed on the path. Walking the path effectively requires that we embrace the truth of God's word. Missing the mark (sin) takes us away from the enlightened path of God in Christ presented in the word. Any missing of the mark, not just sexual sin, but any sin; takes us, if you will, off path, though never out of the love and grace of God. It can lead to consequences...yes, truth or consequences is the way life is for the believer. An unbeliever too, but that is less my concern here.

Well, back to my lament. I truly wish Pastor Hill did not have to present what he does here, but he does so with a genuine heart of compassion for the friends who are walking in a destructive path, and missing the mark. They do this while attempting to communicate that this new and exciting path, (pro-gay and other forms of promiscuity) is what God wanted for us all along.

Sadly, an alternative life style is not "the mark" of the high call of God in Christ, especially expressed in a homosexual life style. Thus, do we (Pastor Hill, myself and other endorsers of this work) gleefully rejoice in our self-righteous, hypocritical, obviously homophobic view of homosexuality? Not in the least, but in fact, are only too aware that we also miss the mark, and in many ways, need great godly help to stay on the path. We weep with the many destroyed lives that have embraced error as truth, whether hetero or homo.

So, I wish I did not see the need for a book like this, but I do, for many of my friends are heading over a cliff, and many others are saying you have every right to do so. In fact, they say that this is the right way to live, in spite the obvious and horrific consequences. Is homosexuality a heaven or hell issue? A life or death issue? Well, certainly the later from my view.

My hope for the reader is, as Moses pleaded with the children of Israel in Deuteronomy 30:19, "...I have set before you life and death, the blessing and the curse. So choose life in order that you may live..." the path is provided by Christ, the choice to walk out the grace of God in truth is ours.

Stan E. DeKoven, Ph.D., MFT
Founder and President
Vision International University
1115 D Street
Ramona, CA 92065

February 1, 2014

Do you know you are loved regardless of age, race, sex, skin color, or religion, & regardless of sexual orientation? It is with love that I see Pastor Jim Hill taking the time and risk to address that those he loves are putting themselves in harm's way. You don't have to be a disciple of Jesus Christ and you don't have to agree with him to find this an important read. At a minimum you will find out why a loving person would address this and hopefully discern & agree with what Jim and I see as the truth leading to a more abundant life in this world and the next.

We are all brothers and sisters and we want the best for everyone. Our Lord tells us that loving our neighbor is virtually as important as loving our God. I see this caring for our neighbor in Pastor Jim's presentation. For virtually everyone, happiness and fulfillment depends on positive loving fulfilling relationships with others. What if we in our best efforts, although truly feeling we have achieved this, have actually missed the mark? What if there are very harmful consequences in this life and potentially the next? Wouldn't you want someone to, in a loving caring manner, share this information?

Jim, in a logical and clear manner addresses relationship, health, and longevity issues and why one should very seriously consider a Christian, biblically based understanding of homosexuality. We all, to various degrees, miss the targets for an abundant life that God has set; this work addresses the gift of sexuality in a loving fulfilling relationship. Within the Lord's Truth and Grace we are in harmony with how we were created and with our Creator, who wants an abundant life for each of us.

Dr. Mel Estey
Captain USN Retired, and
former Psychologist at Donovan State Prison

"This is a courageous book written by a working pastor who has dealt with the homosexual issue for many years. He is convicted and compassionate; informed and inquisitive; biblical and practical; experienced and enlightened. I predict that those who read it and get to know the author will find themselves newly convinced that the issue is not closed no matter how much culture might think it is."

H. Newton Malony, M.Div, MS, Ph.D.
Senior Professor (Retired)
Graduate School of Psychology, Fuller Theological Seminary,
Pasadena, CA , USA

To the Jews who had believed him, Jesus said,
"If you hold to my teaching, you are really my disciples.
Then you will know the truth,
And the truth will set you free."
John 8:31-32

Preface

I have found myself obliged to deal with this theme pastorally now for something like thirty years. It was twelve years ago when I first worked on the manuscript for this book. Things intervened, and I was not able to make revisions I wanted until now. When I first wrote on the theme of homosexuality, its rejection was the standard opinion of society, or "conventional wisdom," although that position was under severe attack. As I complete this revision, the acceptance of homosexuality, as "normal" and healthy, has become the "conventional wisdom" of much of our elite. It is my opinion that this acceptance rests much more upon convenient assumptions, and, sometimes, upon a well-intentioned, though mistaken, desire to be kind, than upon evidence. As I shall note more fully later, I was once a cheerful acceptor of this new "conventional wisdom" of acceptance long before it was conventional, and for some years. Thus, it is not mere habit, nor some old and unexamined prejudice that has led me to the conclusions I shall present here, but rather substantial evidence of diverse kinds.

The evidence is that the great majority of persons who try homosexuality go on to leave it, while this is not at all the case with heterosexuals, which calls into question the innateness of homosexuality. Put differently, the evidence is that most people leave homosexuality behind at some time. There is also substantial evidence that there are common potential causal factors in the childhood histories of adults who identify themselves as homosexual, which suggests that such factors may well have caused homosexual ideation. The evidence also is that there are astronomical increases in health risks and a shortened lifespan associated with homosexuality, which calls into question its healthfulness. There are very great disparities in the rates of anonymous sexual encounters, infidelity in committed relationships, the use of prostitutes, and the use of underage persons in sex acts, as compared with persons who identify themselves as heterosexual, all of which may suggest the possibility of some degree of persistent emotional or psychological disorder in the lives of persons who identify themselves as homosexual.

Furthermore, and this may now be seen as a quixotic personal interest rather than a society-wide concern, but I find that Christianity clearly and explicitly rejects homosexual conduct and that this is not the insignificant matter which our broadly pagan contemporary intellectual culture may now deem it to be.

I find that how one is to respond to persons with a homosexual identity, or to societal concerns of persons sympathetic to such persons, is not quite so simple a matter as has sometimes been assumed, but I will attempt some reflections on that matter too, after we have looked at the evidence upon which we might better evaluate the holiness, healthfulness, and innateness of homosexuality.

It is not only my belief that much contemporary conventional wisdom is based upon casual assertion and little evidence, but also that the truth can be known and that in the knowing of that truth there may be freedom for many who now suffer, many knowingly, others unknowingly. I do believe that truth can set us free. I ask you to pursue truth with me.

Pastor Jim Hill

Table of Contents

12

Part I:

Introduction to The Gay Emperor Is Naked

"But he has got nothing on," said a little child. ... "But he has got nothing on!" at last cried all the people. The Emperor writhed, for he knew it was true. But he thought, "The procession must go on." So he held himself stiffer than ever, and the chamberlains held up the invisible train. – from "The Emperor's New Clothes," by Hans Christian Anderson

Chapter 1:

The Subject of This Book:
We Want to Offer Help

It was nineteen eighty-nine. The place was the First United Methodist Church of Pasadena. Because I had once been on staff there, the senior pastor was willing to allow me and some others to hold a conference there to offer help to folks who wanted help in an area of their lives that was both sensitive and important. We had organized a conference that brought together pastoral counselors, psychological counselors, and persons who had once been heavily involved in homosexuality themselves to tell of their experience, and through it, the possibility of coming out of homosexuality, both conduct and orientation, for those who truly wanted it.

The western jurisdiction of The United Methodist Church is very much what is called "liberal," which means, among many other things, approving of homosexuality. I had given notice of our conference to United Methodist pastors throughout our region. Some told the senior pastor who had allowed us to meet in his church of their disappointment that he was so vile as to have allowed it. One or two wrote me letters declaring that no one should want to know how to change something so wonderful as homosexuality. A small group showed up to protest. They had been uncertain as to how strongly they wanted to protest. At first, they thought they might disrupt the meeting altogether, but then decided to wait for some reasonably appropriate time and then voice their disgust with the conference and their disagreement with the premise that anyone could change, or should.

Andy Comiskey, a former, long-time and committed homosexual, now a husband and father, was our main speaker. He is the founder of Desert Stream Ministries, a large ex-gay ministry, then located in the Santa Monica area. He had just completed his book *Pursuing Sexual Wholeness: How Jesus Heals the Homosexual* (Comiskey, 1989). He replied quietly to the words of reproach from Pastor C. and his group supporting homosexuality. Comiskey said that there were those who found that they did not want to be involved with homosexuality, who wanted to change, but did not know how, and, he said, "We just want to offer help."

At that point, another man said something. I don't know how he got there. The meeting was not widely attended. The idea that Jesus Christ can change lives in any way is not widespread in The United Methodist Church in my part of the country, and certainly not in the area of sexual orientation. A few were present as quasi-official sponsors, there was the group of actual presenters, there was a larger group of opponents, a small group who knew me from a social service agency with which I worked and they came there largely as a kindness to me, and only a few others. This man looked to be in his late twenties, although perhaps in his early thirties. His head had been hung down most of the evening. After the protest, and after Andy Comiskey said that some want to come out of homosexuality, and, that to those who want to come out "We just want to offer help," this man raised his hand and said, "And I'm one of them."

He said that he had never heard before that he could come out of it. He had always been told that was just who he was. He hated it. He hated what he was doing. He hated his lifestyle, but he didn't know, not only *how* to come out, but even *that he could*. To him, it was good news to know that some had come out of life as a homosexual, and that maybe he could too. To him, being told that he couldn't change and that he should not even want to was not good news; it was agony. To him, it was hell. He had accepted it only because he had been told that it was inevitable and inescapable. That night, with tears and joy, he began a journey out of homosexuality. To him, that was very good news. To him, it was grace to hear that he could come out of it.

Six years earlier, or perhaps it was seven, another man brought a concern to my office. At that time, I was Lay Director of Evangelism at the First United Methodist Church of Pasadena. I would not be ordained by the church for another year or two. This was a great time for me then. Many lives were changed there. Young people who used to go to youth group for drugs and sex and had left the church after they got their own cars, began to come back to church, to a healthy young adult group, then they came to what they felt to be a relationship with Jesus Christ, rather than merely membership in an institution, and then they got off sleeping around and doing the pharmaceuticals. New study groups formed, new fellowship groups formed, attendance increased after decades of decline, new social service ministries were begun, and there were many changed lives, among the young, the not so young, and some of the old. These were things which I thought very good.

I was low man on the totem pole: new person on the staff, and with the thinnest credentials. I was willing to talk with folks off the street in part because I was not "in" enough to get an appointment with some of the established members of the church. They did not even want to see me. So, to speak with people off the street gave me something to do. Then too, I was young, naïve, and gung ho for Jesus; so I thought a representative of Jesus Christ ought to want to talk with anyone who showed up. But that was not all there was to it. The other staff members really didn't want to talk to folks off the street. One man was usually mildly irritated with the secretaries when they called on him. Another often had the folks from the street leave in anger or tears or both, and he might sharply rebuke the secretaries if they bothered him with such people. So they began to save these folks for me. I got this young man.

This kid was very clean cut, and he was handsome. He wanted to talk. He was sixteen. He had been stationing himself in a men's room at the mall just down the block from the church and offering to perform sexual services for men who came there. He had told a girl he knew in high school about his actions, and she had told him that it was wrong. He wanted me to tell him if it was.

Some time before this, a man I had invited to speak in the evening service that I oversaw said, much to my surprise, among other things, that he thought the church should welcome homosexual clergy. Shortly thereafter, in the weekly column I wrote for our church newsletter, I staked out a fairly traditionalist position on homosexuality. Others read it, and that was to lead to greater involvement for me with this issue. My point at the moment is that I was already "known" as a traditionalist on this issue. However, if you had overheard our conversation that day, you would not have known where I stood for a long time.

I assumed that this was a very tender and emotionally risky thing for this young man to share with me. It is always an honor to receive the confidence of another, and I intended to honor his confidence. It was terribly important to me to make this be a safe place for him, to give him all the security I could, and to be sure that he knew he was loved whatever I might have to say about conduct. To begin with I did not know what he was going to say. As things unfolded, I did not know, at first, what he thought, what his background was, what his experience had been, nor what he might be ready to hear. Such things do not change the truth, but they may affect what portions of the truth it may be most helpful to express at a given time and how best to express the truth, and I waited and listened before I spoke.

"Yes," I told him. I did think that it was wrong. I didn't think it was good for him. I assured him that Jesus loved him. When we do what we Christians call "sin," and others might call "messing up," it is generally to try to get a legitimate need met in an illegitimate way. It is "illegitimate" because it is bad for us or for others, although we may first *know* it is illegitimate because we understand God said so. He does not say something is bad because He is arbitrary and capricious, but because He loves us and knows us. He knows what works for us. That is *why* He declares some things good and some things bad for us. However, when we do need to make some major changes in what we do, we need a whole lot of God's love *in order to be able to do it*, and we generally need some people to bring us some of that love along the way, when we do right - and even when we don't. Practically speaking, we need what we church folks might call "good Christian fellowship," and others might call "a good support network." I had no confidence that our youth group then was strong enough to help lead this young man in the right way, nor even to accept him with any grace if they knew what he was doing. I invited him to come to our evening services, out of whose regulars I thought I had the best chance of offering healthy fellowship for him. I told him that I would be glad to meet with him anytime. I asked him to please come by again. I wished then I had more knowledge, more wisdom, more help to offer, but I didn't. I never saw him again.

I know that the man in 1989, was in agony, and he looked upon the offer of transformation as help, hope, release, and joy. The boy in 1981, or 2, or 3, was quieter. I will not make claims for feelings on his part which he did not express, but you will not persuade me that his presence in that men's room, offering sexual favors to strange men was a sign of health, a sign of contentment, a proper reflection of a normal sexual appetite. As best I can read him, he was a young boy with no father at home who desperately needed masculine affirmation, seeking it in the only way he knew how to find it, but in a way that would never meet his true need, only mask it, and lead him into more grief. In neither case would it have been grace to tell them, "That is just who you are." To be told "that is just who you are" was not grace, and that was not "who they were." In the short run, the truth might have required them to face some unpleasant facts, and to struggle through to new understanding and some new ways of getting needs met. In the long run, their needs would have been met and their pain alleviated. The "agreeable lie" would have masked their real needs and increased their pain and estrangement. While there is no hope of coming to the truth without grace, it is also true that there is no true grace without truth. It is truth I seek to present here, with as much grace as I can muster.

Once upon a time, in a kingdom far away, there lived a comfortable king with his adoring entourage. He was not extraordinarily good or bad, or wise or foolish, only ordinarily so. There came to his kingdom two clever men who thought to make their fortunes at his expense. They were tailors, they said, the best in the world. They would make clothing of the very, very finest fabric. This was such an extraordinary fabric that only those who were very clever could see it. Foolish, unwise, bumpkinish people could not see it, which means, of course, that those who could not see it were foolish, unwise and bumpkins.

It was very expensive this fabric, as one would expect for a fabric so very fine. From time to time they brought samples to the king's chambers to give progress reports on their tailoring. These two showed it to the king, and he, fearing to be thought a foolish fellow, proclaimed that it was truly magnificent. They offered it for the admiration of the courtiers as well, and they, fearing to be thought fools, proclaimed that it was truly magnificent. And so on went this charade for some seasons. Of course, the tailors required considerable payment along the way for their fine work and very expensive fabric.

Then the day came to show off this fine new suit of clothes to the whole kingdom. There was to be a royal parade. The king would lead the procession in his grand new clothes. The king nodded to the adoring crowds. He walked with great pomp and ceremony. He obviously thought he was wearing the very grandest clothing that ever there was. The courtiers nodded and smiled with very large smiles. They obviously thought this was a great procession and were proud to be part of something so grand that only very clever people could properly appreciate it. The people of the kingdom had heard of the new clothes as well, and they were not to be outdone by the king and his courtiers. They too began to nod and smile and proclaim the great quality of the new clothes. But there was one young boy who just couldn't see it. His eyes got big, and then he proclaimed in a loud voice "But he has got nothing on!" And then all the crowd began to chortle and guffaw and to shout out, "He has got nothing on!" And the Emperor writhed in agony as he returned to his palace. And that is a re-telling of the children's story by Hans Christian Anderson entitled "The Emperor's New Clothes." (Fadiman, 1984, p. 462)

I see "The Emperor's New Clothes" as a parable of our society's current conventional wisdom regarding homosexuality. It is widely believed by clever people of our age that homosexuality is just a normal variation, like having brown eyes or blue, or like being of one ethnicity or another. But that is demonstrably not so. Do you realize that while something like 98% or all persons who ever try heterosexuality go on to consider themselves heterosexual, 75% or more of all persons who ever try homosexuality go on to discover that they were really *not* "gay" after all. Now to the best of my knowledge, you do not find that 75% of persons who think they might be of African ancestry at the age of fifteen go on to discover at the age of thirty that they were really Norwegian after all. Nor do you find that 75% of persons who at the age of twenty thought they were surely Irish go on to discover at the age of forty that they were always Chinese after all. I will give full documentation in the place in which I speak of this more fully. (Michael, Gagnon, *et al*) I do but foreshadow some of my argument here. But homosexuality is *not* a given like being of a particular ethnicity.

It is also often assumed by leading intellectual lights of our day that same sex "marriage" is just like straight marriage. But this too is demonstrably untrue. The most extensive study of gay couples ever made was that by McWhirter and Mattison, and they found that of 137 couples entering into a committed monogamous relationship, only 5% maintained fidelity even for a year, and none, not one, maintained fidelity for five years. This is in sharp contrast to what Michael, Gagnon *et al* found to be true with heterosexual couples. A recent study of same sex married couples in Amsterdam found that patterns of infidelity continue to prevail. (Dallas and Heche) These are but two of many widely assumed notions about the reality of homosexual patterns of thought and conduct which are clearly contradicted by available data. Please, dear reader, do consider the evidence.

In the latter part of the 1800's, the head of the Patent Office of the United States said that we ought to close the Patent Office, because, with the invention of the telegraph and the steam engine and whatnot, why by golly, just about everything that could be invented had been; so there was no need for it. It was only shortly before the Wright brothers flew at Kitty Hawk that competent scientists of the age declared that man could never fly. At one time every good doctor knew that the best, and nearly the only, remedy for nearly everything was to bleed a patient, to cut the patient so as to let out the "bad humors" in the blood. Sometimes they killed their patients with this remedy; rarely did it greatly help. Always it was the best science of their day. There was a time when it was the accepted scientific convention that the earth was flat. There was a time when the best scientists knew that the sun revolved around the earth. This was their conventional wisdom. Not long ago, it was thought that the Soviet Union was enormously strong, would surely be around indefinitely, and might well overtake the United States, and then it disappeared almost overnight. More recently still, it was thought that the world economy had entered some new phase and things would always go up; one could surely give loans for 125% of the value of a home to people who could not afford it because the value would soon go up more; and then the housing market crashed. In each case, the thought expressed was the conventional wisdom of the time. Conventional wisdom is always conventional, but it is only occasionally wise. I want to ask the reader to consider the possibility of things that may be beyond his or her current convention. It was the conventional wisdom of the emperor and his courtiers that the clothes made by their clever tailors were the best in the world, until a child laughed. I do not laugh, but I hope to play such a child.

I assure you I do not want to do this. I do not want to say disagreeable things. I want to be agreeable as much as the next fellow. I have at least as great a need as average to be loved. I want to be thought clever and wise and modern. I would like to be fashionable. Furthermore, some things, though true, still cause discomfort in the hearing. That discomfort, even if it can lead to greater peace at length, is pain, at least for a season, and I have no desire to cause pain. But these things are not my highest goals. It is more important that I speak truth.

I am quite happy to speak truth to those who agree with me, but I want still more, far more, to speak truth to those who *disagree* with me. There's the rub. I do not wish to speak in

Christian-ese to a Christian ghetto. I must speak *as* a Christian, since I am one, but I do not particularly wish to speak *to* Christians. My desired audience is the "general educated public," most of which begins reading, if they begin at all, with the conviction that what I am about to say is obscurantist, ignorant, and foolish at best, perhaps truly mean-spirited, and surely harmful. Of course, I think none of that is so.

I ask one thing of the reader - to read. No, I ask two things: to read and to consider. Consider the evidence. Let me show you the burden I impose upon myself by my title. I do not think that the notion that homosexuality is healthy and an expression of health, spiritual, emotional or physical, to be only slightly mistaken. I think it is greatly mistaken. I do not think that, with your hard reflection, I might "win" the argument "on points." I think that there is a great deal of evidence that bears upon questions we shall consider in this study, and that that evidence points very clearly in one direction. There *is* a great deal of evidence that might serve to answer the question: Is homosexuality holy? There is a great deal of evidence that might serve to answer the question: Is homosexuality healthy? There is a great deal of evidence that can serve to answer the question: Can homosexuality be healed? Yes, there is some evidence that might tend to run in another way, and we shall consider some of that too, but, in comparison, it is not at all what it is widely believed to be. Yes, there are questions that those who disagree with me might raise as a means to try to "explain away" *some* of the evidence I shall offer, and we shall consider some of those as well. Still, I think certain basic conclusions that I shall offer are overwhelmingly supported by evidence that is available. I think that at some point, there will come a time when it will be like the little boy saying "But he has got nothing on!" My burden is to establish my case not "arguably," but clearly. I think I shall.

If I am wrong, then much of what I will have to say *would be harmful*! I do not hide from that fact. Nor do I take that thought lightly. I do not desire to cause even discomfort, let alone pain, and surely not harm. I know that many already think that that cannot possibly be so. I understand those sentiments, but I ask you to consider what follows anyway. After all, if I am so obviously wrong, then it should be obvious, and an easy thing for all those wiser than I, to show it. If I were mistaken, I acknowledge that my argument might well be harmful. I would draw many of the same conclusions as do my initial detractors if I held the same assumptions that they do. On the chance that there might be something of value to note in these following pages, I ask the reader to read them. If nothing else, perhaps it will better enable the reader to correct my errors at some future time, or the similar errors of another similarly foolish person. Of course, if I am substantially right in what I have to say, then that also is a matter of potentially very great consequence, and to know the things of which I shall speak could be enormously helpful to any who wanted help in this area, either for their personal growth or for their further reflections as responsible and caring members of our society.

A few years back, I prepared a booklet-sized version of some of these arguments. With an accompanying letter, I mailed a few copies to various administrative leaders of the church in my part of the world. One replied. He said that he admired my reasoning ability; he had long been impressed by that. He thought the evidence and arguments substantial, but nevertheless, for no reason he could give at all, he chose to see things differently. Another responded when I had occasion to speak with her on the phone, and I asked her for a response. "Well, no," she said, she "hadn't actually gotten around to reading it, but after all, many different scholars think many different things," therefore, she was free to think whatever she felt like, without, apparently, any need to actually consider any evidence. Sadly, I find this to be a common response.

The pastor of a very large church in our annual conference (a region of our denomination) did respond when I asked him to respond in a telephone conversation about another topic. He said that he didn't think what he saw in the booklet fit any of the homosexual persons whom he knew. I am afraid that the problem was that he didn't actually *know* any of the persons that he "knew."

The prominently pro-gay pastor of a largely gay church that I visited one Sunday I had off was delighted to see me in church. He wanted to show me around his community. He showed me the gay bars and the lesbian bar, and he remarked with some contempt upon what he saw as the inability of the gays (male homosexuals) and the lesbians (female homosexuals) to get along. He told me about the other "welcoming" churches (which means churches supportive of homosexuality) in his area which he noted with some disdain only wanted to have gay members and were not as open to straights as he was, applauding himself a little for his unusual openness to heterosexuals. He also told me about the past wars at his church, when the leadership was gay and they did not think the church was gay enough at that time and all left in a huff at one point. None of these things diminished his conviction that homosexuality was a fine thing and much to be applauded. Having been often in conversation with this man, I had asked him to read a couple of books in the field. He declined. He said that he was too busy to read. Busy? I'm sorry, but with what? Many of us who are pastors have fellowship groups that are larger than his congregation. His church survived on subsidies from the denomination, and it has since closed. He knew he wanted to change what had been the established position of the church for thousands of years, and yet he could not take time to read a single book that did not agree with him. I find that incredible, and discreditable.

But it is common. I have given books away to people with whom I wanted to have a dialogue in hopes that they would read them, but apparently nothing that does not fit their preconceptions could be considered. To be fair to you, the reader of the "general educated public" whose attention I seek, *they* should have felt even more obliged than you to read something such as I present here, for they were all leaders in a church whose official position they sought to overthrow. They should have felt some sense of obligation to consider that which they wished to destroy. But, generally, they did not. Still, I ask as much of you. Read. Consider. Consider the evidence. If you find it inadequate, splendid, but then at least you will have considered it. Perhaps you will encounter some things useful here even if you do not accept the whole argument. And, who knows, perhaps you shall find it still more helpful than that. Perhaps I hope for more grace, or responsibility, from you than many leaders of the church have shown! So be it. I do.

I shall divide this study into five sections. In the first part, I hope to introduce the topic and the speaker. In Part II, I shall try to answer the question: Is Homosexuality Holy? I shall do so largely from what I understand to be a Christian perspective. I realize there are many persons, especially among the readers I most covet, who do not count themselves Christian. I shall, a bit further on, suggest some reasons why you might yet wish to consider this section, but I also contend that the rest of my argument should carry the day even without this segment, and still I think the reader's benefit would be much reduced in passing over this section. In Part III, I shall try to answer the question: Is Homosexuality Healthy? There is much evidence that bears upon this question. We will consider some of it, and we will also consider some of the pro-gay proposed answers to some of the problems raised by such data. In Part IV, I shall try to answer the question: Is Healing Possible? See here, the very title implies a perspective; I will not hide that from you. The pro-gay position would not only say that "healing," as they would treat the word, is not only not possible, but also that it is not necessary, wise, desirable or good! As you may by now have surmised, my answers to these three questions would be different. In part V, I shall make some modest attempts to suggest various kinds of possibly appropriate responses based upon what it seems we find as we seek to answer the preceding questions. Responses, plural, is appropriate because there are different needs in different settings.

There are many who have dealt more ably than I with various segments of our discussion. The persons who have come out of homosexuality and who have worked helping others to come out of homosexuality have a much greater wealth of experience upon which to draw in those areas; people such as Andy Comiskey, Bob Davies, Lori Rentzel, Joe Dallas, and David Kyle Foster. James De Young has dealt well with the position of the Bible on our themes. He is probably definitive in the use of other ancient literature and word studies. Thomas Schmidt has done fine work in many of the same fields that I shall enter. Jeffrey Stainover is a doctor and far more qualified than I to speak of a number of the medical and scientific issues with which we shall deal. Ronald Bayer has an excellent history of the views of psychiatry and the APA's (American Psychiatric Association) change of the DSM (Diagnostic and Statistical Manual) in 1973. I shall cite dozens of others along the way who have done fine and helpful work, and, of course, many whose work I may not find so fine but need to acknowledge as a matter of reasonably fair play.

I may have particular strengths in four areas, and I hope for a fifth. First, in my work with the Bible, I shall do much to ask questions which can be truly answered from the Bible itself. Yes, I shall do some word studies too, although not much, but my goal is to make the case clear and overwhelming from data available to all. Second, I do some "cross disciplinary" reasoning not previously much seen. There is data developed in one field that can give more insight when brought together with data from another field. The data is there, but perhaps I see some connections not noted before which can be helpful. Third, I bring a broader range of concerns together under one cover, and there is some benefit to having all these matters dealt with in one discussion. Fourth, by virtue of my experience in spiritual healing combined with my fairly extensive reading in secondary sources, I can perhaps illustrate the human dimension and apparent social consequences better than some who are purely scientists, or counselors, or polemicists. The fifth matter is one of concern to me. I was not always where I am now. I have lived some time in other intellectual worlds, and I hope that I may be able to speak to those who disagree with me, for I once agreed with them. I may speak an awkward word or two just to try to make contact with those "modernists" with whom I want very much to speak.

"*Festina lente*," Augustine used to say. "Make haste slowly." I ask that you not conclude that you know too fully all that will follow, nor all that should follow.

Logically, arguments do not stand or fall upon the histories of their proponents, although in practice they sometimes do. Yet some knowledge of a person may help to make clear, or clearer sooner, the very meaning of what that person says. And so I will share some history of the author's "reflections" upon our theme. I put this word in quotations marks because they were, until recent times, musings or opinions or experiences, but hardly reflections. There is an honorable tradition of the author stating such background, associations or assumptions as might be thought to instruct or influence his words, and thereby the reader can better calibrate his response to the author. So be it. It may be that the reader can find some key that will serve to explain away all my conclusions as mere prejudice, or not. It may be that the reader will see some sign of a journey not altogether unlike his own, at some point in time, and thus perhaps serve to give credence to the things written. The subsequent arguments must stand or fall on the evidence and the reasoning they contain, but still a brief acquaintance with the one who seeks your consideration may not be without benefit.

Chapter 2:

The Author of This Book: Neither Hate Nor Habit, But Hope Offered from Hope Received

There were a number of years when I would not watch Hollywood films. I wanted to be an intellectual. After working all day in the pressroom, I went home and read Milton or Thomas Mann or Tolstoy or Tirso de Molina or Rabelais (very little) or James Joyce (very slowly) or Moliere (not for long) or Thomas Babington McCaully or any of a number of authors often difficult to read. Culture was like a good antiseptic; it had to be painful to be good for you – or so I then thought. And I would only see foreign films. I saw Bergman, Bunuel, Kurosawa, Ray, Truffaut, Renoir, Fellini, and such.

I went to the Los Feliz, the Encore, the Santa Monica, and the Vagabond. One Saturday night, there was a showing of *Last Year at Marienbad* at the Vagabond Theater on Wilshire. There were about a dozen people in the theater, a typical Saturday night crowd for a movie there. The movie was about varying points of view, I guess. After we came out, one man ran up and down the sidewalk in front of the theater screaming. This was an entirely appropriate reaction to that movie. I didn't say it was wise to see only foreign films; just that I did it. This is confessional here, after all.

I also saw some great older American films during this period. About this time, a series of Buster Keaton silent movies was being distributed, such as *The General* and *Steamboat Bill*. I saw Wallace Berry and Marie Dressler in *Min and Bill*, some marvelous stuff with Greta Garbo, such as *Susan Lennox*, and some silent movies, like John Gilbert's *The Big Parade*, Laura LaPlante's *The Cat and the Canary*, and Lon Chaney's *He Who Gets Slapped*. By the way, some of these movies were being shown at the Encore about the time that Troy Perry was starting the Metropolitan Community

Church, also meeting in the Encore, though I only ever attended the movies.

After the show, a friend and I would often go to a coffee shop and talk for about five or six hours. Often we went to Tiny Naylor's on Wilshire, just down from the Vagabond. My friend was terribly literate. He knew plays, movies and novels better than I, though I had an edge in poetry and more than that in history. We had some truly great conversations, one on the element of play in Johann Huizinga's *Homo Ludens* and one on tragedy, calling upon our acquaintance with a bunch of Greeks, Shakespeare, Marlowe, and a few moderns. Much fun. Of course I always sensed that if my life were in danger, and all it took for my friend to save my life was to walk across the street, it would depend upon whether or not he found it esthetically satisfying to do so at that moment. That, too, I think characterizes much of contemporary intellectual life: lifeless, soulless, selfish, and wordy. It is often not so much life, as a way to avoid life, a series of excuses for a lack of life, a way to pretend to disdain the ones of whose seeming comfort with their more normal qualities one is envious. Ah, but I digress.

We went and saw Fellni's *Satyricon*. It was a movie based on the book by Gaius Petronius Arbiter. Petronius was a tutor to Nero. No, don't blame all Nero's failings on Petronius. He is said to have been a fairly good influence on Nero, at least until Nero compelled him to commit suicide. It was considered pornographic for centuries and was read only in Latin. As one Frenchman has said, "On lit Petrone. On ne' le cit pas." "One reads Petronius. One does not cite him." (Petronius, 1965, p. 13) When last I paid attention, forty plus years ago, there were two translations available, Penguin (Petronius, 1965) and Mentor (Petronius, 1959). A prominent part of the book/movie is the main character's search for his runaway, twelve-year old, boy toy, "lover," slave. I distinctly remember arguing with great passion that homosexuality was just like heterosexuality. It was morally the same. There was no reason to disparage it. And, that it was displayed so in the movie/book. My friend disagreed. He was right, but he was not able to present evidence for his opinion then. Later, I re-read the

book. When a main character is called "Crotch," it is possible that
he is being used as the butt of a joke. The main character was
criticized by his friend for his overly passionate desire for his
young, boy lover, and for his inability to move on to heterosexual
love. Then there is the fact that a major theme of the book, in so
far as we have it (for only portions of it remain), is the main
character's need to go to a priestess of Priapus to make the difficult
transition to the maturity represented by moving on to heterosexual
love. But I argued strongly that night for the acceptability of
homosexuality. I did not get to my current understanding of
homosexuality overnight.

I suppose that I had a fairly normal, suburban upbringing in
the late fifties. In sixth grade, when I was ten to eleven, I had
heard about an unfortunate classmate who was supposed to be
trying to buy the friendship of a tall, popular fellow classmate with
money he earned by performing sexual services for men. The
story went that some guy urinated in his mouth. Well, it was a
fairly strong value in our family to discount unkind rumors and not
to believe ill of another readily. Furthermore, in my then current
knowledge of sex, I didn't think that the mouth had anything to do
with sex, and thus this story made no sense to me, and so I
dismissed the whole story. By the way, in this case, and in most
instances that follow, I do remember names, but I don't think it
really helps much to tell them, and so I fear I must deprive the
reader of that bit of titillation. Please forgive me, if you need to.

By late high school time, I was very active in my church.
Among other things, I was a member of both the infrequently
meeting youth choir and the regularly performing adult choir. I
was probably a baritone, but the low bass singer showed up for
choir practice more regularly than the tenors, so I became a low
bass, because I couldn't read music and needed someone to listen
to, to follow. There came to be another fellow in this choir. He
was a church regional official; so, of course, I knew he was a fine
fellow. He suggested that we get together from time to time. We
got together for breakfast before church virtually every Sunday for
a year or two. At some point, he invited me to his home for dinner.

I met his roommate. Around this time, they had just celebrated the anniversary of the day when they bought their house together. His roommate seemed a little gay (well, alright, more than a little), but, you may recall, I had learned not to think ill of anyone readily, and so I would not consciously conclude that they were homosexual, although, at some level, I filed that thought away as a possibility. I don't think I was exactly dense; I just had a high commitment to not assuming evil without incontrovertible evidence.

I went off to college, Occidental College, a "church related school," built by the Presbyterians quite some time before. Among the vestiges of a fast fading Christian faith was a required two-quarter survey of the Bible. There I learned that God had nothing to do with the Bible, but that it was written by J, E, D and P. No, that's not an early rap group; they are different editorial schools, it is supposed. But who they are really doesn't matter just now. The snake had bitten, but the poison had not spread far yet. I was still interested in "the things of God," and so I wanted to get into a class called "Contemporary Trends in Christian Thought." It was for upper division students only. I had to petition my way in. I did. There we read Tillich, Bultmann, Daniel Day Williams, Buber, a very little Barth, and the then very popular John A. T. Robinson's *Honest to God.* So, now I "discovered" that God was dead, that the Bible was a book of fairy tales, expressing profound human truths, but none of it, mind you, really happened. Oh dear.

In high school, my youth pastor, thinking me a very bright fellow, had given me a copy of Rudolph Bultmann's *Kerygma and Myth* to read. Well, in high school, I really didn't make heads or tails out of it. I preferred *The Analects* of Confucius. However, now, when I read it again in college, and gathered that it said roughly that all of Christianity is a myth, and that these other books said so too, and their book jackets said they were the best books by the best people, and I was much too green to know that all book jackets say that about the books within and that everything in print is not necessarily so, and my professors were "doctors of philosophy" in something-or-other, and they were ordained ministers too, and, by golly, come to think of it, my high school youth pastor had promoted Bultmann too, why by gosh, it must be the case that every educated person knows that there really isn't any God! Wow! "What a shame," I thought to myself.

Now Tillich has his rationale for using the language of faith while not meaning it. Among his works, we read *Dynamics of Faith*, and this book drew a distinction between "sign" and "symbol." He said that many ordinary words are just signs, and when you use them, you should say what you mean. But some words are especially important. They are symbols. For example, objects like a scepter or a flag, and words like "resurrection" or "God," are "symbols," and they change their meaning only slowly. Therefore, since they change their meaning only slowly, we, clever, educated people, can use these words meaning entirely different things from what they have always meant, different even from what you know the folks in the pews and other folks in general think you mean by them, and that's okay. You can willingly, indeed willfully mislead, and that's okay. Or, less elegantly, as long as you are a clever, modern Christian, you can lie freely, *and* you also get to look down on the poor dummies who don't know what these things really ought to mean, while you are deceiving them! I suppose that their rationale was that the poor people in the pews needed their "crutches" and so "we" would just break it to them slowly, that what they believed in just wasn't so. I kind of thought that the real reason might be that the folks who paid the bills might not keep doing it if the clever ones let on too clearly what they were up to, and they wanted to protect their livings.

In any case, while I bought the story about the dead God and myths and such, I thought that being a liar was shabby, and so I left the church. (By the way, I still think that such dishonesty is shabby and disgraceful and that there are many clergy who ought to come clean with their congregations, or, perhaps better still, surrender their orders.) I was a young buck in college, now maybe eighteen or nineteen, in my sophomore year of '64-'65. The new trinity was sex, drugs, and rock and roll. More than one wag has said that "the theologian of the '60's was the Playboy Advisor." I was never the wildest child of my age, after all, I was a little bit socially inept, but I was a child of my age. I never much liked drugs, although I did inhale, but I did rather like booze. Jack Daniel's with a beer back or Wild Turkey, straight, came to be my preferred poisons. There came a time when I had a wine cabinet stocked with Italian reds, German whites, Portuguese rosés, and French champagne, but that was later, when I had more money.

Overlapping some of the above chronicled developments, in a later quarter, in my sophomore year, I took a class on Christian ethics. The only text I recall was a slim volume by the good Bishop of Woolwich, John A. T. Robinson, in which he espoused "situational ethics." This means that Christian ethics are not hard and fast, but what is ethical at any point in time depends upon "the situation," which, of course, you evaluate since God doesn't know anything about it. Now I am sure that the good bishop thought that only highly educated, nicely dressed, very well scrubbed young people, who were really not too terribly young, and who had wisdom enough to always use "protection," and who would never sin in any unseemly, sordid or truly ugly manner, and who really cared for each other and indeed might very well get married later - that only these people would apply his new standard, and thus that he could be confident that his standard would be applied in a manner of which he would more or less approve or of which he would disapprove only slightly, but he did two things by his whole system that made this most exceedingly improbable: 1) He said that the only absolute is that there are no absolutes – there are no clear rules, and 2) He said that you decide – just like Eve and Adam, you do your own thing. Well, once you prop open the barn door, there is no guarantee that only the one horse you don't greatly care about will run away.

I was a young buck, with the new freedom of college, whose new motto was "Never let your studies interfere with your education," who had also just discovered that all "educated" people knew that God was dead, who was also taking a course in do-it-yourself ethics. So for my term paper, I wanted to write on sex. And for my main source of study on Christian ethics on sexuality, I read Kinsey, Pomeroy and Martin's little book *Sexual Behavior in the Human Male* (Kinsey, 1948). Well, "read" is probably a bit much; maybe I skimmed it.

Somewhere in there, Kinsey said, "The only unnatural sex act is one you can't perform." Oh, I thought that was clever. It's not true, of course. It consists of a play on words, relying on the fact that, in ordinary language, we use the word "natural" in two ways: 1) to mean "what occurs in nature," and 2) to mean "that which seems to be in accord with some design in nature." "Nature is brutal" refers to the fact that Mary's little lamb may be eaten by a big bad wolf, that Mickey Mouse's cousin may be gobbled up by a hawk or a snake, and that Bambi's baby may be torn apart by a pack of Wiley coyotes. "He's a natural born leader" refers to the sense that one person seems to take a leadership role easily, as if particularly fit for it, as if he were a "natural." But I didn't know that at eighteen or nineteen. Thank God I didn't do everything I thought it was okay to do, but I am even embarrassed to think of what I thought it was okay to do, oh, and I did some things that are embarrassing too, about most of which I have no intention of telling you. Also, I was protected by my naiveté.

One fellow I had met at college invited me to his place for dinner. He and a couple of other guys had rented rooms upstairs in a private house. After dinner, the other boys took away the dishes and began to clean up. The door was shut to our dining room. My friend and I were going to smoke cigars. He suggested that his way was to smoke a cigar after dinner, and, being full from the dinner, to loosen his pants, and sit there leaning back with his pants open. The other boys gave me a slightly strange look as they took away the dishes. Jealousy? I don't know. But look, I kid you not, I didn't even realize he was trying to nudge me towards something more intimate until I thought back on it years later! Oh well, sometimes stupid is good. By the way, this guy was gay, and he was a nice guy so far as I knew him, and I heard later that he died trying to save someone in the ocean only a year or so after that.

I transferred to UCLA for my junior year. I got a bachelor's degree in history, and MA in East Asian History, was, for a very short time, a fair haired boy in the history department, got the chairman mad at me, got sick, left in '69. Overlapping this, I worked in a pressroom. It was not a Sunday School picnic. One guy was the horse bookie, another guy ran the football cards, one guy sold pot, another sold pills, a couple loan sharked, some smuggled people across the border, one did a little occasional pimping, another got clothes at a great discount from his girl friend who worked in a clothing store, and another had a steal-to-order business. Every third word was a curse word, and we spat on the steel plank floors. It was hot, dirty, just a little dangerous, especially when guys came to work drunk, and it was, in many ways, great fun! I enjoyed the camaraderie of the pressroom a lot until I became a supervisor, at which point the pressures of managing people and the many hours of OT I was asked to get out of them began to get to me. It paid well, it was secure. I was viewed as an up-and-comer by the bosses, but I had known all along it wasn't what I wanted to do. I saved up some money, and in January of 1978, I quit work to write the great American novel.

I never did that. Some short stories and poems were okay. I consoled myself with the fact that the *New York Review of Books* guy wrote extra words of encouragement on the standardized, mimeographed rejection slips he sent me for some poems. Later, I did get a nice letter of rejection from them for something else. I got a nibble at Macmillan from a couple of editors for a different collection of poems, but they decided that they couldn't sell enough to make it pay for them.

Meanwhile, God had begun to get my attention. Across the years, not too long after I left the church, I began to go to church again. This time I went to a big church, to hide! I figured if I went to a small church somebody might ask me what I was doing there, and I didn't know. I went to First United Methodist Church of Pasadena. I cursed the traffic on the way to church! I scammed, in my mind's eye, on a gal in a pew three rows in front of me. I went more religiously to brunch at the Huntington Sheraton, but I went to church, maybe thirty Sundays out of fifty. First Church was a great place to hide; there was no danger of anybody talking to me there. One old guy, bless his heart, Lambert Baker (when I have only something positive to say, I'll give the real name), came over and said hello from time to time. Our conversation was pretty superficial, but that was about all I was ready for at that time.

Eventually, I heard a man who sounded honest and sounded like he believed in something. I went to the evening service that he had started. It was held in the smaller chapel. The first time I went, they had some special group doing something. This group brought out a lot of extra people, and I felt it was too much like being in a small church again, so I left! Later I went back. The leader recognized I was searching for something. He suggested that we get together from time to time to chat. We did. Our last breakfast together, before he returned home after he had completed the studies at nearby Fuller Seminary that he had come for, he suggested that I was more of a Christian than I wanted to acknowledge. I felt, internally, that he was right, but I did not tell him that.

Not long before mentor number one was to leave, mentor number two came along. He was a young guy. He was baby-faced, and my first thought was to disdain this young fellow. His first sermon in the evening service started off badly, but then he dropped his clever plans and spoke from his heart, and I began to love the guy. [I hope I can use that word without folks misreading it.] We talked. He turned me on to Pannenberg and C. S. Lewis. I began to acquire the intellectual understanding of faith that I wish I had had back in college, but another book was more important.

These guys liked the Bible. I wanted to be their friend. "So, what the heck, I'll read the Bible," I said to myself. And things began to happen. It was never when I expected it. I had read this book some before, and sometimes I said to myself that I was going to be moved when I got to a certain point, but no, it *never* happened like that. And sometimes I was moved when I was in a sort of hazy state as I was just beginning to read but before I was really focused and aware of what I was reading. When I looked at what moved me, it was always on things that affirmed the reality of God and the divinity of Christ. Those were the questions that I had, and those were the questions I got answered. There were a lot of things that went together to lead me to ask Jesus Christ to be my Lord and Savior, but I'll not share that tale now, including a neat story about a little time spent in the chapel at St. Bernadine's Hospital in San Bernardino when my mother was there dying of cancer and a story about a hike in the mountains and a baptism in a mountain stream on the Mt. Wilson trail above Sierra Madre, for I am writing this for hard nosed "worldly" people, and maybe you don't want to hear about all that namby-pamby stuff.

However, from about 1964 until about 1978, I thought homosexuality was fine. The church official, who I had known in my church in high school, later went to the big church where I went to hide. I had met him there. Then I saw that he was not there for a season. Suspecting that the vicious church people had scurvily chased him out with their rejection of him for his proclivities, I was prepared to be angry with "the church" for what I supposed to be its harsh anti-gay stance. I found fault with it for a fault they never committed. He showed up later. He had just been out of town with a new job for a while. But my point is that I largely shared the belief in polymorphous perversity that is now the accepted orthodoxy among our educated elites. To be honest, Norman O. Brown always irritated me, and I was never totally at peace with "polymorphous perversity," even when it seemed to be the wisdom of the age, but I sort of accepted it, in principle. It was later, in this pagan period, I saw Fellini's *Satyricon* with that literary minded friend of mine.

By these bits and pieces, I mean to say that I had long believed that homosexuality was okay. I had gone through the transformation out of "old fashioned" Christian faith to the "modern," "self-actualizing," hybrid, do-it-yourself "faith" of our age. So then, my current conclusion that homosexuality is unhealthy, is not a continuation of custom, but it is a conclusion based on considerable evidence.

That in and of itself does not mean that my new conclusions are correct, but it should help to take away one means the reader may be accustomed to use to avoid dealing with the arguments to be presented below. What I shall say is not an accident, not an old, unconsidered habit, not obscurantism, not unreflective, not knee-jerk reaction. Disagree if you will, but wrestle first.

It is not from hate, for I have never hated those caught up in homosexuality, although there have been times when I have been a little testy with those who promote it. It is not from habit, for I long ago left the habitual opposition with which I grew up, and after that left also the new habit of accepting the way of the world. I myself found something new, oh, thirty plus years ago now. It gave me some new joy. Another digression: An agnostic Jewish, actor-director friend of mine with whom I was palling around about the time I was coming to Christ said something to me that pleased me. We were having something to eat at a coffee shop one time and chewing the fat, and he said to me, "Jim, Jim, you are the first guy I ever met who got religion and became funnier!" For me, coming to Christ was freeing. I did get funnier because I was not trying to scam anyone. I wasn't trying to get into the girls pants anymore, and so I could be more relaxed. I didn't desire to hurt anybody, so I didn't have to analyze my words before I said them quite so much. Now getting into ministry is a different thing. A church is much like a convoy and only moves as fast as the slowest ship, which does not necessarily always make for the most fun. But Christ is fun! If you are not reasonably happy, you probably are not really holy! And holiness is really all about how to be really happy, so to speak. And I have found something that made me happy. Well, alright, so happi*er*. So maybe I'm still a little morose at times, but not like before; not hardly. And I know there is something that can make others happier too. I know because I've seen it many times. So then, it really is not from hate, nor from habit, but it is with hope that I speak. Of course, I could still be wrong.

Part II: Is Homosexuality Holy?

The Lord said to Moses, "Speak to the entire assembly of Israel and say to them: 'You must be holy because I, the Lord your God am holy." Leviticus 19:1-2

Chapter 3:

Introductory Reflections on a Moral Consideration of Homosexuality

In this section, I want to answer this question: Is homosexuality holy? That question means is homosexuality godly, or approved of God. Differently put, I might ask this question: Does Christian faith reject homosexuality? Does it approve of it? Reject it? Ignore it? Say nothing about it? Be ambivalent about it? Does Christian faith have clear teachings on related matters that might reasonably be said to reflect upon a response to homosexuality? Does it speak clearly about homosexuality? Does it address the kinds of concerns and claims made in the discussions on homosexuality today? Can it be said to be outdated, and if so, what consequences, if any, would that have for our understanding of Christian faith? What role, if any, should Christianity, or any religion, have in reflection upon social policy, notions of right or wrong, or conduct to be encouraged or discouraged by governmental action or inaction?

I will not attempt to speak of the positions of other faiths. I know that many claim that other faiths have a position. There are those who say that all monotheistic faiths reject homosexuality, thus including Christianity, Judaism and Islam. I know that the Dali Lama is reported to oppose homosexuality. However, I have not made myself knowledgeable in the positions of these faiths regarding homosexuality, and I expect to say nothing further about them, excepting this brief note about the possible position of Judaism.

Since some of my discussion will deal with what we in the Christian faith call Old Testament scriptures, and since these scriptures are common heritage of both Judaism and Christianity, then I would expect that persons of Jewish faith might find that some of these discussions speak to some specific concerns of theirs. However, there are many questions about the manner in which such scriptures might be used to attempt to ascertain God's will by persons of the Jewish faith that I not only have not answered, but do not even know. Furthermore, the interpretive or instructive role of other Jewish writings of a holy but somewhat less holy character than the Bible, such as Mishnah and Talmud, is another matter with which I am not conversant. Therefore, let me point out that I make no claims for my reflections in this section other than that they attempt to discern and convey a Christian understanding of homosexuality.

Note also, that while much of the discussion about homosexuality overlaps in various segments of the Christian body, there are also some denominational distinctives, and I do not intend to try to deal with all of those. Specifically, I do not intend to attempt to deal with any distinctively Roman Catholic discussions on this matter. To be sure, I expect that some of the psychologists whose writing we will consider are Roman Catholic, but I am not dealing with them *as* Romans Catholics. They also deal with some sources of instruction in a way that we in the Protestant tradition might call instructive or illustrative, but not authoritative. Of course, I would expect that all of the matters which I do consider, persons in the Roman tradition would also find appropriate to consider. Further, I fully intend that my argument speaks compellingly to all persons of the Roman tradition. I simply mean to say here that there may be some specifically Roman Catholic concerns with which I may not deal.

Mind you, there are varieties of positions among what are called Protestants. I will give considerable attention to various pro-gay positions. Whether or not some of those positions are properly called "Christian" will be one of the main concerns of this segment of our discussion. What I hope to lay out before you is what I offer as *the* Christian position. While there will doubtless be matters of interest not dealt with, the conclusions reached ought to be such as to lead all observers to conclude that they express Christian positions on the matters with which they deal.

I acknowledge that there are large numbers of bishops, seminary professors, clergy, and lay persons who *no longer* hold the conclusions to which I have come and for which I shall lay out my reasons in the following chapters. I am aware of that. It is my position, however, that they are wrong.

In anticipation, let me note some things that I have concluded. Then I will ask you to follow the arguments for these conclusions to see if they are sound or, should you so desire, to see if you can *reasonably* overthrow them. The arguments that I shall take up in this section are these:

1. The Bible does have a theology of sexuality, and it is clearly heterosexual.

2. The Bible does speak specifically about homo-sexuality, and it clearly rejects it on each occasion when it does so.

3. The Bible has a massive concern for sexual morality, arising from God's concern for the well being of people. The extent and nature of the expression of this concern is supportive of the general rejection of homosexuality.

4. The Bible has a theology of an ordered creation, and a number of physical facts taken in conjunction with the belief in an ordered creation are also strongly supportive of the rejection of homosexuality.

Realize that this argument is not purely scriptural, and the reader might find my facts in error. The reader may, for example, wish to argue that the vagina and the rectum are really *not* different structures physiologically, or that the differences are not meaningful, but then that would be his or her task to argue.

The reader will doubtless have noticed that, at each point, I spoke of what the Bible would have to say. Even Protestants may, in some manner, at least in some traditions, consider other evidence. Among Methodists, for example, there has arisen something called the Wesleyan Quadrilateral. I shall, later, deal more with this, but the reader needs to know that many of the attempts to use other interpretive schemes are, shall we say, "creative" and often seem to be attempts to obscure truth, not reveal it. Furthermore, there is *no faithful* Protestant tradition that does not accept the word of scripture as authoritative when it is clear, and the attempts to declare it unclear in this matter are generally logically unsound. Finally, it is a common touchstone for all Christian traditions. Even our Roman and Eastern brothers and sisters, who may have a faith in tradition, or clergy, or one particular bishop, or the church in council which we Protestants do not precisely share, do still themselves revere the Bible and, I think, would find clear argument from it compelling.

However, I shall deal, slightly, with other sources of Christian instruction. I shall also deal, in short space, but as a matter of considerable importance, with the authority of the Bible, *and* the serious questions that a reflective reader should answer if he wishes to deny the authority of the Bible.

Before that, there is one other question to which I should like to give an answer: Why should the reader be concerned with "a Christian position" on homosexuality? Why worry about what God says? Why should the reader even wish to look at the question: Is Homosexuality Holy?

Chapter 4:

Why Make Any Moral Considerations?

"Holiness" refers to something in accord with the will of God. Why does it matter? Why does God's opinion matter? Perhaps it does not.

Rudolph Otto in *The Idea of the Holy* attempts to evoke the sense of the transcendent, something like the "wholly other" of Barth. He specifically seeks to draw attention away from "holy" as a moral quality. I adore his concern for an awareness of a transcendent God, but I confess that here I am indeed dealing with a moral quality. The reader may say he does not wish to deal with such a quality. Fine, but then he must forswear the right to speak of any right or any wrong; and that, I think, he is not willing to do. So then, we deal with one approach to determine the moral. Deal with it for a moment, before you try to claim another approach.

Do you believe in God? Most Americans say they believe in God. Some say, "Everybody's got to believe in something; I believe I'll have another beer." Our notions of God may be fairly fuzzy, and many may mean no more than that they believe "God exists" when they say they believe in God, which is a grossly inadequate understanding of Christian belief, but it is a place to start.

Ninety-three percent of Americans say they believe in God, in some way. (Barna, 1992, p. 74) Seventy-three percent say that "God is the all-powerful, all-knowing, and perfect Creator of the universe who rules the world today." (Barna, 1992, p. 74) If you believe in God, certainly if you believe in God with the kind of understanding held by 73% of Americans, then by virtue of that alone, you ought to be concerned with God's opinion on any matter on which you could discern it. Nearly all people, at all times, in all places have believed in God in some sense, in something or some things supernatural. The modern, Western world is an anomaly in terms of human history. While granting that much of Europe may be even more agnostic than we, over all we are on an historic low period in terms of awareness of and belief in God. Still, even in our slough, the great majority of Americans believe in an all-powerful, all-knowing, and still ruling Creator God. Those who believe in such a God ought to be concerned about what He thinks. AND others ought to ponder this fact that so many people here and now, and so many others in so many other places at so many other times have believed in this God whose views many are now ready to discard casually.

Let us suppose that you are still quite comfortable in your rejection of the idea that God exists. Think that through. First of all, be quite sure now, are you ready to say that God does not exist? If you are, then consider some further thorny problems. You might read Phillip Johnson's *Darwin on Trial* or *Reason in the Balance: the Case Against Naturalism in Science, Law & Education*, but I don't want to argue the matter with you now. I want to ask you questions. If you deny God, don't try to assume moral constraints or explanations of worldly realities buttressed by a God in whom you say you do not believe; be consistent.

If there is no God, where did the world come from?

If there is no God, where did order in the world come from?

If there is no God, upon what basis do you assert that *anything* is right or wrong? Oh, go back over that one. Don't try to say, "Well, every body knows x, y, or z." First of all, they don't. Second, they don't agree. Third, why should they? Try it again: Upon what basis do you assert that anything is right or wrong? Convenience? But it might not be convenient for someone else. Convention? But conventions vary, and they also fade when the force that gave birth to them is abandoned. Majority? But the majority has often been wrong too. Indeed, the majority has sometimes been corrected, but not because there was no standard to which to call it! Might? Ah, there you have it. "Might makes right," is not a new saying, but is it true? And can you live with it?

"Why, the very idea of right and wrong is old fashioned and false," you might wish to say. Really? "Yes. Whatever is, is good." Okay. Then, by that standard, war is good, famine is good, murder is good, disease is good, gay is good, but so is gay bashing. If "everything is everything," then nothing is really anything, and anything goes, but, you know, you really may not like just where it goes.

If you say there is no God, then you say that you know better than nearly all people in nearly all times. Then you say that nearly all Americans now are fundamentally wrong about the most important things. Then you say that God, since He did not exist, according to you, did not deliver Israel from Egypt, did not raise Jesus Christ from the dead, did not raise up the Church, has not changed history, has not brought healing to people, has not changed lives, and has not established any right or wrong. Then the early Christians who died for their faith were fools. Then Augustine and Aquinas and Luther and Wesley were fools. Niemoller and Bonnehoffer were fools to risk their lives to oppose Hitler for a God who does not exist. The list of persons whom you now declare fools, is really quite long, if you say there is no God. If you say there is no God, then you say there is no standard, no right or wrong, or no right and no wrong. If you say there is no God, then there is no purpose, no hope, no direction, and no meaning – all these are but words to express vague feelings to which we mere human animals, by your understanding, falsely ascribe reality and importance, words which have no more real meaning in our lives than they would if applied to the cockroach or an amoeba. Unless....

If you say there is no God, but you find that you cannot tough it out with the disorder that declaration brings with it, then you might make one "slight" alteration. You might say there is no God but you. You are God. Is that what you really want to say? Can you really live with that? Is that a role you think you can handle? Do you think such a claim by you is reasonable? Makes sense? Can be defended intellectually? Would be appealing to other people? Would lead to a better ordered life on earth? That is not a new thought either. It is as old as Satan. You as God? Do you really think you are up to it?

Alright, dear hearts. If you want to claim there is no God, then do your homework and think through the consequences of your conclusions. Can you live with what that would mean? I don't think you can. You can live with it, uncomfortably and fretfully, only because you assume benefits derived from beliefs by others that you deny, and even then, only for a season.

Richard Dawkins in *The God Delusion* says that he can. (Dawkins) He says that the fact that he can look forward to having lunch is equivalent to a faithful Christian looking forward to eternal peace with God in heaven. First, I think that is a trivial and enormously superficial attempt at disparaging humor. Second, he speaks as one who knows not, but who knows not *that* he knows not. Even so, he ought to realize that those who disagree with him here mean a good deal more than he seems to realize. Furthermore, he consistently acknowledges that his explanations of the existence of many things are wildly improbable, but he alleges that since, as he also alleges, his theories are less improbable than theistic theories, his are to be declared correct, but the lesser improbability of his theories is supported only by his assertion, and not by any evidence he presents. "B" is wildly improbable, acknowledges Dawkins, and in fact his "B" goes against various established physical laws, requires belief in many things never seen, and regularly contravenes things which are seen, but, since he declares "A" to be impossible (declares, mind you, not proves), then, he says, we must prefer his theory, and since we must prefer it, then we must also declare it to be proven. I find him neither intimidating nor persuasive. Indeed, I understand that his recent work is not much applauded even by his own tribe. (McGrath) I trust that the average reader will be less blinded by Dawkins' "religion," or *a priori* assumptions, than is Dawkins.

Here I argue that there are good reasons for believing that there may well be a God, and if there is it may well be important to know His will about things if it can be known. It does not establish that the Christian God is God, nor that His will can be known, nor what His will is with regards to homosexuality. I hope to do some work with these themes as we continue.

Chapter 5:

Why Consider the Christian Position on Homosexuality?

Sometime in the reign of Chairman Mao, oh, it must have been in the '60's, it was determined that sparrows ate a great deal of grain. Feeding the people was an important goal. The sparrows ate grain. Therefore, a large campaign to kill sparrows should be begun. At Chairman Mao's direction, it was. Many sparrows were killed. However, after a season, it was discovered, the sparrows ate some grain, but they ate far, far more bugs, and these bugs ate far, far more grain. Now that the sparrows were killed, the bugs were not. More bugs meant less grain, and more hunger for the people.

It is true that I think all people should be Christians. I believe that Jesus Christ is the way, the truth and the life, that no one comes to the Father but by Him, that He is the very image of the invisible God, but I want to speak to people who do not believe that just now. Is it still possible that there are reasons why one might take seriously "the Christian position" on an issue even if one were not a committed Christian? It's possible.

If Christianity is responsible for some significant things that the reader finds good, admirable, valuable, or helpful, then it might be the case that the reader should not casually dismiss a system of thought which has brought him things that he finds good. You don't want to "jump out of the frying pan into the fire." You don't want to "kill the goose that lays the golden eggs." You don't want to "cut off your nose to spite your face." You may not want to be like a child who rejects the reasonable discipline of a parent and, being upset or petulant or childish, "runs away from home" only to find great trials in the "wide world." You may not want to kill off all the sparrows until you know if they eat more bugs than grain. You may not want to write off Christianity if there is any good that has come from it. If, of course, there is anything good which has come out of Christianity. Is there? Oh yes.

Now there are many works written to "lead people to faith in Jesus Christ." I will mention some of them, but that work is not what I want to do here. There are other books meant to equip Christians to support their faith. That also is not my goal here. Lee Strobel has written two fine books in this vein: *The Case for Christ: A Journalist's Personal Investigation of the Evidence for Jesus* and *The Case for Faith: A Journalist Investigates Objections to Christianity*. I recommend them. Read them. I found C. S. Lewis' *Miracles* and *Mere Christianity* very helpful some years ago. By all means, read them. A recent, slightly more heady work than some is *Why I Am a Christian: Leading Thinkers Explain Why They Believe*, edited by Norma L. Geisler and Paul K. Hoffman; fine, read it. Josh McDowell has written in this field for years. Read his *Evidence that Demands a Verdict* and *Evidence that Demands a Verdict Volume II* and *Answers to Tough Questions: What Skeptics Are Asking About the Christian Faith*. Paul Little also has written *Know Why You Believe* and *Know What You Believe*. These are all useful, but my goal here is more limited.

I want to argue that there are some things that you do now believe to be profoundly good, that are the result of Christian influence upon human history (I would prefer to say "the result of the Spirit of Christ at work in the world," but I fear that would sound too churchy to the dear reader's ear), and that in light of this you might want to take another look at the matter of homosexuality from a Christian perspective, just in case there was something of value there too. That is the burden of this small chapter.

It was many Christmases ago now. My best friend in the neighborhood was a Jewish guy who married a non-practicing Catholic woman. She loved to decorate at Christmas. She had a beautiful tree, shining, brilliant and many other decorations. My neighbor's relatives had no particular place to go on Christmas day. After all, they were Jewish and did not celebrate Christmas, but the rest of the world was at least nominally Christian, everything was pretty well shut down on Christmas, everybody else had family celebrations, and they had no particular place to go, so they went to Ernie's. (That's not his name, but it will do for this little story.)

Ernie and I sometimes exchanged modest gifts at Christmas, a plate of cookies, a bottle of wine, something. I went over to his house with something-or-other, and he introduced me to his relatives (maybe I met them a time or two before at Christmas). Then he invited me to stay and chat a bit. I did. At some point in the conversation, a younger sister of his told why she fell away from going to synagogue right after Hebrew school. She said that among the prayers the students were taught was one that said something like this: "I thank Thee, God, that I was not born a slave, a gentile, or a woman." To her, being thankful for not being a woman was not encouraging. I think I told them a little bit of what I am going to tell you, but hesitantly and oh so gently. After all, I do place a high value on being a good guest and so I was not there to twist anybody's arm. Although maybe I want to twist yours just a little.

Every Protestant kid (Catholics too?) who ever warmed a pew for very long has heard what I am about to tell you. Paul, once a prominent Rabbi himself, wrote a letter to the church at Galatia. In what has been marked as the third chapter, verse 28, he said, "There is neither Jew nor Greek, there is neither slave nor free, there is neither male nor female; for you are all one in Christ Jesus." People have been saying the prayer my neighbor's sister was taught for a long time. Paul was speaking with that prayer in mind. He wanted to say that for those who were now in relationship with Jesus Christ there was now a relationship that transcended and was altogether more important than these other three socially very important relationships. I contend that the Spirit of God, let loose in the world through the work of Christ, has profoundly affected these relationships in ways that virtually all my readers would say are beneficial. The great reduction in slavery that we find in the world today is a result of the work of Christ. There is in Christ a capacity to transcend ethnic barriers. Imperfect? Oh yes, but the imperfection is not new; it is the striving for perfection which is new in human history. The status and welfare of women has been enormously improved by the effects of the Christian faith. If there is truth to these assertions, and I say there is, then the abandonment of Christianity is perhaps something not to be taken so lightly.

In the Old Testament, it is clear that slavery of a brother Israelite or fellow believer in Yaweh was not good, even if accommodated. (See Leviticus 25:39 ff.) In the New Testament, it is much clearer that everyone is at least potentially a "brother," and thus the seed of the idea that slavery is wrong was planted. (See Galatians 3:28, but also II Corinthians 5:17, I Corinthians 12:13, and Ephesians 6:8) The New Testament church did not urge the outlawing of slavery. In a world where the majority of persons were slaves, the instant abolition of slavery would probably have been incomprehensible and surely seen as a threat to the whole society, but the church did clearly argue that slaves were of equal spiritual worth, itself a revolutionary idea. In Philemon, Paul is arguing for a slave owner to set free a runaway slave whom by law he could have killed. It is the spirit of that argument which was to prevail, with much travail and across much time.

Christianity was responsible for much increased manumission of slaves in Roman times and much improved conditions (Latourette I, 1975, pp. 245-246). The spirit of the Christian faith continued to work improvement in the condition of slaves and work towards the abolition of the slave trade and slavery throughout the middle ages (Latourette I, 1975, p.558). It was an evangelical Christian impulse which led to the abolition of the trade of African slaves and then of slavery itself in most of the western world. (Latourette II, 1975, pp. 948-949, 1019, 1032, 1200, 1228, 1250, 1269, 1279, and 1336. See also Pakenham, 1991, p. xxii and p. 117. See also Davis, 2006, pp. 231-267, Thomas, 1997, pp. 449-590, and Simms, 2013, p. 257 and pp. 145 ff.) Yes, others not particularly Christian joined in, and some stoics had objected to it, but it was a Christian movement that had effect, eventually. Slavery was endemic throughout the world. In Africa, it was a Moslem and African institution. That Christians joined in was not new; that some among Christians came to object to and oppose the business and the institution of slavery was. Of course, you know that there remains slavery today, of black Christians and fetishists by Moslems in the Sudan, and to a lesser extent in Mauritania, and to some extent of various peoples who come to Arabic lands as servants only to find themselves enslaved. Christians do not have clean hands, because we all grow slowly in Christ, but it is from the Christian faith that the impetus to end slavery has come, and not from any other spiritual source.

"Greek" stands for all the other people around them, all who were not Jewish. To say that in Christ there "is neither Greek nor Jew" is to say that in Christ there is no difference between one ethnic group and another. Have Christians ever failed to live up to this ideal? Oh, of course. Anyone who says otherwise should be met with gales of laughter. But there is nothing unique in ethnic strife. That is common. That is universal. The Greek term for foreigners is the word from which we get our word "barbarian." It was used because it was thought to imitate their speech, "bar-bar-bar." In other words, all non-Greeks just made nonsense sounds and did not really have a language. In more than one language, the words for the group that uses that language means "the people," implying that others are not people. Group identity and ethnic strife are universal. It is the ideal of a relationship in Jesus Christ that can transcend such barriers that is new, revolutionary, consequential, and very good. It is a commonplace that the ability of Christianity to give people of various ethnic groups a new identity in a time when their ethnic identities were weakened by the conquest of their local regime and incorporation into the Roman Empire was one of the reasons for the growth of Christianity.

We speak of Hinduism having a "caste" system. We use the word "caste" because we have taken it from the Portuguese word "*casta.*" However, the Hindi word so translated is "*varna,*" and it literally means "color." Apparently an Aryan people conquered a Dravidian people and they organized people by a color code. There was some mixing over the centuries and there is much more to Hinduism than this one feature, but it appears that the "caste system" is very much a system to keep people "in their place." Not so many years ago, the Vice President of India was an untouchable; he dedicated a monument in some place; and immediately after he left, the persons of a higher caste went and washed off the monument since they understood the vice president to have defiled it by his presence. Christianity has an attraction to some untouchables in India because, in part, it says that they are persons of sacred worth too, that all persons are. Not every faith system quite says that.

Have there been ethnic related conflicts among persons who were supposed to be Christians? Absolutely. But conflict is the world norm. What is different is that among Christians there is this notion that this really shouldn't be so. America is a flawed but good example of the Spirit of Christ at work in just this way. Surely there have been conflicts, and some remain, but the remarkable thing, the thing that is different from most times and places, is the degree of unity. Surely the reader knows that the Ainu have not felt welcomed in their homeland of Japan. Surely you know that Koreans are not highly esteemed there either. Surely you know that the Han Chinese do not always look with affection upon the Turkic peoples of their western regions. Surely you know that the Montangards of Vietnam were not always highly esteemed by the majority. Surely you know that there are tribal peoples in India, Myanmar and Thailand who feel uneasy in their minority status. Surely you know that each rival independence movement in Angola, of which there were three, represented a different tribe, or ethnic group. Surely you know that Rwanda, Burundi and the Congo have been convulsed by ethnic slaughter. The list could go on. Ethnic animosity is an ancient problem, and exists not only in ancient times. It is not a peculiarly Western, or Christian, or American problem. What is peculiarly Christian is a discontent with this strife. What is peculiarly Christian is an ideal that it ought not to be so, and out of that ideal has arisen the impulse to eliminate ethnic hatred and the slaughter to which that impulse has given birth; and also, with all their flaws, this impulse has given birth to such things as the United Nations, the World Court, and numerous secular "helping" organizations which have their inspiration and model in Christian missionary activities across the ages.

Something does not come out of nothing. Not even ideas. It is not the case that "everybody just knows that." It is not the case that "every thinking man agrees." The sentiment that ethnic hatred is wrong is now held by many, but it was largely birthed by the faith that says that in Christ "there is neither Greek nor Jew."

Women. Is any argument needed? Please, dear reader, survey the world in your own mind. Where are wives burned to death at their husbands' funerals? This has been so in India, in very recent times, in the pagan north of Europe many centuries ago, but not in lands that once were in some sense a part of Christendom. Where are women covered head to toe? Where are they not allowed to leave the house? Not allowed to be educated? Not allowed to work with the skills and abilities that God has given them? This has been so in many times and in many places, but it has been in lands touched by Christ that things have much changed. And those lands with few who call themselves Christians have also been much influenced by the values of the nominally Christian lands. There may well be excesses and follies within the movement called feminist, and there may well yet be flaws in the treatment of women in those lands influenced by Christ, but no reasonably honest observer can deny that women live better, live longer, have more opportunity, and breathe more freely in lands affected by Christianity.

It is a pernicious falsehood that Christianity is opposed to science. It is a commonplace among our elites, but it is untrue. Christianity gave birth to science! Alfred North Whitehead is no Christian, but he points out some useful things. You do not look for order in the universe if you do not think that order exists. Many faith systems did not think there was order. What Whitehead calls the Judeo-Christian worldview did. It is a Biblical notion that this world is made and ordered by God. That idea had consequences. You do not look for order in the world if you think this world does not matter, and the highest good, and only real good, is to escape it. God looked over all His creation, according to the Judeo-Christian view, and he said it was "Good." (Whitehead, 1953) Not all belief systems have believed these things, and it is not in all places that the scientific method has arisen. There have been great discoveries in many places. Paper, printing, and gunpowder are a few of the contributions of China to the world. But a methodical procedure, and an expectation that methodical inquiry would bear fruit, that is a western invention. If that is so, and there is much evidence of it, it may be that this goose that lays so many golden eggs should not be summarily killed. As the title of Richard Weaver's famous book says *Ideas Have Consequences*.

Scientism is not science. There is much that is promulgated by persons who are professionally some sort of "scientist" but who speak on matters that are not under their purview as scientists. They are quite at liberty to have their own belief systems, but to claim as a scientific conclusion that which is only an assumption, or a postulate, or leap of faith, is to be dishonest. So, dear reader, do not suppose that everything any "scientist" says is science. It often is not. And some of them are not strong enough to resist taking advantage of the idolatry with which some persons sometimes bestow on those called "scientist." Just as a rock star may be corrupted by adulation, so also may be the scientist who speaks *not as* a scientist but with the mantle of "the scientist." If the cobbler cannot stick to his last, at least he should acknowledge that he is no longer making shoes.

Have there been those in Christendom who have opposed something which has turned out to be sound science? Of course. So what? If you think occasional obscurantism remarkable, you are not very knowledgeable of the failings of mankind. The allegation of peculiar Christian opposition to science is ignorant. Consider Bryson's *A Short History of Nearly Everything* or even John Gribbin's *History of Western Science*, and the reader will find that the initial rejection of new ideas is a common *human* failing, most emphatically also among scientists. The overarching

Christian distinctive is belief in the presence of a godly truth to be pursued even in the face of difficulties. It is a commonplace among scientists that a new view often does not so much win converts as wait for the former leaders to die off. Take a larger perspective. Where has science arisen? Among peoples of what faith? Is it possible that is not mere coincidence? I think so.

Max Weber is perhaps most famous for his contribution to the Weber-Tawney Thesis, relating Protestantism to the rise of capitalism. (Weber, 1958; Tawney, 1954) He has written extensively on various topics within the sociology of religion. He, Weber, points out that industrialization is very much hindered by a caste system in which persons of one group cannot even stand to have persons of another group walk by and cast a shadow over them or over their food. He also notes that enterprise is hindered by a cultivated disdain of useful labor, and a religious commitment to long fingernails which shows that you are superior since they prove that you could not do any manual labor. (Weber, 1963) So then, it would seem that our economic development must owe some substantial debt to Christianity.

It is probable that many readers prefer the material comforts of our age to those of prior centuries. I am told that the wine froze in winter on the table of Louis XIV, the Sun King of France, in the Palace of Versailles, because, unless you were directly in front of the fireplace, there was no heat. I understand that in this most magnificent palace, there was no plumbing, and, it being a large place, there were six thousand chamber pots to empty each day, a great encouragement to the business of perfumes.

Do you know that all of the charters of the thirteen original colonies of the United States declared their authority founded in God? Do you know that for much of our history, we have seen ourselves as a "city set on a hill," as very consciously a Christian experiment? Do you know that we had established state churches in three states after the bill of rights was adopted? The last one to be disestablished was in Massachusetts in 1833. Did you know that our Declaration of Independence speaks specifically of our Creator? Did you know that the Treaty of Paris of 1784, by which

Great Britain acknowledged our independence, begins, in an oversized hand, "In the Name of the Most Holy and Undivided Trinity"? Did you know that throughout the sixteen hundreds, seventeen hundreds, and halfway through the eighteen hundreds, virtually all schooling in America was in the hands of the clergy? Did you know that, while our nation was founded in a time of relative spiritual decline, compared to the times just before and just after, our founding fathers still regularly spoke of the possibility of democracy working only in a godly land, of the need to teach the Bible, of the need to live by the ten commandments, of the need of Christian faith? Is it possible that there is some relationship between our having been a Christian land and our having been successful at setting up a democracy?

Where do you see democracies? What faith system have they come out of? Christian. Yes, there have been some democracies which have arisen after World War II which are in non-Christian lands, but as a rule of thumb, the more successful a country has been as a democracy, the greater had been their prior involvement with a Christian country. Is it possible that the ideal of the sacred worth of each person, a view not held by all faiths, is necessary for democracy to work? Is it possible that values such as honesty, truth telling, honest weights and measures, which are, ideally, to transcend nuclear family and clan and race, simply because "you must be holy," and, which are espoused in part by some others, though not by all, are important for the successful functioning of a democracy? Is the lack of such a faith in some societies a factor in the difficulty with "nation building" which the United States has encountered in recent years?

None of these are offered as adequate reasons for faith in Jesus Christ as your personal Lord and Savior, although I proclaim Him such, and urge you to give Him serious consideration as well. However, here my only task is to suggest that Christianity is not without some fair claim to a number of virtues, and that the wise citizen might be well advised to consider its wisdom on homosexuality before rejecting it out of hand. I submit that a historical survey will support the claim that Christianity has been significantly responsible for: 1) the abolition of slavery; 2) the improvement of opportunities for women, children, and all persons less able to fend for themselves physically; 3) an increased ability for people to transcend ethnic barriers; 4) the rise of the scientific method; 5) the rise of industry; 6) the ideal of universal education, and 7) the rise of democracy. I submit that these are things without which very few would wish to do. For these reasons, it might be appropriate to consider the Christian view of a matter before rejecting it out of hand.

One more thought in this vein. The whole of western history and much of world history for a century or two is really incomprehensible without a serious knowledge of Christianity. Oh, one can have some superficial knowledge of some things, but have no capacity to understand what a thing means or where it came from or what it might lead to or what similar things have looked like elsewhere. I'm all for studying Wittfogel or Wittgenstein, and I am fine with studying Levi-Straus and Malinowski. One can derive some benefit from Freud and Fanny Hill, from Tirso de Molina or Rabelais, from Li Po, Tu Fu or Tao Yuan Ming. But the idea that one can understand western civilization without thinking deeply on Christianity is shallow, and mistaken. It is a common idea; it is also wrong. True, as a Christian, I think that each person at some point must do more than think; one must also submit, must come to say to Him, with Thomas, "My Lord and my God," but I do not ask that now. However, I do ask that you consider this "goose" that lays golden eggs a bit, before you try to kill it. Perhaps you will find it still has some things of worth to say.

Chapter 6:

Is It Even Legitimate to Consider Anything from a Religious Perspective?

Well, of course it is, but in recent times in America, there has been a great hue and cry raised about the alleged impropriety of viewing or discussing matters through a religious perspective. It is more specifically alleged that religious considerations should not have any influence in moral judgments, social policy considerations, or, most importantly, law. This is ignorance and bigotry.

The prefix "re" in religion means "again" or "again and again," as in return (turn again) or revolve (turn around again and again). The root of the word lig- relates to our word for ligament, and it refers to that which binds things together. It comes to us from the Latin *religo, religare*, which meant to fasten or bind, and came to refer to scruples and commitments. So, "religion" is that basket of ideas by which one makes sense of things in general. It answers such questions as these: Where do we come from? Where are we going? What do we do while we are here? What is our purpose in life? By what principles should our conduct be guided?

There are those who falsely allege that they have no religion and that they only speak from scientific fact. First of all, that is nonsense. No one does that. They are only deluding themselves. Secondly, note that it is an exceedingly common custom for each proponent of each new idea to say that theirs is the best, and that it is qualitatively different from its preceding alternatives. We Christians tend to say that pagan religions had myths, while we have truth. Now I may believe that, but our saying it is a part of a common pattern of promoting one's own belief system. More kindly, perhaps, Moslems tend to say that Judaism was a somewhat good oasis in the bleak desert of life; Christianity was a slightly better such oasis; but Mohammed rode on and found not a mere oasis, but the true city, and all ought to join him there. Increasingly in the twentieth century and continuing, there are those, including some nominally among the Christian tribes, who say Christian notions, just like prior pagan notions, and all other religious notions for that matter, are all also myths! These are simply our peculiarly western human ways to attempt to assign meaning to something and to sort out how we can or should live. From Darwin's time there have come others, bolder still in this area, with their *alternative religious notions*! But their notions are also religious, however much they attempt to claim a scientificity, which they do not have.

They answer the question, "Where do we come from?" with the answer "Nowhere," or "From a primordial soup of basic elements" (the origins of which they cannot explain), or "From some infinitely dense and infinitely small bit of energy, which at some point, for no reason, and with no outside direction or input, turned *instantly*, at some point in time, into billions and billions of planets, solar systems, and so on." But these are only theories. They are not provable. They are their postulates, perhaps, or, better still, these are their articles of faith, but they are not scientifically verifiable, and they have no particular reason-based claim to one's faith.

Their answer to the question "Where are we going?" is "Nowhere," or, perhaps, for some, "To be recycled as our bodies rot and help to fertilize the ongoing trees, flowers and grass." But again, this is at best a theory, not a demonstrable fact.

Their answer to "What do we do while we are here?" is problematical. Because there is no overarching moral authority in their religious system, pretty much anything might be okay, and reasons for any one action being better than another will have to be made up "on the run," so to speak.

It is a common practice for a disputant to try to find some succinct way in which to invalidate an opponent for some perceived flaw. If he can do that, then he can save himself the difficult work of really thinking through his opponent's ideas. But many who seek to claim the title of scientist do, by no means, work *as a scientist* when they make sweeping claims about the true nature of the world. They may be philosophers, if you prefer, they may or may not be insightful in one or more ways, they may be good or bad, and they may be true or false, but they often speak in areas wherein they are not being scientific: they are not then acting *as* scientists.

In recent years, after World War II, American courts have been increasingly eager to bar any *public* discussion of religious notions on the basis that our Constitution forbids the Congress from making an "establishment of religion." An "establishment of religion" is what one sees in many countries of Europe and in many Moslem lands where the state does have a state supported, official religion. We never have. However, we did once have establishments of religion in various states after our Constitution was in effect. We have had government supported chaplains in circumstances where required employment might make difficult one's regular attendance at worship (in the military, for example). We have freely employed religious institutions to serve government desired ends (in teaching and social work, for example). And such things were initiated by the very same Congress that proposed the first ten amendments to our Constitution, including the prohibition on an "establishment of religion." Therefore, much of the current reading of the unacceptability of religious life in the public square is *not* based on our Constitution but on the waning Christian faith of our social elites, or perhaps more accurately, on their slow conversion to a new paganism.

Now then, drawing upon the influence of such new directions in our legal discussions, some social commentators have attempted to try to bar any consideration of any matter *with which they did not agree* on the grounds it was religious and that no matter could properly be evaluated from any religious perspective. One could have a religious opinion, they might say, but only if you kept it to yourself! But, of course, they are never consistent. It is a moral sentiment to disapprove of bullying, a very fine one, but that is a moral, and thus religious, issue. It is a moral value that tells us not to disparage persons for no good reason, such as their ethnicity, also a fine value. One point here is that these anti-moralists are so only when and where it suits their current fancy. A second point here, and one more important, is that they are still arguing from a religious perspective, which is quite fine, but they ought to realize and acknowledge that they do that and they ought not to be quite so quick to disparage others for doing that which they so regularly do themselves.

Christians do make extraordinary claims; they have always acknowledged that. Based upon our understanding of our guidebook, the Bible, we conclude many things about these basic questions. Shortly I shall share with the reader some of what I think our guidebook says about certain aspects of sexuality. *In a later section*, I shall present massive quantities of evidence which I think tend to confirm the wisdom of our guidebook. My point in this section is that *everyone* does in fact *have* religious ideas. They may be fuzzy or clear, they may be right or wrong, they may be helpful or not, but *everyone*, in many areas of life, speaks *from their own religious* perspective, and thus it is hardly unreasonable to consider a religious perspective.

Chapter 7:

Why Use the Bible to Make Our Moral Considerations?

It is of value to consider the Bible because it is a source of authoritative teaching for all Christian denominations. It is reliable, in the authenticity of current copies, and in the accuracy of that which it records. It is a source accessible to all persons. Its contents are rather clear on the matter before us. It is the primary source of authority for persons in the Protestant denominations. It is a book that has massively influenced and given shape to the development of western civilization in general and American society still more especially. It is the book which once was, and still ought to be, foundational for the education of all educated persons in the English speaking world. I also say that it is of God.

Once upon a time, when my finances were fairly flush, I got a set of *The Oxford Illustrated Dickens*. Then, from time to time, I would pull down one of the volumes and read it. One time I pulled down *Nicholas Nickleby*. Each volume has an introduction by a person of, presumably, some note. This one had an introduction by Dame Sybil Thorndyke, of whom I had never heard, but whom I thought it probable was an actress, from some of her comments. I noticed some other things in her comments. She spoke of Naaman the leper (Thorndyke, 1987, p. xii), a Syrian general who went to Elisha to be healed (II Kings 5:1-19). Then I noticed that she also spoke of "irredeemable evil, and the badness that is only human," a character who seems "the incarnation of sin," "real Evil," (p. vii), "this warning from God to the children of evil," "it is the Christian attitude – hate the sin, love the sinner, but do not tamper with the Evil one," (p. viii), "the Saving Grace," (p. xii), and more. She did not argue *for* anything particularly Christian; she *assumed* a general knowledge of the things of which she spoke. She did not explain *them*; their use explained what she was saying about

Dickens' book, and she could rely upon a common store of knowledge of the Bible as a means by which to do that.

I came to find out that Dame Sybil was an actress of considerable note in the earlier part of the twentieth century. She toured America in a Shakespearean repertory company from 1903 to 1907, in 1914 she became attached to the "Old Vic" company in London, she played Hecuba in *The Trojan Women*, and Joan of Arc in *Saint Joan*, among other roles, and was made a D. B. E. (Dame Commander of the Order of the British Empire) in1938. True, her father was the Reverend A. J. W. Thorndyke, a canon of the cathedral at Rochester, therefore, she may have been more thoroughly acquainted with the Bible than some of her peers, but not so very much so. Other introductions in this Oxford set of Dickens make use of the common store of Biblical knowledge upon which one could once rely, a common store that is now almost entirely gone.

That alone is a loss. Among an educated few, a knowledge of classical literature once also served at least the purpose of providing a common store of references by which to make thoughts more readily known, but that body of knowledge was never so broadly known, nor so educational, nor so intimately related to the society in which man lived, nor served so many purposes, as the Bible. McGuffey's readers were full of the Bible. The flyleaf of Webster's dictionary was full of verses. All English speaking public speakers knew, and made reference to, the Bible. *The* book in every American home was the Bible, and the second most widely owned book was Bunyan's *Pilgrim's Progress*. Under the authority of the somewhat deistic Thomas Jefferson, the Washington D. C. school board, of which he, as President, was then chairman, had two texts in its classes: the Bible, and the hymns of Isaac Watts, read for their theology. In our day, our education has not *pro*gressed; it has *re*gressed. We have suffered a great decline. We have *no* common language by means of which to speak of moral issues. Having disdained the Bible, we have vastly less knowledge of God, of man, of rise and fall, of the consequences of actions, or of the sweep of time. We not only have less knowledge of moral truth, we have less awareness of it as a category of concern. To suppose that the snippets of blather from the anthologies of passing fashions with which we have replaced the Bible in our educational institutions is progress is ludicrous, risible, and contemptible. No doubt many are the readers who think that we should not construct anything, but only deconstruct. Many suppose that, since there is no truth, why, any lie will do nicely – so long as it accords with our momentary impulses. Yet I am hopeful that there remain those who think there may be such a thing as truth, and that if there is, then it is worth seeking and knowing and doing, and it is my hope that this diatribe may shake the modern, or post-modern, reader's confidence, in *his* pieties, enough to at least consider mine. Of the eight reasons I gave for a consideration of the Bible in my opening paragraph, I have now spoken to number seven.

Number one was that the Bible is authoritative for all Christians. I have argued that above, or rather asserted it. I do no more than that here. It is a commonplace. Though our Roman and Eastern brothers and sisters may raise up other authorities beside it in ways that discomfort Protestants, they also place great store in the Bible.

Number two is that the Bible is reliable, in copy and content. We have more extant ancient copies of the Bible than we have for any other similarly ancient document. Time and again, debunkers who have thought to undercut the reliability of the Bible have been unhorsed by new archeological discoveries. Science is not an enemy to faith; good science is one of the many defenders of the faith! Soldiers in the twentieth century won battles based on statements given in the Bible! "Scholars" declared that Moses must be a myth because there was no writing in his times, only to be proven false by the discovery of whole libraries nearby, centuries before Moses' time. "Scholars" declared that the gospel of John must be a late second century document, responding to a Gnostic writer of that century, only to have a portion of the gospel of John discovered, in Egypt, and dated to between 95 and 125 AD, long before the Gnostic writer and thus establishing the time frame the church always claimed for John. There is an ocean of such evidence; a few of the islands in this ocean are noted in the bibliography. (Barclay, 1975; Keller, 1981; Strobel, 1998; Strobel, 2000; Bettenson, 1975; Wilkins and Moreland, 1995)

Number three is that the Bible is accessible to all persons. There are many who make arcane arguments from various historical sources. By means of these things they attempt to say that what appears to be obviously one thing really is not that at all. Generally, this is not true. This poor scholarship can be overturned, too, and I shall point out some of its flaws, and I shall note others who deal more extensively with such flawed arguments, but one goal of the dealers in such material is to try to make things sufficiently murky, unclear, or uncertain, so that people who desperately want to maintain a lie can more readily do so. One virtue of the Bible is that it *is* comprehensible. I shall argue *about* it, but I shall also argue *from* it, and in that endeavor, the reader can join.

In point number four, I declare that the Bible really is rather clear on homosexuality. That is a matter that shall be one of the burdens of the next several chapters. Let the reader decide.

In argument number five, I have stated that the Bible is uniquely authoritative for Protestants. First, that is simply true. Second, that is known to all persons knowledgeable in the field. It arises in fair measure from Luther's doctrine (doctrine simply means "teaching") of *sola scriptura*, Latin words which mean "scripture alone." Protestants were called "Protestants" because they protested certain abuses in the church of the day. Some who shared many goals of reform remained within the Roman Catholic Church; others did not. Many things we in the Protestant tradition have felt were errors were justified upon the basis of the *magisterium*, or "teaching authority" of the church, which claimed some special authority apart from and not subject to scripture. In an attempt to escape errors arising from what were felt to be no more than personal opinions, the Protestant tradition has generally followed Luther in looking to scripture for authoritative and definitive teaching on all matters essential for life and faith.

Wherein there are creeds, among us Protestants, they are generally viewed as summaries of faith which are bound to and can be argued from scripture.

You know the old adage that "figures don't lie, but liars can figure." Well, it holds true in many fields. Among Methodists there has arisen something called "the Wesleyan Quadrilateral." "Quadrilateral" means "four-sided," and this system of "doing" theology asserts that Wesley used four kinds of input ("four sides") in his theologizing: scripture, tradition, reason and experience.

First, this system did not come from Wesley. It came from Albert Outler, a very able John Wesley scholar. Second, it is substantially true that Wesley did take these four things into account when he reflected upon the things of God! Indeed, I would say that, in some sense, anyone must! Having said that, let me say that Wesley never used them the way many "modern Methodists" have often used them.

With regard to these four elements, as Wesley used them: First, scripture was first and foremost and, when clear, final! When scripture was clear, that was the end of it. Scripture was *never* one among equals, not even first among equals; it had no equal for Wesley. He, who was an Oxford don, read most extensively in many various languages, and wrote many volumes, declared that he was "a man of one book," and that one book was the Bible.

Second, tradition meant "tradition of the early church," or "tradition of the church since the early days of the church." If scripture was ambiguous on the role of a bishop, for example, but they had been around in some form roughly as known at his time since the early days of the church, then it could be supposed that their use was consistent with the meaning of scripture since that use overlapped the earliest knowable days of the church. (By the way, I confess that this is an interesting choice of example since Wesley came to feel a need to re-think how bishops are made, but when he did so, he did argue it from scripture.) Nowadays, "modern Methodists" will speak of "traditioning," by which they mean "making your own traditions." But when you make your own, they ain't traditions! Reverend So-and-so may have a "tradition" of cruising the red light district, but that is not what Wesley meant by consulting tradition.

In passing, let us note that the tradition of the church has been in solid opposition to homosexuality. Despite Boswell's attempt in his second book on this subject to claim the acceptability of homosexuality for a season, that thesis is simply without foundation and is everywhere debunked, by gay and traditionalist scholars alike. (DeYoung, 2000, Licata, 1981, Mondimore, 1996)

Third, reason was never something in opposition to scripture. Largely, "reason" meant reasoning *from* scripture and *about* scripture. Surely illustrations could be drawn from the natural world, but it was to illustrate biblical truth, never to oppose it. Wesley never saw that "reason" was opposed to biblical truth, nor do I. It never is! When it is so used, it is not true.

Fourth, "experience" did not mean just any sort of experience. It meant experience of life in Christ. After one came to new life in Christ, one often found that things that had not previously made sense now did. After I began working in a church, there came a time when I recognized that I had a conflict with a secretary at the church. From my background, I had learned to deal with conflict by ignoring it! By being very nice to the conflicted one and hoping the problem would go away! That wasn't working. I sat at my desk in the office at church and tried to figure out what God would have me do. I gathered that He would want me to speak with the woman and try to reconcile whatever the problem was. I did not want to. I saw all sorts of reasons why that might not be good, but it was clear to me that that was what God wanted. I thought of all the things that I had done that might possibly have offended her, three of them. I went to her and apologized if any of these three things had offended her; sure enough all three had. We reconciled, and became good friends. Then, I had some experience of new life in Christ in that area. I have prayed for people and have seen physically inexplicable and beneficial things happen right after prayer in Jesus name. That is another kind of experience in Christ. When your "heart is strangely warmed" or you are "lost in wonder, love and praise," then you may have had some Christian "experience." But if it is "your experience" that doing the right thing is hard and therefore you want to change your definition of "the right thing," well, that very likely is not *Christian* experience. Don't forget, as we leave this digression, that, with Wesley, if it is clear in scripture, that's it.

Point number six I have argued in some measure above in my discussion on the influence of Christianity in the world. Why do we have twelve members of a jury? Because, there are twelve tribes in Israel. Washington, Adams, even Jefferson and Madison, Lincoln, Martin Luther King and legions more could not possibly have been the people they were had it not been for the role of the Bible in their lives and in the lives of the society around them.

Point number seven I spoke of when I began the story about Dame Sybil Thorndyke. Whether well or ill, I have made my point there.

Ah, point number eight: "Of course, I would also say that it is of God." You don't? Splendid, but I still have something for you. If you do not say the Bible is authoritative, very well, let us pursue that. What, then, is? If the Bible is not authoritative, what is? Is anything? Let's suppose that you say that nothing is authoritative, but, you see, you don't really believe that. No, however much you may say it, you do not believe it. Do you in actual fact ever make pronouncements on right and wrong? Do you? Come on now; try to be honest. If you do, then you are presuming that something is authoritative.

First, some of you may want to say that you really do not think that there is any right and wrong, but that is nonsense. No, no, I am not disputing here the point itself, although I would do that too, I am disputing the idea that you even believe it! Do you never descry world hunger? Slaughter in Burundi? Traffic jams? High prices for energy? "Those awful kids"? "Those awful police"? "Those awful whatever"? If you do, then you are presuming to find fault with something, or someone, or some thing. And to do that *is* to declare something wrong. Upon what basis do you do so? If not the Bible, then what? "Well, it doesn't have to be the

Bible," you may say. Fine, but then what? It is not a trivial question, it is not unimportant, and it is not inconsequential.

What is your authority for declaring something good or bad, right or wrong? State it. Then apply it. Is it consistent, or, rather, can you be consistent in using it? Does it cover the ground you need to live life? Poke around in a few different areas. Does it still work? As you apply it, do you find you are actually using the standard(s) you have previously stated, or are you importing new "principles" as you go? If the latter, what does that say about your moral system? At the moment, I am not objecting to some other standard, I am simply asking you to find out what standards you are actually using, where they come from, how they work out in practice, if others are likely to find them appropriate, and so on. If you discover that you are importing all sorts of bits and pieces as you go, don't feel like the Lone Ranger; people do that all the time, but that doesn't mean it works very well. Many "Christians" do the same thing. They say they use the Bible plus "X," or "Y," or "X, Y, and Z." But what that ends up meaning is that they use "X," or "Y," or "X, Y, and Z" as their authority, and not the Bible. Just know what "X," "Y," and "Z" are all about, whatever they are. You may not find them as tidy or agreeable as you had thought. One more question.

Do you discover that in the process of discerning your standard(s), you in fact make yourself to be "God"? I had a poster in my garage once. It said something like this: There are two foundational facts of human existence: 1) There is a God, and 2) You are not Him. Of course if there is (were) no God, then the job is (would be) open. Can you fill it? Do you want others to fill it? Do you want everyone to be his or her own God? Do you think there might be any problems with that? Reject my standards, if you like, but then do some fairly serious reflection on what standards you intend to use. You see, I suspect that many people want to continue to draw the benefits of a moral code they want to scorn. I don't think it works that way. Not for very long. Give it a thought.

Chapter 8:

Notes About the Literature that Deals with the Christian Faith and Homosexuality

(If you are pressed for time, this is a good chapter to skip.)

The first prominent work that attempted to support a pro-gay position on homosexuality was by Derrick Sherwin Bailey in 1955, *Homosexuality and the Western Christian Tradition*. (Bailey, 1955). It was a serous attempt to overthrow the Christian consensus that had long been held on homosexuality. While it caused something of a stir at the time, I don't think its message gained great currency then. More recently a man largely followed Bailey and got great mileage out of his work. I speak of John Boswell and his 1980 book called *Christianity, Social Tolerance, and Homosexuality: Gay People in Western Europe from the Beginning of the Christian Era to the Fourteenth Century*. (Boswell, 1980) Boswell was heavily and favorably reviewed in the popular press. I recall that the *Newsweek* reviewer was much taken with Boswell. I also recall that an article in *The New York Review of Books* fairly thoroughly debunked his history, though I was quite upset that the author did not debunk his philology. Specifically, his work with Greek words that can be used to refer to homosexual acts is a study in special pleading. In fair measure, it is arguments from these two that I will address; especially in my chapter dealing with the specific scriptures which are generally thought to disallow homosexuality.

There are others who have written in this vein. L. William Countryman has written *Dirt, Greed, and Sex: Sexual Ethics in the New Testament and Their Implications for Today* (Countryman, 1988), Martti Nissinen has written *Homoeroticism in the Biblical World* (Nissinen, 1998), Robin Scroggs has written *The New Testament and Homosexuality* (Scroggs, 1983), and Letha

Scanzoni and Virgina Mollenkott have written *Is the Homosexual My Neighbor: Another Christian View* (Scanzoni, 1978). I am afraid I do not recommend any of these works for their reflection or faithfulness. In my opinion, unless the reader is engaged in considerable research in this field, she or he can safely omit most of this body of work. However, it is easy to get parochial, provincial, narrow, or blind. Therefore, the moderately serious student of this subject no doubt should read at least some of the works from this pro-gay perspective in order to be sure that he or she has been exposed to their thoughts and that his or her rejection of their arguments is his own, and not merely borrowed from another. Unless the reader has a profound personal, emotional need to find their conclusions satisfying, I don't think he will.

There are several Christian works which I do recommend that deal with the kinds of materials to be considered in this section: *A Strong Delusion: Confronting the "Gay Christian" Movement*, by the ex-gay Joe Dallas (Dallas, 1996), *The Complete Christian Guide to Understanding Homosexuality*, by Joe Dallas and Nancy Heche (Dallas, 2010), *Straight and Narrow: Compassion and Clarity in the Homosexuality Debate* by Thomas E. Schmidt (Schmidt, 1995), *Homosexuality: Contemporary Claims Examined in the Light of the Bible and Other Ancient Literature and Law* by James B. De Young (De Young, 2000), and *Homosexuality and the Christian*, by Mark A. Yarhouse (Yarhouse, 2010). Each of these works does a number of things well, and I recommend their consideration. The De Young book is pretty well definitive in the area of word usage and other ancient literature that reflects upon the meaning of scripture.

Both Schmidt and De Young place much heavier emphasis on marriage than I do. I think that marriage is a profound symbol of the image of God and of God's relationship with the church in general, and Christian people in particular. I also think that marriage is a great blessing and a great means of fulfillment, and even normative for human beings. An ex-lesbian friend of mine told me, some years ago, of the new things she was learning in her then recent marriage to an ex-gay whom she met in ministry. I rejoice in that for her, and I do not doubt the joy and the meaning for a moment. Nevertheless, and having said all that, I still think there is more to being male and female than procreation, and even more than marriage. I have found some marriage focused discussions consider too little the plight of the homosexual and deal too shallowly with the many important elements of marriage, which, of course, means "heterosexual marriage." I do not claim to have a grand statement that puts all in order here; I merely note a modest disagreement in tone.

Our Roman brothers and sisters tend to put a high emphasis on procreation in marriage. That is the reason why they find contraception so objectionable; it willfully interferes with what they believe to be an essential purpose of God in marriage. And they have the support of Genesis 1:28, wherein God said to mankind, "Be fruitful and multiply." We in the Protestant tradition rejoice in the procreative ability, but tend to find that Genesis 1:26-31 was a more general statement, and that the material in Genesis 2 is more specific and developed, and upon that basis look to Genesis 2:18, wherein God said that "it is not good for man to be alone." Thus, we tend to view the personal completion as more of the essence of marriage. For that reason also, we tend to be less discomforted by the use of contraception, something which prevents conception, and view that as an altogether different matter from abortion, an act which terminates the life of a child who has been conceived.

Pro-gay theorists will try to undercut arguments that emphasize procreation with the argument that a consistent application of such a principle should bar people beyond the age of conception from marriage, and people who intend to use contraception or in some manner wish to avoid having children should also be barred from marriage. It is assumed, and rightly so here, that their traditionalist opponents will not like that conclusion, and then will be weakened in their hold to anything unique about male-female unions. There are a number of rejoinders that one might offer to such pro-gay argumentation, but in some ways it is beside the point. While I personally emphasize the sense of completion of each, which heterosexual union offers to each partner because of their bringing their unique male and female contributions to the marriage, my primary concern here it to try to discern God's will regarding homosexual ideation and conduct, and that can be done without answering all the secondary arguments into which one might wish to go concerning marriage. God has a theology of sexuality which is clearly heterosexual. I'll take that up next.

Chapter 9:

The Bible Has a Theology of Homosexuality, and It Is Clearly Heterosexual

In the first chapter of the first book of the Bible, basic statements about the creation of the universe by God are given. Several things relevant to our discussion are stated or implied there:

1. God is. (Genesis 1:1)

2. The universe did not exist before God created it. (Genesis 1:1-2)

3. God created the universe. (Genesis 1:1 and 3-31)

4. A part of that creation was the creation of human beings (Genesis 1:26-30)

5. Mankind was a key or unique part of God's creation. Mankind and only mankind was made in God's image. (Genesis 1:26-27) Mankind was given dominion over all the other creatures. (Genesis 1:28) Mankind was given the fruit of the land for food. (Genesis 1:29)

6. The creation of mankind, along with the rest of His creation noted in chapter 1, or Genesis, was declared "very good." (Genesis 1:31)

7. **And in the original creation of mankind, He created them "male and female."** (Genesis 1:27)

8. **It is apparently male and female <u>together</u> which reflect, or most fully constitute, the image of God.** (Genesis 1:27)

If the reader wishes to contend that God does not exist, and should the reader's contention be true, which, I claim, it is not, that would undercut the weight of the discussion here. We have dealt with that contention elsewhere, and we are not going to deal with it again. However, if the reader has imported that thought into his reactions to these reflections, then please note what you are doing and do think through the consequences of your denial of God.

Alternately, if the reader wishes to contend that his "God" does not really know what He is talking about, or was just not up to modern levels of understanding "back then," then the reader should know that he has declared a faith in a very weak and limited God. That is not the standard definition of God. That is not my definition of God. And that is not a biblical understanding of God. It may be an attempt by the reader to maintain some claim to faith in God while not actually having such a faith. In any case, the reader needs to be clear about the eviscerated "God" he has created and, again, think through the consequences of his own "faith system."

If the reader wishes to claim that the Bible, while being a pretty good book, or one useful book for moral reflections, or some other such limited entity, then again the reader should realize that we have dealt with reasons for consideration of the Bible elsewhere. We are not going to do that again, and, also again, the reader needs to realize just what authority he or she is granting to the Bible, and just what authority or authorities he or she has chosen to put in its place or above it. The reader must realize that he cannot reasonably declare the Bible to be without real authority in one place and then presume to claim it has real authority in another. He cannot readily claim to speak at some other point, on some other matter, upon the authority of the Bible, when he has denied its authority here.

I have laboriously reviewed these considerations since it is my experience that persons often wish to speak unclearly, or without acknowledging the assumptions they have made and not working through to the conclusions which would follow from their unacknowledged principles, and I wish to diminish such confusion.

I am quite content with the reader rejecting my principles, if he clearly sorts out his own, since I am persuaded that he will then find difficulties which will, at length, push him back to mine. Now then, whether you personally and truly accept this principle or merely accept it for the moment as a working hypothesis, we will proceed with the assumption that the Bible, if clear, can speak to the subject with which we deal.

I reiterate point 7 and 8 made above. Point 7: God made them male and female. Again, assuming that the Bible expresses the mind of God and assuming that God knows what He's doing, then it is relevant to note that God made them "male and female," and not "male, female, gay, lesbian, bisexual, transgendered, and questioning" (LGBTQ), which list includes the customary pro-gay litany of alleged genders. These verses in Genesis would strongly suggest that in so far as these *additional* categories of "gender" actually exist, their existence was not a part of God's creation. Please, do not suppose that I wish to trivialize the deep feelings of sexual identity which these terms hold for some people, but at the moment, the task is to discern what theology of sexuality, if any, is declared by the scripture. Genesis 1:26-27, says that the division of human beings into male and female is a key and essential part of God's plan and mankind's creation.

In my Point 8, I declare that what Genesis 1:27 says would suggest that male and female together do in some way constitute a reflection of the image of God, which neither male alone, nor female alone, nor male and male, nor female and female, would so constitute.

This passage would further suggest that there is the likelihood that males in general and females in general bring to creation some unique qualities necessary for the expression of God and for the fulfillment of God's purposes in creation.

This would further suggest the possibility that men and women need interaction with each other in some way or ways for their completion, that man may not be fully man without some interaction with woman, and that woman may not be fully woman without some interaction with man, or that in one or more ways, each may not fulfill God's purposes for them without some interaction with the other. Other scriptures may or may not reflect upon this matter in some way, but these are reasonable inferences from the material in Genesis 1: 26-31.

Chapter one of Genesis gives an overview of creation. The first three verses of chapter two speak of the institution of the seventh day as a day of rest. The remainder of chapter two, verses 4 through 25, deal with the creation of humankind more specifically. This is an extraordinary devotion of attention to human beings, and this devotion of attention implies a radically different understanding of the importance of human beings in the mind of God than that which is held by some other faith positions. For our purposes, the focus on Adam and the arrival of Eve is key.

All the other creatures were brought to Adam (vv. 19-20), but none of them were satisfying (v 20). Adam went through goldfish, and hamsters, and frogs from a nearby canyon; he went through parrots and pythons and cats and dogs. They were all fine in their way, but they were inadequate to fulfill the man. So God made for Adam, Eve (vv. 21-22). And then Adam said, "Wow! Thanks, God. Uh, hi, hi, Eve? My name is Adam, would you, uh, like to have a malt or something, and maybe take in a movie, or we could just have a Coke, that would be okay. I mean just if you'd like to." And mankind was off to the races.

Take another look. In verse 18, "The Lord God said, 'It is not good for man to be alone.'" There we have a problem. Man surveys the animal kingdom. That is good in many ways, but it does not fulfill man's need. We are told in verse 20, "But for Adam, there was not found a helper comparable to him." So the problem remained and had to be solved. The solution was Eve. The solution for man's aloneness was woman. The means to complete and fulfill the life of the man was a woman. Again, you may wish to reject God, Christianity or the Bible, but this is what the Bible clearly says. The solution for Adam was not another Adam, and the purpose for Eve was not to find another Eve.

This is extremely clear. This is foundational. In chapters 1 and 2 of Genesis, we have a description of God's original intent. It is not until chapter 3 that we get to "the fall," a description of the broken condition of mankind, a description which is sketched out in chapters 3 through 11, when God will begin to intervene in history to start work on a plan to restore human happiness and well-being, or to "save" them. There is nothing before these two chapters. There is nothing after these two chapters that overturns the things said in them as an expression of the ideals of creation.

Many try to create a false dichotomy between the Old Testament and the New Testament. While it is true that some things in the Old Testament are not clearly understood until seen through the mind of the New Testament, both remain authoritative. If one wishes to dismiss some things in the Old Testament, as indeed we Christians in some ways do, then one must have some clear authority in the New Testament by which to do this. With regards to these ideas: 1) that God created two sexes, male and female, 2) that it is the two together which constitute the image of God, 3) that fulfillment for each is to be found in the other, 4) that it is a union of man and woman which is ordained, and 5) that this union is especially holy – all this is reconfirmed in the New Testament, and by Jesus Christ.

Jesus said, "From the beginning of creation, God 'made them male and female.' 'For this reason a man shall leave his father and mother and be joined to his wife, and the two shall become one flesh'; so then they are no longer two, but one flesh. Therefore, what God has joined together, let not man separate," as is recorded in Mark 10:6-9. These words of Jesus are also recorded in Matthew 19:4-6. This is a fairly clear statement. Jesus is quoting Genesis chapters one and two. His words are recorded in two different gospels, and most people consider Jesus Christ to have the authority to define the Christian faith, even some bishops and seminary professors.

The primary task of many contemporary intellectuals often appears to be the use of their intellect to obscure truth and not to reveal it. One of their devices is to dash from one point to another, hoping to keep clear attention from any one point, sensing that to allow close attention to a point is to lose the argument, and so I am sure that many will wish to rush to chatter about divorce. After all, these words of Jesus are set in a discussion of divorce.

One pro-gay clergywoman of my acquaintance said that the Bible said that divorce was wrong, she was on her third marriage, and she was an ordained minister, therefore, that proved that homosexuality was okay! I suggested to her that perhaps the church was too cavalier about divorce. There are several flaws in her argument.

First, even if the church did not handle divorce well or consistently, that would not mean that there was no statement about homosexuality here in Jesus' words. Second, the church does not declare divorce a good, but rather some portions of the church declare that persons who have been divorced may be able to deal with their past sins, learn from them, repent (which means "turn away from") that which was wrong (which is what "sin" means), and grow in Christ. Such repentance and restoration is offered to all persons, including persons who engage in various kinds of sexual sins, as well as many other kinds of sin. Thus, for example, a person who had been in homosexuality could repent of it, and be at one with God quite as easily as one divorced. Third, there is a difference between repenting of sin and reveling in it. Now, dear reader, there are answers to *every* complaint the proponents of homosexuality would offer, but if we are to run after every one of them, it will be difficult to keep the pieces of the main argument in order, so I shall not always make such digressions, and, please, do not let possible side chatter deflect your attention from the main arguments.

Genesis one and two and the words of Jesus in Mark 10 and Matthew 19 make it abundantly clear that God's plan was for human beings to be male and female, and for male and female, at least potentially, to be in relationship with each other in ways not intended for male with male, nor female with female. If there were nothing else in scripture about our subject, from these verses alone, one could reasonably conclude that *hetero*sexuality was God's plan, that homosexuality was at the very least beside the point, or that homosexuality was less than a fulfillment of God's intended plan, and possibly an abomination and contrary to God's plan, or a perversion of His intent - again, assuming you accept the Bible as an authoritative expression of the will of God. If you do not, then do your homework about your own "god" or "bible" and the consequences of your rejection of God, Christ and the Bible.

There are hundreds of positive references to heterosexual marriage in the Bible. Of course there are numerous references to various sexual sins. After all, as Genesis chapters 3 through 11 point out, the human condition is fallen, or troubled. As the scriptures also state "all have sinned and fall short of the glory of God." (Romans 3:23) However, there are numerous references to the benefits of marriage, references that imply it is good and a blessing. There is *no* such kind of statement for any homosexual relationship. The only general discussion of homosexual relationships are those among the people surrounding the Israelites, which are abhorrent to God's people and which they are absolutely to eschew. The only specific instances of such activity are revealed as occasions for the destruction of an entire community. (See Genesis 19 and Judges 19 both of which will be discussed later.)

Some of what must be discussed in this book is unpleasant to consider, and it is disagreeable even to make reference to some pro-gay arguments to which I will now make reference. There are those who assert that the relationship between David and Jonathan and that between Jesus and John were homosexual. This is rank nonsense, and there is no evidence for it in the text. This assertion arises not from any evidence but, apparently, from the need of some to grasp at any straw, however imaginary, and the obsessive sexualization of so many things that now pervades segments of our culture.

In mourning the death of his friend Jonathan, David did say, as recorded in II Samuel 1:26: "I am distressed for you, my brother Jonathan; you have been very pleasant to me; your love to me was wonderful; surpassing the love of women." The same word used in this context for "love" is also used in describing God's love for Israel. Do you wish to argue that God had carnal relations with Israel? It is used of many different kinds of relationships. It refers to affection. While it may be used to refer to a relationship in which there could also be carnal relations, such as a husband and wife, it is not to intercourse that the word refers, but to affection. The attempt to imply that any relationship of affection must involve sexual intercourse is wrong, and possible only because so much of our contemporary culture is debased. It is only a relatively recent development in our culture that such an argument could have been conceived, for it arises, not from the text of II Samuel, but from three other things: 1) the elevation, perhaps deification, of sexual intercourse in our society; 2) the devaluing of all relationships not involving sexual intercourse; and 3) a profound need on the part of those who argue it to escape the truth of scripture.

Much the same can be said of the argument for Jesus and John. There is nothing in the text that gives rise to such a thought. Yes, Jesus did spend more time with Peter, James, and John. That means nothing, as anyone who has ever spent more time with some friends, or co-workers, or students, or mentors than with others can readily attest. Yes, John came to be known as "John the beloved," but that nickname was in no way related to John's sexual activities, but to the graciousness he displayed in his gospel and letters. It was in years after Jesus' death when he acquired a reputation for a loving spirit. During Jesus' ministry on earth, he was known as one of the "sons of thunder"! He was a loudmouth, not a lover. To reason as the proponents of homosexuality do here, you must suppose that when we are told to "love one another," that means to "have sex with one another." This may say something about the mind of the disputants, but nothing about the text of scripture. Furthermore, in each case, to argue for such unholy relationships, one must entirely ignore the social code of the societies in which David and Jesus lived, the fact that it was unalterably opposed to homosexuality.

We have the clear words of Genesis one and Genesis two and the words of Jesus in Mark 10 and Matthew 19 and many other passages consistent with those words that make the point that *heterosexuality* was and is God's plan. We have the supporting evidence of hundreds of *clear* positive references to *hetero*sexual relationships and *no* such references for any other sort of sexual relationship. From this evidence, I submit that the Bible has a theology of sexuality and that this theology of sexuality is clearly heterosexual.

Chapter 10:

A Note on the Word "Sex"

The English word "sex" comes from the Middle English word *sexe*, which comes from the Old French word *sexe*, which comes from the Latin word *sexus*, which came from the Latin word *secus*, (Webster, 1967, p. 1663) which came from the Latin verb *seco, secare, secui, sectum*, meaning "to cut," or "to divide" (Simpson, 1968, p. 541), as reflected, for example, in our English word "section." "*Sexus*" means "the state of, or specific qualities associated with being male or female," or "those belonging to one sex or the other." (*Oxford Latin Dictionary*, 1982, p. 1751) "Sex" refers to the fact that human beings are <u>cut</u> or <u>divided</u> into two sexes. "Sex" means "male and female."

The word "heterosexual" is a tautology. Its prefix is redundant. "Sex" means "heterosexual." In a sense, there is no need to use the word "heterosexual" since whenever it is used, the word "sexual" could be used alone. The word "heterosexual" is of later coinage, arising *after* the legitimation of the word "homosexual," which will be discussed later. However, since the word "homosexual" has gained currency in the last century, there is now a need to use the word "heterosexual," even though it does nothing more than re-iterate the meaning of the root word "sex."

Words are not necessarily magical. To know the etymology of a word is not necessarily to know its "true meaning" as currently used. However, to know a word's origins may be instructive. Language can, and often does, reflect truths about man or life or the world. The word "sex" refers to the fact of the division of mankind into male and female. There is such a thing as *a*sexual reproduction in some other creatures. An amoeba, for example, just divides, but that refers to a circumstance in which there is not a variation into male and female of the members of a species. The root meaning of the word "sex" necessarily refers to the differences between male and female and to reproduction by means of this male with female coitus. Whatever the word "homosexual" means, it is not exactly "sex." Whether it is good or bad, it is still not exactly "sex." Whether or not this fact is significant (signifies something), or is meaningful (has some relevant meaning), or is important (is a fact of some weight, or import), it is a fact that "homosexuality" is not "sex."

The word "sex" is not in the Bible, but then there are many words not in the Bible. The Bible was written primarily in Hebrew for the Old Testament, and in Greek for the New Testament. Every language slices up reality differently. While the word "sex" is not in the Bible, the idea of sexuality that is conveyed in the origins of this word is. This particular point about language is *not* compelling evidence that the understanding of the biblical theology of sexuality is "heterosexual," as I have argued above, but it is suggestive and does tend to confirm that that understanding is a reflection of something perceived by Latin, Old French, and Middle English cultures as well as by ours, and by the Hebrew and early Christian cultures as well. And, of course, the scriptures in Genesis one and two, in Mark 10:6-9, and in Matthew 15:18-20, and many other passages, do speak clearly of a biblical doctrine of heterosexuality.

Chapter 11:

There Are Several Specific Scriptures That Clearly Reject Homosexuality

There are seven passages in scripture that specifically condemn homosexual conduct: Genesis 19:1-28, Leviticus18:22, Leviticus 20:13, Judges 19-22, Romans 1:18-32, I Corinthians 6:9-10, and I Timothy 1:10. There are five others that condemn certain specific homosexual activities: Deuteronomy 23:17, I Kings 14:24, 15:12, 22:46, and II Kings 23:7. There are a number of passages that condemn homosexual activities by implication, of which nineteen are noted here: Deuteronomy 29:23 and 32:32, Isaiah 1:9-10, 3:9, and 13:19, Jeremiah 23:14, 49:18, and 50:40, Lamentations 4:6, Amos 4:11, Zephaniah 2:9, Matthew 10:15 and 11:23-24, Mark 6:11, Luke 10:12 and 17:29, Romans 9:29, II Peter 2:6, and Revelation 11:8.

I will deal most heavily with the first seven passages mentioned, in the order in which they appear in the Bible. I will consider some of the pro-gay arguments that attempt to undercut traditional understandings and give the reasons for the conclusions that I draw from them. In the course of dealing with these passages, I will also deal with some material in Ezekiel 16, which some erroneously claim undercuts traditional interpretations of the Biblical view on homosexuality. I shall deal with the groups of five passages on homosexual temple prostitution in a group, and with the nineteen that use "Sodom" as a by-word either for evil or for judgment as a group.

Before we continue, let me point out that here we are trying to find out if the Bible views homosexuality favorably or unfavorably, or is neutral. We are dealing with the biblical view on homosexuality; we are not dealing at this point with any possible response to persons who engage in it, nor to societal actions that might or might not relate to the matter. In so far as we do that, we shall do that at a later point. I make this note here because I find that many persons commonly jump from the apparent rejection of homosexuality that we shall discover in scripture to conclusions about *either how we should* respond, *or* how it is *supposed* that some would have us respond. Some try to jump to an exceedingly ungracious presumed response in the hope that, because the presumed response is unacceptable, the conclusions in this section will be rejected. Others may jump to an inappropriate response because they have not thought through the issue of a response upon a Christian basis. However feebly I may do so, I will sketch out some elements of a response in a later section, not here, and the reader should not let those considerations influence his reading of the arguments in this section. Do these passages indicate a rejection of homosexuality, or not? That is our question for the next several pages. At each passage, I invite the reader to get out his or her own Bible and read them over to see if my conclusions seem sound or otherwise.

The story of Sodom and Gomorrah is the first one that shows God's rejection of homosexuality. It is found in Genesis 19, and it is a story of the destruction of a whole community because, at least in significant part, of its practice of homosexuality. It is from this biblical story that the English language has long used the words "sodomy" and "sodomite" to describe homosexual conduct and those who engage in it. That this is properly so understood has been disputed in recent decades.

In Genesis 18:20, the Lord says of Sodom and Gomorrah "their sin is very grievous." However, it may not be clear there what "their sin" is. The Lord tells Abraham that He plans to destroy Sodom and Gomorrah. Abraham argues for God to spare the cities for the sake of some who are righteous. It is agreed that if even ten righteous persons can be found, the cities will not be destroyed: then begins the story in Genesis 19. Two angels come to Sodom at evening. Lot was apparently a man of prominence in Sodom, for he was sitting at the gate when they came, as was the custom of the men of some prominence. Lot went to the visitors and asked them to stay at his house. There were very few, if any inns at that time, and offering visitors his hospitality was the proper thing to do. They, being polite and independent minded reflections of this time, at first declined, but as Lot pressed his invitation, they accepted. Before they could get to bed, "the men of the city, even the men of Sodom, compassed the house round, both young and old." (Genesis 19:4) The men of the city said, "bring them [the visitors] out that we may know them." (v. 5) Lot went out to speak to the men, shutting the door behind himself. (v. 6) He said to them "do not so wickedly," (v. 7) or more colloquially, do not do such a wicked, or evil, thing. Next, Lot offers them his two virgin daughters in an attempt to placate the crowd. (v. 8) The townsmen start speaking ill of Lot, descrying his judgmental attitude toward what they want to do. (v. 9) The angels then pulled Lot back in, struck the townsmen blind, never gave up the daughters, and told Lot and his family to get out of town for they are going to destroy it. (vv. 10-13) After Lot had a chance to get his family out of town, the Lord destroyed the city. (vv. 24-25)

The traditional understanding is that when the townsmen said they wanted to "know" the visitors, they wanted "carnal knowledge," that is, to have sex with them. Bailey in 1955 (Bailey, 1955, pp. 2-3) and Boswell in 1980 (Boswell, 1980, pp. 93-94) have argued that that was not it at all. The men were visitors to the town. They simply wanted to "know" who they were. They note that there are hundreds of uses of the Hebrew word used here for "know," the word *yada*, and that very few of them are used to mean "to know sexually," therefore, Bailey and Boswell argue, it was probably not so used here. All the townsmen went to Lot's house simply to find out who the visitors were. They simply wanted to "know who they were." Their actions had nothing to do with desiring homosexual contact.

Is there any way to sort this out? Yes, of course. A number of ways:

1. All scholars accept that *yada* can mean "to have sexual relations with." It is clearly used that way in Genesis 4:1, 4:17, 4:25, 24:16, 38:26, and in several other verses.

2. There is <u>no</u> known use of *yada* with the sense of "to identify an unknown person." To suspect that *yada* is used here to mean "to identify" in this way relies upon supposition from English usage, but such a usage is without support in the Old Testament.

3. In Genesis 37:32 there is the use of a word to mean "to identify a known object." However, this word is an entirely unrelated word, *nakar*.

4. Perhaps there is no other instance of a request to identify persons in the Old Testament. Is that the case? No. In Joshua 9:8, Joshua asked of some strangers come to him, "Who are you?" An interrogative pronoun, *miy*, is used, not *yada*.

5. In Genesis 19, verse 7, Lot said that the men should not do so evil a thing. The evil thing they wished to do was "to know" the visitors (v. 5). If the word here means "to identify," or "to get to know who they are," then that must mean that identifying them was evil. Is that found to be so elsewhere in the Bible? No.

6. Is that because there are no other instances of identifying people in the Bible? No. There are many; one has just been noted in Joshua 9:8.

7. There is no known instance in the Old Testament when a request to identify someone was considered evil, as this "knowing" was in Lot's story.

8. Is there any instance when seeking to find out who someone was is found to be justification for destroying an entire community? No.

9. Whatever is meant by "know" is a matter of very great evil for it was found to be justification for destroying the whole community. Are there other instances of destroying an entire community in the Old Testament? Yes, there is one that is similar, but that also deals with a

case of desired homosexual relations, as we shall see when we look at Judges 19-22.

10. In verse 8, Lot offers the townsmen his virgin daughters to do with as they wish. That suggests that the townsmen's desires were sexual. Bailey argues that one may try to placate someone with a substitute of a different sort, and thus that this offer of his daughters is not compelling. It is true that one may offer some alternative. A man may offer a robber his watch if he has no money, for example, or a man may offer money in lieu of a beating perhaps. This means that Bailey thinks Lot was offering the rape of his daughters in lieu of the visitors being obliged *to say who they were*. First, do you think that probable? If a policeman were to stop you while driving and ask to see your driver's license, would you offer him sex with your daughter in the back seat instead, rather than show your driver's license? I think not. Second, while one *could* offer a substitute offering of a different sort, it is not altogether a *compelling* argument here. The fact the he offered the men his virgin daughters is still a strong argument in favor of the idea that their desires were of erotic gratification, and the proposed alternative is wildly improbable.

   Lot offered the men his daughters because there was a very high value placed on safeguarding persons who had come under one's protection, and, perhaps, because there was an insufficiently high value placed on women. Do note that the angels did not accept Lot's plan, and they did not allow the daughters to be so used. Lot was only relatively righteous, or righteous for his time. However, Lot's flaws need not obscure God's condemnation of homosexuality here.

11. There is yet more. In verse 8, Lot does not say that his daughters are "virgins." He says that they have not "known" a man. He is using *yada*, the same word used

three verses earlier by the townsmen when they said they wanted to "know" the visitors. It is improbable that the same word would be used with a radically different meaning in so short a space.

12. In the similar story in Judges 19, we see *yada* used in an obviously sexual manner in Judges 19:25, where it says that the townsmen who do take a man's concubine in lieu of "knowing" him, "knew her and abused her all night." As a result of this "knowing," she died. I think it unlikely that she died as a result of thorough examination of her driver's license. The similar use in a similar situation is supportive of the same meaning here.

13. In Jude 7, the sins of Sodom are identified as "sexual immorality" and "perversion." (NIV) This, too, confirms the traditional understanding of this passage. It is also inconsistent with the idea that the townsmen merely wanted "to identify" the visitors, "to know who they were."

14. In II Peter 2:6-10: The sins of Sodom are characterized as "filthy conduct" (v. 7), and "walking according to the flesh in the lust of uncleanness" (v. 10), which also tends to confirm the sexual meaning of the passage.

In summary, there is no known Old Testament use of the word *yada* for "to identify him." There are several acknowledged instances when it means "to know carnally." There is no instance of destruction of an entire community for a desire to say "Hello" to someone. There is another instance of such similar destruction for a similar desire "to know." There are also other instructions to completely eliminate peoples when they represented a spiritual threat to the community, but never for a desire to get acquainted. The nearby use in v. 8, of *yada* for carnal knowledge of his daughters, increases the likelihood that the use in v. 5 also means "to know carnally," and the desire to have that carnal knowledge was their great "wickedness," evil itself, and the best symbol of their wickedness. I believe that no serious scholar now argues that *yada* in Genesis 18:5 meant "to find out who they were." Indeed, many proponents of homosexuality have since given up this false claim.

It is also claimed by some proponents of homosexuality that the real sin of Sodom was a lack of hospitality. This, too, is untrue. My brother took a trip to Alaska as a young man in 1959. The car he and his buddies were driving in had problems and broke down somewhere between Whitehorse and Fairbanks. Folks driving by readily shoved over their families in the back seat and offered a ride, saying, "We've got plenty of room," when in the lower forty-eight no one would have thought of trying to make room. I suspect that in places where a lack of hospitality is deadly, hospitality becomes a higher value. It was certainly a high value among the peoples of biblical times. Generally there were no inns, no restaurants, few public watering places, and no public restrooms. The custom was to go to the town center, usually by the city gates, and wait for someone to invite you to stay with them. Now let us consider the relevant text in Genesis 19 again. Did Sodom reveal a lack of hospitality? Generally, no, but with one possible exception, which is an exception without a distinction, and with which I will also deal.

1. Lot was a resident of Sodom, and he *did* offer the visitors hospitality, (Genesis 19:1-3), therefore, hospitality was *not* denied the visitors.

2. There is *no* rebuke of Sodom in Genesis 19 for a lack of hospitality.

3. There *is* a rebuke of Sodom in Genesis 19:7, but that rebuke is for the townsmen's desire "to know" the visitors.

4. There is no rebuke of Sodom elsewhere in the Bible for a lack of hospitality. (Ezekiel 16 does *not*, I repeat does not, contain a rebuke of Sodom for a lack of hospitality, and I will deal with that in due course.)

5. There *is* a rebuke of Sodom in Jude for sexual immorality and unnatural sex acts.

6. Now let us deal with the exception without a distinction. If one wishes to argue that the townsmen were "inhospitable" because of what they wanted to do to the visitors, one is quite right. They did not come as the welcome wagon of Sodom to offer a free fly swatter from the local cleaners and two for one coupons to the local pizzeria. However, what they wanted to do that was objectionable, as is quite clearly indicated, was their expressed desire "to know" the visitors. This means that the expressed desire to have homosexual relations with the visitors was abhorrent to God. That this is "inhospitable" is quite right, but that hardly takes the onus off homosexuality in this passage.

Others have argued that the only real problem with the events in Sodom was violence. This, too, is unsound. Again, let us consider the text as we try to determine its meaning.

1. There is no mention of violence in the rejection of the proposed acts of the men of Sodom.

2. There is something explicitly mentioned, and that is of their desire "to know" the visitors.

3. This rejection by Lot of their proposed actions as "wicked" (v. 7) precedes any indication of possible violence by the townsmen. The threat of violence does not arise until verse nine, after Lot's rebuke. Lot, although a foreigner in Sodom was a man of considerable standing there. His brother Abraham had saved the city in the recent past (See Genesis 14). It was not necessarily inevitable that this crowd would threaten violence at the time that Lot rebuked them for their stated desires.

4. The rejection that is given is complete; it is not qualified in any way. Theoretically, had homosexual conduct been acceptable to God, the angels might have said any number of other things: a) "Hey, thanks for coming. We didn't know how to find the gay clubs, and Lot is kind of square. We appreciate your invitation;" or b) "Hey, not so many.

We like gay sex too, but only a few at a time;" or c) "Hey, no rough stuff now. We like gay sex a lot, but we're not really into S and M;" or d) "Gosh, we are the straight angels. The gay angels are coming next week. Sorry, you'll have to wait for them." But they didn't. The stated rejection is of their desire "to know" these visitors, *not* of any *aspect* of that knowing.

5. Violence is common in the Old Testament, but it is not thought grounds for destroying an entire community. There is another occasion when the destruction of an entire community is called for, but that, too, is an instance of offering homosexual acts.

Certainly it is worth noting that virtually the whole town came to their door. That shows the pervasiveness of their sin. Had it not been so pervasive, then God would have spared the town, according to His word to Abraham. (See Genesis 18:16-33.) The presence of the crowd emphasizes pervasiveness, not violence.

Still others argue that the only real problem was that this was rape, that it was not consensual. This, too, is not supported by the text. Heterosexual rape is also abhorrent, as is made clear in Deuteronomy 22:22-29, but homosexual activity *per se* is objectionable. Some of the elements that indicate that are noted below.

1. Why was it not consensual? It was not consensual because it was not acceptable to the visitors. If these visitors had found the activity acceptable, then they could have participated in it willingly.

2. Why was it not acceptable to the visitors? The most probable reason is because it was abhorrent to God.

3. Again, the rejection in the text of their expressed desire "to know" the visitors was complete, not partial. There is no indication that any sort of homosexual encounter would have been acceptable.

4. While the penalty for rape in heterosexual intercourse with a married or betrothed woman is death for the willing party, as indicated in Deuteronomy 22:22-27, the penalty for heterosexual rape of a woman who is not betrothed in Deuteronomy 22:28-29, is a fine to the father and marriage to the woman, not death. In no case is the response the destruction of an entire community, which strongly indicates that the homosexual act *per se* is very objectionable to God.

5. A kind of rape is once used to *solve* a problem. In Judges, an Israelite tribe that has tolerated unacceptable activity is punished by the whole nation, at great cost to the whole nation, but almost to the extinction of the one offending tribe. The one tribe is left with only a few survivors, and no wives. The other tribes had sworn not to give their daughters to them since they had tolerated vile conduct, but now they wished to have compassion on them. They arrange with community leaders for a group of women to be seized by the survivors for wives. Thus no one has "given" them their daughters, and yet the tribe is not exterminated.

The angels of God did not allow Lot's plan of giving his daughters to the townsmen to occur, Deuteronomy does prescribe death for certain kinds of rape, and I am not happy with all aspects of this illustration from Judges 22, but it does serve to reinforce the idea that homosexual conduct *per se* was highly objectionable to God.

Leviticus 18:22 and 20:13 contain perhaps the clearest and most sweeping rejection of male homosexual conduct in the Old Testament. Leviticus 18:22 states: "You shall not lie with a male as with a woman. It is an abomination." (NKJV) and Leviticus 20:13 states: "If a man lies with a male as with a woman, both of them have committed an abomination. They shall surely be put to death. Their blood shall be upon them." Many proponents of homosexuality grant, or at least assume, that these passages condemn homosexuality, but they argue that these passages are parts of an old holiness code that includes things that other Christians generally do not now accept and therefore they are also free to dismiss these prohibitions. I will look at one bishop's more elaborate version of this argument shortly. Some also argue that these prohibitions were for temple use only, and thus, presumably, the same things prohibited here are acceptable if not performed in temple worship services. Mind you, they do not claim this is their personal opinion but rather that it is the meaning of the text. I find serious flaws in both kinds of arguments. As we consider the matter further, bear in mind that the texts do clearly state that the act is wrong, that it is an "abomination," and that it is of such severity that it is worthy of death. There are many things in the Bible that are deemed wrong, not all of them are called abominations, and not all of them are deemed worthy of death.

One bishop of my acquaintance, who has publicly stated his approval of homosexuality, has privately argued his biblical understanding on homosexuality as indicated below. He has stated his general position publicly, and he has acted upon the basis of the following arguments, but at the time he expressed these views in my presence, he requested confidentiality, and so I grant it. Among his unstated, but clearly understood assumptions, were the claims that he did accept the Bible as authoritative and that he was simply arguing from the Bible. His argument went like this:

1. These codes were established in a time of turmoil for the Israelites after the return from exile.

2. There was a great premium placed on re-establishing God's order.

3. That is why there are prohibitions on such things as planting the same field with two kinds of grain and having two kinds of material in one garment (in Leviticus 19:19) and for males sleeping with males (in Leviticus 18:22 and 20:13).

4. The essential element is the establishment of God's order.

5. Since science has shown us that homosexual orientation may be innate, therefore that is a part of God's order.

6. And therefore, he is compelled by scripture to approve homosexuality.

This is quite a chain of reasoning. One problem here is that his argument rests upon several unacknowledged, unproven, and unsound assumptions. It is, as much pro-gay argumentation is, charming in its presumption and demonic in its deceptiveness. Let us deal with his unstated claims and assumptions first. His statement that the Bible was written in a time of turmoil after the return from exile means that he assumed or concluded, though he never acknowledged it, that the Bible was written only after the return from the Babylonian captivity some time after 538 B.C. This means that he *denies* the authority of scripture when it itself claims to have been written at any earlier time. Therefore, it is already clear that he accepts the Bible as authoritative only *when* and *how* he wants it to be. He wishes to exhort action from others, the approval of homosexuality, based upon the authority of the Bible, whose authority he regularly denies, although he did not acknowledge this fact. Now to his arguments in order:

1. These codes were established long before the return from the Babylonian captivity. Some "liberal" scholarship (Or is it "scholarship" I should put in quotation marks?) once claimed (Ah, perhaps both.) that Moses was just a myth, that all of the Old Testament must have been written after the Babylonian captivity since they didn't have any written language in the presumed days of Moses. Since that time, whole libraries have been discovered from times prior to Moses in regions nearby. The primary impetus for the declaration of late authorship for the Old Testament is the temperamental horror of and disavowal of anything supernatural. Since, by these scholars' assumptions, there is no supernatural, then there could be no prophecy and thus anything sounding like prophecy must have been written after the fact. This is an issue with which I cannot

begin to deal fully here, but let me note that it is dissembling to claim an authority you deny when it suits you, and deceitful to fail to note your denial. Many able scholars accept an authorship for Leviticus preceding the time after the Babylonian captivity. However, as to there being turmoil, why, I suppose that might be said to fit nearly any time in Israelite history!

2. You will hardly get a rebuttal from an evangelical Christian about the appropriateness of establishing God's order. However, there are many things in the Bible which speak to God's order in matters sexual; for example, Genesis 1:26-31, Genesis 2:18-25, and Mark 10:6-9. So now our good bishop must ignore the things of scripture that speak most clearly to the theme with which he purports to deal.

3. The matters he cited in Leviticus 19:19 are not called "abominations" (*toevah*), as is the lying of male with male in Leviticus 18:22 and 20:13.

3a. Also, there is no penalty indicated for the offenses of which he spoke in 19:19. The penalty for the adjoining and sexual offense in Leviticus 19:20 is a scourging and a trespass offering. The penalty for male lying with male is death (Leviticus 20:13), a severity which suggests that there may be some important distinction here.

3b. Furthermore, his "solution" to the problem of "outdated" laws is to throw out the whole code. In Leviticus 18:6-18, there are laws about incest. Do we now eliminate all prohibitions on incest? In Leviticus 18:20, adultery is prohibited; in Leviticus 18:21, burning your babies in offering to Molech; and in Leviticus 18:23, having carnal relations with animals. These verses immediately surround the verse condemning homosexuality. Are all these things now to be approved? Such would follow from the good bishop's argument. The same problem presents itself with the verses surrounding Leviticus 20:13.

3c. It is not a matter of each one picking as each one wishes. The general rule has been that Christians are no longer bound by ceremonial and ritual laws, but are bound by moral laws enumerated in the Old Testament. This principle is guided by specific statements in the New Testament, such as that of Jesus recorded in Matthew 15:1-20, where he notes things that are ephemeral and things that are a reflection of the heart of a person and thus are of lasting importance, such as "sexual immorality" (Matthew 15:19), and Peter's vision and experience in Acts 10. Many Christian denominations have specific doctrinal statements dealing with this very issue, such as that in Article VI of the "Articles of Religion of the Methodist Church," which states: "Although the law given from God by Moses as touching ceremonies and rites doth not bind Christians, … yet notwithstanding, no Christian whatsoever is free from obedience of the commandments which are called moral."

Furthermore, the use of "the abominable" in Revelation 21:8 seems to be a quotation from Leviticus 18:22 and 20:13, and thus, is a New Testament reiteration of strong rejection, "for they shall have their part in the lake which burns with fire and brimstone, which is the second death" (Revelation 21:8).

4. Again, we would quite agree that establishing God's order in the world is one of the Bible's concerns, but the good bishop quite ignores what the Bible says about God's order with regard to sexuality, including in the very passages which, theoretically, he is "analyzing" Leviticus 18:22 and 20:13.

5. Now here he shifts to an argument from science. I will deal with scientific matters in a later section. For the moment, let me point out that "innate" does not necessarily mean "congenital." "Congenital" does not necessarily mean "God ordained." AND, it is *not* proven

that homosexuality is innate. Indeed, the evidence shows that the determining factors are environmental, not genetic, although there may well be some factors that are pre-disposing, or not!

If the bishop wished to pursue this line of reasoning, setting aside the actual science of the matter for the time being, he should here acknowledge that he found the Bible to be inadequate on the matter of God's order, and that he felt obliged to look elsewhere for authority. Theoretically, that is an intellectually legitimate exercise. He has failed to note his shift in authority. Further, he has assumed that "innate" meant "God ordained" and "good," which is not necessarily so. If alcoholism is innate, that does not necessarily mean that it is "God ordained" or "good." A clubfoot may be innate, but not good. So his assumption is, at best, unexamined.

6. At this point he is certainly not compelled *by scripture* to approve of homosexuality, although he said as much. He apparently feels compelled by other considerations to reject scripture with regards to homosexuality. That may or may not be wise, and I would say it is not, but while the approval or disapproval of homosexuality is certainly a legitimate intellectual consideration, it is not legitimate to claim that the compulsion came from scripture when it did not.

His argument was more sophisticated than many in this vein. Generally, the argument, for those who wish to make it, runs that we do not hold to some other parts of the old holiness code and thus we cannot feel bound by the parts of it that reject homosexuality. The basic reply is that Christians do not pick and chose at will in this matter but are instructed by the New Testament, wherein, if at all, they may re-interpret the Old. The general cautionary note to be raised, is to ask if one wishes to throw out prohibitions on adultery, bestiality, incest, and child sacrifice as well, since that would reasonably follow from an application of the pro-gay understanding of scripture.

Some argue that the prohibitions on homosexuality in Leviticus are intended to apply only in temple worship. Now this is quite extraordinary and requires a studied avoidance of examining the text. So let us take a look at the surrounding text.

Leviticus 18 begins with: "Then the Lord spoke to Moses saying, 'Speak to the children of Israel, and say to them: "I am your God. According to the doings of the land of Egypt, where you dwelt, you shall not do; and according to the doings of the land of Canaan, where I am bringing you, you shall not do; nor shall you walk in their ordinances. You shall observe My judgments and keep My ordinances, to walk in them; I am the Lord your God. You shall therefore keep My statutes and My judgments, which if a man does, he shall live by them: I am the Lord."'" (Leviticus 18:1-5)

1. God has told Moses to tell this to all of "the children of Israel," not just to those in worship at a given time.

2. God points out that people did things differently in Egypt, not in Egyptian temple worship, but in Egyptian life, but God's people are not to do what the Egyptians do.

3. God points out that the people in Canaan do things differently, not in Canaanite temple worship, but in Canaanite life, but the people of God are not to do what the Canaanites do.

4. The people of God are to do what God wants, to keep God's ordinances, statutes, and judgments, and to walk in God's way.

5. There is every indication that this is about life in general, and not about temple worship.

6. God tells us to do this because "if a man does, he shall live," *not* "if a man does this in worship, he shall live."

There is nothing in the following verses that suggest any narrowing of focus. The admonitions are about things related to life in general, not to temple worship. Various kinds of incest prohibitions are dealt with in verses 6 through 16. It is highly improbable that this is intended to mean one shall not commit these incestuous acts only during temple worship; it is vastly more probable that these are instructions for life. Verses 17 and 18 are guidelines for avoiding grief in the taking of an additional wife. Verse 19 deals with avoiding relations with a woman during her period. Verse 20 reminds one not to commit adultery. Is this to be considered acceptable outside of worship services? Verse 21 prohibits the offering of your children by fire to the god Molech. If you burn your children in the privacy of your own home, but not in temple, is this okay? Verse 22 says that one is not to lie with a male as with a female; it is an abomination. Verse 23 says that one is not to have sexual intercourse with animals. Is one to suppose that there was a serious problem of persons wanting to lie with animals in temple worship?

Again, it seems vastly more probable to suppose that these are guidelines for life, and not just for temple worship, and there is nothing in the text to suggest the more limited focus. The chapter closes with verses 24-30 saying not to "defile" oneself with any of these things. The other nations did these things, and that is why God is casting them out to make a place for Israel: Don't do these things or you may be cast out too. If anyone does these things, they are no longer of God's people and are to be cut off. "Keep My ordinance, so that you do not commit any of these abominable customs which were committed before you, and that you do not defile yourselves by them: I am the Lord your God."

In chapter 20, we have the same set of circumstances. It begins: "Then the Lord God spoke to Moses, saying, 'Again, you shall say to the children of Israel.'" It is not limited to worship practices; it is about life. This time, penalties are prescribed. If Israelites, or a stranger among them, gives a child to Molech (meaning to burn them as an offering to Molech), "he shall surely be put to death" (v. 2). You are not to turn to mediums (v. 6), you are not to curse your father or mother (v. 9), you are not to commit adultery (v. 10), and you are not to commit incest (vv. 11-12). In

verse 13, you are not to lie with a male as with a woman. If you
do, both are to be put to death. Again, there is nothing in the text
that suggests that these prohibitions apply only to worship services.
Such a notion can arise only from a profound need for denial, and
can be maintained only by not reading the surrounding text.

**In Judges, chapters 19 through 22, we have a story with
some similarities to that in Genesis 19, illustrating the horrific
nature of homosexual conduct to the biblical mindset.** A
traveler came to the town of Gibeah, intentionally bypassing
possibly more convenient non-Israelite towns so as to avoid
spending the night with foreigners, non-Israelites. An old man
invites the stranger and his concubine to spend the night with him.
Men from Gibeah, described as sons of Belial (Judges 19:22),
roughly meaning evil minded persons, came to the house and told
the old man to bring out the visitor that they might "know him."
The host goes out to the crowd and begs them not to act so
"wickedly" (v. 23) and calls their proposed acts an "outrage" (v.
23). He offers the men his virgin daughter and the man's
concubine. The crowd is not happy with that. Then the visitor took
his concubine and thrust her out to them. The townsmen "knew
her and abused her all night" (v. 25). In the morning, the woman
came to the door of the house, where her master found her dead.
He cut up her dead body into twelve pieces, distributing one to
each of the twelve tribes of Israel, and calling them to
accountability for what had happened in an Israelite place. The
tribes gather, and try to call the tribe of Benjamin to account for
what has happened among them, asking them to surrender the
"sons of Belial" responsible for this. Benjamin refuses, and there
is war between Benjamin and all Israel. Israel suffers greatly, but,
at length, Benjamin is nearly exterminated. Having punished them
sufficiently to make the point that such conduct is not to be
tolerated; Israel relented and allowed the remnant to live. Having
sworn not to give wives to them, they arranged for them to take
wives for themselves from among the daughters of Shiloh during a
festival. This is a synopsis of the story given in Judges chapters 19
through 22.

There are many evils here, but our task is to examine these materials to see if they reflect upon a biblical acceptance, or rejection, of homosexuality. The other issues, important though they are, are beyond our current scope.

Proponents of homosexuality argue that the townsmen simply wanted "to identify" the new guy in town. That is all, they argue, that their stated desire to have the man brought out so that they might "know" him, meant. First, I would suggest the reader review the discussion about the Hebrew word *yada* offered in the prior section dealing with its usage in Genesis 19.

1. The word *yada* is used for carnal knowledge many times in the Old Testament.

2. The word *yada* is nowhere used in this way in the Old Testament to ascertain identity.

3. In Judges 19:25, it is said that the men of the town "knew her [the man's concubine] and abused her all night." By morning she is dead. We have two possibilities offered here with regards to the meaning of the word "to know": a) "to identify" and b) "to have sex with." Which seems to best fit the context? Was it a vigorous examination of her passport that led to her demise, or is it more likely that it was a long night of rough sex? I think most readers will conclude that "to have sex with" is the more likely meaning of *yada* here.

4. If that is so, is it not also likely that the request to "know" the man noted three verses earlier (v. 22) was also a request to have sex with him?

5. These men who came to the house were described as "sons of Belial," a term of reproach associated with impurity. Sometimes the phrase is translated "perverted men." If their desire was only to know who the man was, is it likely that they would be called "sons of Belial," or does that not tend to support the idea that they wanted impure sexual contact?

6. The host immediately called their act "wicked" and an "outrage" (v. 23). Again, is that the most reasonable characterization of a reasonable request to identify a visitor, or is it more likely to characterize a request for an impure sexual contact?

7. This act, whatever it was, is viewed as something so horrible that the whole nation is willing to suffer many thousands of casualties and the near extinction of a brother tribe to protest it. Is it likely that a request to know who someone was would be so viewed, or is it more likely that a desire for impure sexual conduct would be so viewed?

I do not see how any reasonable person can doubt that "know" in verse 22 meant "to know carnally," "to have sex with."

It might be objected that it was the rape of a concubine that was so objectionable. It was indeed objectionable. There were penalties against it. But it was not the most horrific thing here. Sex with another man's wife was a capital offense (Deuteronomy 21:22). The rape of an unmarried woman required a payment to the girl's father and for the man to marry the woman (Deuteronomy 21:29). The rape of a concubine, although clearly wrong, was not the most horrific act involved here from the Old Testament perspective. Women in general did not have the highest status in pre-Christian societies, and concubines in particular had a somewhat lower status; it is likely that something else had to be involved to arrive at the war that ensued. By the end of this war, the victors arranged an act of mass heterosexual rape to provide wives for the defeated survivors, without breaking their own vow to not give them wives, which, I suppose, might have been seen as a somewhat unusual arranged marriage. For all their possible moral error, it still supports the notion that homosexuality *per se* was horrifically objectionable.

It has also been argued that this story is so similar to the story of Sodom that it is only a re-telling of it, and, thus, it has no independent weight.

1. Such an argument must assume that the Bible is not authoritative, that the reader may pick and chose, may omit portions as he or she wishes, and, for this segment of our discussion, I have asked the reader to accept as a working hypothesis that the Bible *is* authoritative. If it *is* authoritative, then its inclusion here would be important even if it were only a re-telling by some later editor.

2. There is nothing in the text itself that says that it is a re-telling of the same story. In one tale, the city is non-Israelite; in the other, it is Israelite. In one, there are angels visiting; in the other, it is just an ordinary traveler. In one, the offer of the daughters is thwarted; in the other, while the daughter is not given, the concubine is. In one the townsmen are struck blind; in the other, that is not so. In one, the city and a region is supernaturally destroyed; in the other, a very bloody, but very natural, war is fought. The only apparent reason to suppose that the story in Judges is only a re-telling of the one in Genesis is that it is thought by some to help diminish the weight of the biblical opposition to homosexuality, if it were so; there is no reason for such a conclusion in the text.

3. When a story, the same story, is told in multiple gospels in the New Testament, that repetition is usually taken as a sign of its importance. Therefore, even if it were merely a re-telling, for which there is no evidence and much evidence to disabuse one of that notion, then it would still mean that the matter spoken about was of increased importance, not diminished of importance.

Some argue that Ezekiel 16:49 disestablishes the standard view of the story of Sodom, and establishes a contrary view. I have heard a Metropolitan Community Church leader proclaim this view, and have seen a United Methodist pastor's article espousing it as well. At first glance, it looks explosive, but if you do more than glance at the text, the argument disintegrates.

Let us look at the pro-gay evidence and argument first. The evidence comes from Ezekiel 16:49: "Look, this was the iniquity of your sister Sodom: She and her daughter had pride, fullness of food, and abundance of idleness; neither did she strengthen the hand of the poor and the needy." The argument: 1) There you have it! What could be clearer?! There is no mention of sexual sin. The sins were pride, abundance of food and idleness, and, most of all, a lack of hospitality to the "poor and the needy." 2) It is the homosexuals today who are the "poor and the needy." 3) Since the *real* sin of Sodom is a lack of hospitality to the "poor and the needy," and since it is homosexuals who are today the, or among the, "poor and the needy," *then* it is those who oppose homosexuality who are the *real* Sodomites! Voila! And take that!

I laugh, I smile in wonder, I applaud, after a fashion, the *chutzpah*, but again, to maintain the argument requires a careful avoidance of the surrounding text and any reflection. My special emphasis is not word studies, but looking at the text, asking questions of it, and seeing what, if anything, it says in reply. Does the Bible elsewhere say anything that speaks to the pro-gay argument above? Does the text surrounding this single verse say anything that speaks to the above argument? Yes, on both counts.

1. The sin of Sodom is clearly noted in Genesis 19. It is the desire of the townsmen to "know" the visitors. Thus, the sin of Sodom must at least have included sexual sin, even if Ezekiel did not know it, which, by the way, he did.

2. The sins of Sodom are clearly labeled in Jude as "having given themselves over to sexual immorality" and having "gone after strange flesh" (v.7). Thus, the sins of Sodom clearly must have at least included sexual sins, even if Ezekiel did not know it, which, by the way, he did.

3. In II Peter 2:6-10, the sins of Sodom are also indicated to be sexual, and not a "lack of hospitality." Thus, the sins of Sodom must clearly have at least included sexual sins.

4. There is no reference to "a lack of hospitality" in Genesis 19.

5. There is no reference to "a lack of concern for the poor and the needy" in Genesis 19.

6. There is no reference to such as a lack of concern in Jude or elsewhere in the Bible.

7. Sodom had become a byword for evil and for judgment. Among the instances of the use of Sodom as an example of evil see the following verses: Deuteronomy 32:32, Isaiah 1:9-10 and 3:9, Jeremiah 23:14, Matthew 10:15 and 11:23-24, Mark 6:11, Luke 10:12, II Peter 2:6 and Revelations 11:8. Among the instances of the use of Sodom as an example of God's judgment or punishment read: Deuteronomy 29:23, Isaiah 13:19, Jeremiah 49:18 and 50:40, Lamentations 4:6, Amos 4:11, Zephaniah 2:9, Matthew 10:15, Mark 6:11, Luke 17:29, Romans 9:29 and II Peter 2:6.

   At first glance, it is entirely possible that Ezekiel was simply using Sodom as a byword for wrongdoing. Upon further consideration, that this is the case becomes obvious.

8. In this same chapter, 16, but in verses before and after the verse (49) cited by the proponents of homosexuality, we find many uses of the names of various groups used as words of imprecation, used to criticize those to whom he spoke, just as he was using the name of Sodom. Consider the following: Hittite and Amorite (v. 45), Samaria and Sodom (v. 46), Samaria (v. 51), Sodom and Samaria (v. 53), Sodom and Samaria (v. 55), and Syria and the Philistines (v. 57). If one reads the larger context, the meaning is clear and obvious.

9. In verse 47, Ezekiel specifically says that those to whom he is speaking did *not* do what the Sodomites did. I repeat that, they did *not* do what the Sodomites did.

10. In verse 48, Ezekiel specifically says again that Sodom did *not*, I repeat, did *not* do what those to whom he was speaking did.

11. In verses 51 and 52, it is slightly less clear what difference there was, but it is clear that the sins of Samaria were also different from those of the Israelites to whom he spoke.

12. The whole of chapter 16 is saturated with sexual imagery, strongly suggesting that Ezekiel knew well what Sodom was known for.

13. Verse 49, cited by the proponents of homosexuality, does not mention the destruction of Sodom, but verse 50 does, and gives a reason for that destruction: "They were haughty and committed abomination before Me; therefore I took them away as I saw fit." The word "abomination" was used in Leviticus 18:22 and 20:13, in reference to a male lying with a male as with a woman. Surely Ezekiel knew that. This is a clear reference to the sexual sin of Sodom.

14. "A lack of concern for the poor and the needy" is not what is usually dealt with under the rubric of "a lack of hospitality." The pro-gay argument chooses to conflate two issues. Both are important. Neither concern means that homosexuality is approved. Hospitality was offered to the visitors to Sodom, therefore, that does not seem to be an issue there. It is not raised either in Genesis 19, nor, nor, nor in Ezekiel 16! One should, of course, be hospitable. (See Hebrews 13:2)

15. A lack of concern for "the poor and the needy" *is* a concern expressed by Ezekiel. That is a good and godly concern. If no other scripture spoke of it, and many do, this word alone in Ezekiel would be sufficient to establish it as a godly concern. It is apparently a problem for the community he addressed in his time, but he specifically said that their sins were *not* those of Sodom. It has nothing to do with the story of Sodom and Gomorrah.

16. The position I advocate is *not*, I repeat *not*, unconcerned with those caught up in homosexuality. They are God's children, just like all the rest of us. I would desire that they be offered help just as all of us need help in different ways and at different times. One of the best ways to help them *may be* to help them know that homosexuality is not God's perfect plan for their lives.

To maintain the pro-gay position with regards to Ezekiel 16:49 requires several errors: 1) not reading to the end of the sentence, which is in the next verse, verse 50; 2) not reading the verses just before verse 49, such as 46 and 47; 3) not reading the verses after verse 49, such as 51-60; 4) not reading the whole of chapter 16; 5) ignoring the primary text dealing with Sodom, in Genesis 19; 6) not dealing with other scriptures in the Bible that speak of the sin of Sodom; 7) not considering the widespread use in the Bible of Sodom as a byword for evil; 8) conflating "lack of hospitality," which has a specific meaning in biblical times, with a lack of concern for "the poor and the needy," also an important value, but neither of which had anything clearly to do with Sodom; 9) making a questionable assumption that today's homosexuals are the true "poor and the needy;" 10) making the still more questionable assumption that acceptance of wrong is helpful to the wrongdoer; and 11) supposing that those who do not find homosexuality to be a blessing are necessarily hateful – among other errors.

As a general rule, reading portions of scripture larger than one verse will often improve one's ability to understand a text. Seeing parts in relation to a whole is also, often, helpful. Finally, assuming that I have more or less fairly represented the pro-gay argument at the beginning of this discussion of Ezekiel 16:49, and now taking into account the subsequent discussion, does not the apparent inadequacy of their reflection leave one with doubts about their ability, their capacity to think fairly or thoroughly about things touching upon homosexuality? Does this difficulty suggest that something may be obscuring their vision?

I will offer only a very brief note about *qadesh* or *qedeshim*, "male prostitutes." There are several references to male temple prostitutes used in worship in various cultures surrounding the Israelites. The reference is always negative, and strongly so. You may find references to them in Deuteronomy 23:17, I Kings 14:24, 15:12, 22:46, and II Kings 23:7.

These references are largely left out of discussions about the biblical attitude towards homosexuality. The Bible is also opposed to female temple prostitutes, it is argued, thus the opposition can be seen as merely opposition to prostitution and not necessarily to homosexual acts that do not involve prostitution. This is true. In so far as it does speak to our theme, these passages do show a horror of this conduct. Taking this rejection of these homosexual acts together with the absence of positive reference to any homosexual acts, when such positive references do exist for heterosexual acts, tends to confirm the picture of rejection of homosexuality throughout the Bible. It has also been argued that these passages do not speak of homosexual acts at all, but that is quite unsound (For that, consider De Young, 2000, p. 125-133).

Let us review where we have come so far. In the preceding chapter, I argued that the Bible has a theology of sexuality and that it is clearly heterosexual. I pointed to the statements in Genesis one, Genesis two, the word of Jesus recorded in Mark quoting those two passages, and the fact of numerous positive references to heterosexual marriage throughout the Bible and the absence of anything like that for homosexual relationships. In this chapter, I have begun to point out several specific rejections of homosexuality. This discussion has been as elongated as it has, *not* because the texts themselves required it, but because of the extensive pro-gay argumentation claiming that the apparent meanings were not the real ones. To deal with a number of such arguments, we have had to look more closely at the texts, and see what evidence they gave about their meaning. I re-iterate that it is clear that the story of Sodom and Gomorrah in Genesis 19 does clearly imply a massive rejection of homosexuality. I submit that the story in Judges 19 through 22 does also indicate a horrific objection to homosexuality. The passages in Leviticus 18:22 and 20:13 are so clear that most proponents of homosexuality have not attempted to undercut them, but have accepted that they do reject male homosexual acts and have tried instead to say that they are no longer authoritative for one reason or another. Attempts to undercut these traditional understandings have not, I believe, held up to scrutiny. Thus do we review the discussion of specific rejections of homosexuality given in the Old Testament. After a brief digression on the word "homosexual," we shall resume the theme of the Bible's specific injunctions against homosexuality, next time, in the New Testament.

Chapter 12:

A Brief Note on the Word "Homosexual"

In a moment, we shall get to a consideration of the New Testament. The objection might have been raised about the Old Testament, but it has not been so. It has been raised about the New Testament. It has been objected that the New Testament never uses the word "homosexual," that in fact, it has no word for it at all. Therefore, it can hardly be said to have an objection to it! Interesting, isn't it, that this objection is not raised in the Old Testament, where it would be closer to the truth, though still misleading.

In an early lecture in my cultural anthropology class, some forty-nine years ago, I recall that the professor said that the Eskimos had no word for snow in their language. They had thirty-two of them, such as, two-day-old-snow, powder-snow, and, perhaps, yellow-snow. They had more words for snow than we do because snow was more important to them than it generally is to us. Every language slices up reality differently.

Latin declines nouns and conjugates verbs, and most of us English speakers think that "declining" is what Bible people did at the dinner table and "conjugation" is what parents tell their teenagers not to do. French and Spanish conjugate verbs a lot, but decline nouns only a little. German declines nouns more than French or Spanish, but not so much as Latin. Different Chinese dialects use the same characters, but pronounce them differently. In English, we do conjugate verbs some: I am, you are, he is – but not too much. And we decline nouns a little: actor, actress, and actors – but very, very little. In Greek, and several other languages, you often do not need a pronoun since the ending of the verb gives you the same information that we English speakers usually get from pronouns.

Each word, in any language, often has a range of meanings, and the right word by which to translate from one language to another may vary depending upon the more precise meaning indicated by the context. In all languages, one word often has multiple meanings. In "I love my children," "love" does not have the same meaning as it does in "I love strawberries," or at least so I would hope. We can understand it, but we might have to translate "love" with two different words in another language. It's no big deal; it's just the way it is; languages express reality differently.

I am reminded of a story a Latin teacher of mine once told. A woman came to her one day and wanted very badly to get into her Latin class. She said that she had to take Latin right then. Since she had such a sense of urgency about her request, the professor asked her why there was this urgency. She replied that she was going to take a trip to Latin America soon and she wanted to be able to speak the language before she went. Sometimes the apparently significant is untrue; they didn't speak Latin in Latin America.

Is it true that the word "homosexual" is not in the Bible? Why, yes. "Gay" isn't either, and probably no word on this page is either! You see, the Bible was basically written in two languages: Hebrew for the Old Testament and Greek for the New Testament. Back in the days of the Bible stories, they did not use any English at all. They did not even have the King James Bible! (Please don't tell the Baptists I said that.) In fact, English didn't even exist then. However, if you want to ask, was there homosexual conduct in those days, the answer is: Why, yes there was. And if you want to ask, did the Bible speak of it, the answer is: Why, yes it did. And did people perform those behaviors? Why, yes, they did. And did the Bible speak of them? Why, yes, it did. And it still does.

Not only did the Bible not have the word "homosexual" in it, the English language didn't either! Uh-huh, not until quite recently. Let's talk about that for a moment, and then we'll get back to some Bible words.

The origin of the word "homosexuality" is in the German word "homosexualitat." This word was invented in 1869 by

Karoly Maria Kertbeny (Dynes, 1990, p. 555 and p. 558). The word was first used in English in the 1890's (OED, 1989, vol. VII, p. 345). It did not become standard in English for quite some time. Many other words were used in English to speak of homosexuality across the years. Sodomite was long the most common. Catamite was used for some period of time to refer to a receptive partner in a homosexual act. "Invert" and scores of other words have been used at one time or another, in various ways as well. Though the word is often used to refer only to male homosexuals, gay activists would generally now prefer "gay" as the main word for homosexuals. It is currently felt by many homosexuals that the word "homosexual" is not affirming enough, but it was itself a word of advocacy when introduced.

Kertbeny was gay and an activist for his day. The word was devised to change the image of homosexuality, then most commonly called sodomy. It is composed of two parts: a Latin root, and a Greek prefix. The Latin root is *sexus*, meaning "sex." See the prior discussion about this word. Sex refers to the division of human beings into two sexes, male and female. "Homo" is from the Greek word *homo*, which means "same." The invention of this word was an attempt by Kertbeny to say that "homosexuality" was just the same as "sexuality," only different. It was after the word "homosexuality" gained acceptance that the word "heterosexual" became necessary. Prior to that, "sex" meant "heterosexual." No more, no less.

If one wanted to be a stickler, one might say that "homosexuality" was a contradiction in terms, that since "sex" means "different sexes," "homosexuality" is saying "same-different," but, while there is a point to saying that, it simply is not helpful. The word homosexual is established, and it is perhaps the most easily understood term for our subject today. It is, however, a result of a victory of a prior advocacy effort begun by Kertbeny and carried on by many others.

Greek did not have *one* word by which to express homosexuality. In one passage alone in the Bible, there are *four* words used, each of which, on some occasions, were used to refer to persons who engaged in homosexual conduct. In the context, I think that two of them referred to heterosexual acts, and two of them referred to homosexual acts. I'll refer to them when we discuss I Corinthians 6:9-10.

Some claim that the *kind* of homosexuality which "we have today" is something new, and something which the New Testament could not comprehend, and to which it made no reference. First, I would question whether or not what some think "we have today," we have. Second, I would ask if the contemporary condition of homosexuality did not exist in antiquity, is it then a universal, on-going human condition? Third, I would ask since the word "homosexuality" didn't exist until 1869 in German, and still later in English, does that mean that homosexuality did not exist until then? Fourth, it is simply untrue. The ancient world was familiar with many expressions of homosexuality. As De Young puts it "the ancients knew virtually all forms of homosexuality, including orientation, centuries before Paul" (DeYoung, 2000, p. 157).

Chapter 13:

What Does the New Testament Seem to Say About Homosexuality?

In the New Testament, there are three primary passages which specifically address homosexuality: Romans 1:18-32, I Corinthians 6:9-11, and I Timothy 1:10. There are other passages that speak of it clearly but indirectly, such as in Jude, II Peter 2:6-10, and Revelation 21:8. There are other questions that some have raised and with which we should deal in this chapter.

It is in Romans 1:18-32, that we encounter the first explicit statements about homosexuality in the New Testament. There are many things with which Paul deals in this passage, but homosexuality is prominent among them. I have before urged the reader to go to his own Bible to confirm or deny my readings of things, and I do so again, but this time I shall also include a longish quotation. You decide if it speaks approvingly of homosexuality. For some readers, it is too much, but there are multiple elements brought out in this passage. The question, at the moment, is not whether or not you agree with Paul, but what did Paul actually say here. Now follows Romans 1:18-32 (NIV):

(18) The wrath of God is being revealed from heaven against all the godlessness and wickedness of men who suppress the truth by their wickedness, (19) since what may be known about God is plain to them, because God has made it plain to them. (20) For since the creation of the world God's invisible qualities – his eternal power and divine nature – have been clearly seen, being understood from what has been made, so that men are without excuse. (21) For although they knew God, they neither glorified him as God, nor gave thanks to him, but their thinking became futile and their foolish hearts were darkened. (22) Although they claimed to be wise, they

became fools (23) and exchanged the glory of the immortal God for images made to look like mortal men and birds and animals and reptiles. (24) Therefore God gave them over in the sinful desires of their hearts to sexual impurity for the degrading of their bodies with one another. (25) They exchanged the truth of God for a lie, and worshiped and served created things rather than the Creator – who is forever praised. Amen. (26) Because of this God gave them over to shameful lusts. Even their women exchanged natural relations for unnatural ones. (27) In the same way the men also abandoned natural relations with women and were inflamed with lust for one another. Men committed indecent acts with other men, and received in themselves the due penalty for their perversion. (28) Furthermore, since they did not think it worthwhile to retain the knowledge of God, he gave them over to a depraved mind, to do what ought not to be done. (29) They have become filled with every kind of wickedness, evil, greed, and depravity. They are full of envy, murder, strife, deceit and malice. They are gossips, (30) slanderers, God-haters, insolent, arrogant and boastful; they invent ways of doing evil; they disobey their parents; (31) they are senseless, faithless, heartless, ruthless. (32) Although they know God's righteous decree that those who do such things deserve death, they not only continue to do these very things but also approve of those who practice them.

First, does this passage seem to speak approvingly of homosexuality, or disapprovingly?

Second, please note that just before this Paul had spoken of his joy in "the gospel of Jesus Christ, for it is the power of God to salvation for everyone who believes, for the Jew first and also for the Greek. For in it the righteousness of God is revealed from faith to faith; as it is written, 'The just shall live by faith.'" (Romans 1:16-17 NKJV) Paul is not trying to *bring* gloom, but to *dispel* gloom, but first some may need to know that gloom is gloomy.

Third, please note that immediately after this discussion, Paul will go on to criticize those who are quick to judge, especially those who practice the same or spiritually similar things, in Romans 2:1 and following. Paul is not going out of his way to pick on some people in particular.

Fourth, Paul is dealing with the realities of the pagan world into which he had gone to bring a word of hope that was to change many, many lives. In Romans, he is making more general statements about the human condition than he did in some other letters.

Now let us look at some of the things Paul had to say.

1. He said that some things can be known about God "from what has been made," and, therefore, everyone has some responsibility before God for his or her actions. (v. 20)

2. He says that since they could not recognize God in His creation, they created their own things and declared them gods: "images made to look like mortal men and birds and animals and reptiles." (vv. 21-22)

3. There is a progression, or a regression if you will: a) people do not honor God (v. 21); b) they chose to honor their own creations as "god" (v. 23); c) then, in a sense, God gives them over to their own desires (vv. 24 & 26); d) which leads to shameful conduct (vv. 24 – 27), and e) the "progression" continues on to ever greater evil (v. 29-31), and even beyond the doing of what is wrong to the *approving* of it as well (v. 32).

What are some of the things the text seems to say about homosexuality? It is 1) a result of idolatry, 2) a sign of the rejection of God, 3) a sign of a false claim to be wise, 4) foolish, 5) a "sinful desire," 6) a result of exchanging the truth for a lie, 7) a "shameful lust," 8) "unnatural," 9) "indecent," 10) "perversion," 11) part of a spirit which can lead to a host of other sins, and 12) leading to death. Altogether it is a horrifying list. Please, dear reader, do not despair. Paul points out the darkness of things to lead us to redemption, not to leave us in darkness. Now, review the text and see if I have fairly drawn these twelve inferences from the text? If so, then I think that the point is made that this text does not approve of homosexuality.

My friend Don grew up Jewish and gay in New Jersey. (Again, this is not his real name, but he is a real person, and this story is real.) The police caught him in the vicinity of a gay party one time when he was a boy, and took him home to his mother and told her. Don hadn't actually had any homosexual affairs yet, but he knew that he was attracted to guys, and he had begun to think that he might be gay. I don't think father was told at that time, but mom took him to a psychiatrist. The shrink said, "Yep. This kid is a true homosexual. That's what he is. That's what he will always be. And you should help him to feel good about that," – or something like that. So Don knew he was gay. Then he had affairs.

Years pass, and Don moves out to the west coast. He starts dating a young guy who is an associate pastor at the Metropolitan Community Church, the big gay church in L.A. Since his boyfriend is involved in this church, Don attends its meetings. One time he hears an invitation to accept Jesus Christ as his Lord and Savior, and he does. Don gets "saved" in a gay church! Well, as a good Jewish boy, he had never read the New Testament before, but now that he has become a Christian, he starts to read the New Testament. He comes to this passage in Romans, and, wow, it says that guys having sex with guys is unnatural! He had never heard that before. He's new to this stuff, and he thinks he must be the first guy who ever noticed this passage. He takes it to the senior pastor, Troy Perry.

Troy Perry tells him something like, "Oh, yeah. Well, that's just for folks who are 'naturally heterosexual.' That's not for folks like us who are 'naturally homosexual.'" Don didn't buy it then, but he wasn't confident enough yet to argue with the pastor. Perry gave Don the most common argument offered by the proponents of homosexuality to rebut the evident meaning of Romans 1:26-27: It only opposes homosexuality for those who are "naturally" heterosexual, assuming that some, such as themselves, are "naturally" homosexual. One early use of this was in Cory. (Cory, 1951, p. 29) Karl Heinrich Ulrichs, a German gay activist in the

1800's may have set the pattern. He said, "There is no such thing as unnatural love. Where true love is, there is nature also." (Mondimore, 1996, p. 28) Could that also be translated, "If it feels good, do it"?

By the way, Don, a then life-long homosexual, came out of homosexuality, started an ex-gay ministry, got married, had a good marriage to a woman who has since died of cancer, has worked with other ex-gay ministries, and continues life as a Christian and a former homosexual.

There is nothing in the text to support the notion that Paul is speaking only of some sub-group of males or females. Nothing.

1. Paul had been a Pharisee. If there were to be such a revolution in his thinking on sexuality, there would be something about it in his letters. There is something about his revolution from "works righteousness" to "salvation by faith," something about associating with gentiles, and something about eating non-kosher food. There is much about sex, too, but it all is supportive of traditional sexual morality.

2. The text speaks of "degrading their bodies with one another," (v. 24) and in that there is no limitation as to for whom these acts would be degrading.

3. The text says, "Even their women exchanged natural relations for unnatural ones." (v. 26) It does not say, "their straight women." It says, "their women."

4. The text says, "in the same way the men also abandoned natural relations with women and were inflamed with lust for one another" (v. 27). It does not say, "the straight men." It says "the men."

5. Nor does the text say "men with boys," but males with males, thus this is not a reference only to pederasty.

6. It speaks of "leaving the natural use," or "abandoning it." This implies that there is a clearly discernible use that those engaging in this activity have left, and that there are

some acts which can be discerned as "natural" and others which can be seen to be "unnatural."

7. In verse 16, just preceding this passage, Paul says that his gospel is "for the salvation of everyone who believes." In the absence of contrary evidence, that would suggest that the following passage would also apply to everyone.

8. Now, if you want to argue that Paul didn't know what he was talking about, that is a different argument. It may or may not be sound, and I would say it isn't, but in any case, such an argument would not affect the meaning of what Paul said, and it is poor logic. No, it is dishonest, to try to say that Paul didn't "really" mean what he said because you think he *ought* to have said something else!

It is quite clear that Romans 1:18-32, and specifically, vv. 26-27, offer a rejection of homosexuality, among many other statements.

Another important New Testament passage dealing with homosexuality is in I Corinthians 6:9-11. Paul has been addressing a number of problems throughout this letter to the church at Corinth. He speaks against breaking up into hostile groups in chapter 1:10 to 17, not getting puffed up and thinking too highly of yourself in 1:18 to 2:16, returns to oppose the sectarian spirit in 3:1 to 15, and so on. In chapter 5, he speaks against sexual immorality. In chapter 6, from verses 1 through 7, he protests that Christians should not need to take each other to court, but should be able to judge things rightly among themselves. Christians should not take things to the courts because all of the courts at that time would be run by non-Christians, and, he reminded them, it is the righteous, not the unrighteous, who are to be able to judge. Then he notes that the unrighteous will "not inherit the kingdom of God," and lists some of those whose actions establish that they are unrighteous. Chapter 6, verses 9 and 10, reads:

Do you not know that the unrighteous will not inherit the kingdom of God? Do not be deceived. Neither fornicators, nor idolaters, nor adulterers, nor homosexuals, nor sodomites, nor thieves, nor covetous, nor drunkards, nor revilers, nor extortioners will inherit the kingdom of God (NKJV I Corinthians 6:9-10).

Here are some factors to note:

1. There are many "sins" named.

2. There are other sexual sins listed.

3. There are non-sexual sins listed.

4. The list is not said to be exhaustive, but is illustrative.

5. There are homosexual acts listed as sins.

6. The consequence of having a spirit inclined to do these things is said to be that one is so out of right relationship with God that one will "not inherit the kingdom of God."

It is here that some say the word "homosexual" is never used. Regarding that assertion, see also the preceding discussion about the word "homosexual." In fact, there are four Greek words used here, each of which *sometimes* was used to refer to persons who engage in homosexual acts. The common reading is that, in this setting, two of them refer to heterosexual acts, and two of them refer to homosexual acts. I think that is sound. The four Greek words are: *pornoi, moichoi, malakoi*, and *arsenokoitai*.

"*Pornoi*" is here translated "fornicators." Wherever you see "sexual immorality" or "fornicator" or slight variations of those words in the New Testament, it is generally a translation of one form or another of *pornos, pornoi*, for the person, or *porneia*, for the activity. In the New Testament, the word *porneia* is generally used to refer to sexual immorality in general, and thus, *pornos*, or the plural form *pornoi*, refers to persons who engage in it. In other ancient Greek usage, *pornos* is most commonly translated as "catamite," which is a boy used in pederasty, or "sodomite," which is a more general reference to one involved in homosexual acts (Liddell and Scott, 1968, p. 1450). *Porneia* most commonly meant male and female prostitution. In translations of the New Testament, these words are commonly understood to refer to sexual immorality of every kind (Bauer, Arndt and Gingrich, 1979, p. 693). I fully accept the traditional translation of "sexual immorality," or, as in the translation used above "fornicator," but I think it highly improbable that these words could have lost altogether the sense of reference to homosexual acts that they most commonly carried in Greek literature outside of the New Testament. Therefore, any time a variation of this word is used, and they are used some fifty-five times in the New Testament (Brown, 1975, p. 499), it must, it seems to me, at least imply some element of rejection of homosexuality as well. However, I am *not* counting it here as one of the two used in I Corinthians 6:9-10 to refer to homosexuality.

Nor am I counting the next word in this series, *moichoi*. This word is used here to mean "adulterer." Quite so. It commonly means a paramour, which would also be an adulterer. However, in other ancient Greek literature it commonly means "the paramour of a sodomite." (Liddell and Scott, 1968, p. 1141) Thus it is one of the four words that I noted could be used to refer to persons who engaged in homosexuality.

Now we come to the two words that are used here to refer to persons who engage in homosexual acts. The first one is *malakoi*. NIV translates it as "male prostitutes." NKJV translates it "homosexuals." "*Malakos*," when used of persons may mean "soft, mild, gentle, morally weak, or lacking self-control (Liddell and Scott, 1968, p. 1077), or may mean "soft and effeminate, especially of boys and men who allow themselves to be used homosexually" (Bauer, Arndt and Gingrich, 1979, p, 488).

The second is *arsenokoitai*. This word is one that seems to have been invented by Paul, which he does from time to time. It is a compound formed from two other words: *arsen*, which means "male," and *koitai*, which means "bed," and from which we get our word "coitus." The version of the Old Testament most widely distributed in Paul's day was in Greek. It is called the *Septuagint*. In Leviticus 18:22 and 20:13, both these words are used in the prohibition of men lying with men as with a woman. Paul is quoting the *Septuagint*, Leviticus 18:22 and 20:13. It says, and Paul says, and this word says, a male (*arsen*) should not take a male to bed (*koit-*). Boswell notes that Paul was apparently the first to use the word (Boswell, 1980, p. 341), but then discounts the possibility of the word referring to homosexuality since he does not find that it was so used by other previous or contemporary writers (Boswell, 1980, p. 345). He tries to claim that *arsenokoitai* simply means male prostitute. Boswell's attempted explanation simply fails to deal with the *Septuagint* (Boswell, 1980, pp. 107, 114, 338-339, 341-342, 344-52).

The most likely reading of these two words in this passage is that they did refer to persons who engaged in homosexual acts. It is the most likely reading in view of the customary range of meanings for these words. It is the most likely reading in view of the historical opposition to homosexuality of the people of God. It is the most likely reading in view of New Testament and Pauline concern for sexual morality. It is the most likely reading in view of the historical and sociological factors of the day. Most of the pro-gay argumentation is special pleading, arising from their felt need to obscure the meaning of the text, not from the text. To maintain the pro-gay position requires regularly accepting the least probable meaning and turning an occasional blind eye.

Before we leave this discussion of I Corinthians 6:9-10, I want to call the reader's attention to the following verse, verse 11. In some ways, what it says is better discussed in the later section of this study that will deal with transformation, but I cannot pass over it without some notice. I Corinthians 6:11 says: "And that is what some of you were. But you were washed, you were sanctified, you were justified in the name of the Lord Jesus Christ and by the Spirit of our God." And that is what some of the church members in Corinth, to whom Paul was writing, *were*, past tense. They were that no more. It needs to be noted more than once that the goal is *never* condemnation, but *always* release from condemnation, and that that goal can be achieved.

The next New Testament passage that contains a specific injunction against homosexuality is I Timothy 1:10. There is one key word given here in the context of verses 8 through 11:

But we know that the law is good if one uses it lawfully, knowing this: that the law is not made for a righteous person, but for the lawless and insubordinate, for the ungodly and for sinner, for the unholy and profane, for murderers of fathers and murderers of mothers, for manslayers, for fornicators, for sodomites, for kidnappers, for liars, for perjurers, and if there is any other thing that is contrary to sound doctrine, according to the glorious gospel of the blessed God which was committed to my trust (NKJV).

I want to thank my non-Christian readers who are unaccustomed to wading through so much scripture for their perseverance, if they have come this far with me. I know that it must seem to you a burden. Indeed, such examination is a burden to me as well! I lead us through it only because what has long been thought to be established has been challenged in recent times. Many have assumed that the challenge was sound, and others have concluded that since commentators were alleged to have disagreed, then one was free to ignore all evidence and believe whatever one wished. I do not find that the challenge has succeeded, intellectually, and I want the reader to be able to have some basis for drawing his or her own conclusions.

True, *pornos* appears again, and the reader might review the discussion of this word above, but here again I grant that it is used as a term referring to sexual immorality in general. The key word is *arsenokoitais*, which we have also encountered in the prior discussion of I Corinthians 6:9-10. The two parts of the word, its origins in Leviticus 18:22 and 20:13, its setting in the early church, its setting in Paul's work, and its setting in the world of the early church, all serve to confirm its traditional meaning, here given in the NKJV as "sodomites," and referring to persons who engage in homosexual acts.

There are three other New Testament passages that indirectly reject homosexuality. One is in Jude. I will note a few verses, that we might have a basis for our reflections:

(4) For certain men whose condemnation was written about long ago have secretly slipped in among you. They are godless men, who change the grace of our God into a license for

immorality and deny Jesus Christ our only Sovereign and Lord. ...(7) In a similar way, Sodom and Gomorrah and the surrounding towns gave themselves up to sexual immorality and perversion. They serve as an example of those who suffer the punishment of eternal fire. (8) In the very same way, these dreamers pollute their own bodies, reject authority, and slander celestial beings (NIV).

Bailey and Boswell (Bailey, 1955, p. 11-16; Boswell, 1980, p. 97) try to claim that this passage depends upon an Old Testament passage for it's meaning, and that this Old Testament passage refers to having sex with angels or alien beings, and, that since this makes no sense to us, we can therefore safely ignore this passage in Jude. But it was meaningful to Jude, so let us see if we can discern which meaning might be more likely.

Verses 4 and 8 make it clear that whatever the problem is, it is current in the church of the day: "certain men ... have secretly slipped in among you," and "in the same way, these dreamers pollute [present tense] their own bodies." His letter is not abstract; it is very practical. Based upon your knowledge of the Mediterranean world in the time of the early church, what was the more widespread activity with which Jude might have been concerned: 1) sex with aliens or 2) homosexual sex? I think it rather more likely that the issue was, at least in part, homosexual acts, rather than anything to do with sex with celestial beings. The whole point of Misters Bailey and Boswell bringing that material in was, I think, to try to muddy the waters, not clarify them.

Whatever these men were doing, it included changing "the grace of our God into a license for immorality," and giving "themselves up to sexual immorality and perversion," and "pollut[ing] their own bodies." Whatever they were doing it was just like what Sodom and Gomorrah did. So then, this passage tends to confirm that the sins of Sodom and Gomorrah were sexual, that the sins of Sodom and Gomorrah were perverse, or unusual in their sexuality, and that such things were proposed by some who had entered the church in Jude's day (some things never change), and that what these persons proposed was doctrinally and morally wrong. Therefore, while this passage may be less direct than some others, it also affirms the fact that the New Testament rejected homosexuality.

I have dealt more with Jude because it was so much fun to look at the Bailey-Boswell argument against it. Read also the passage in II Peter 2:6-10, which identifies the sins of Sodom as "filthy conduct" (v. 7) and walking "according to the flesh in the lust of uncleanness." See also Revelation 21:8, the "abominable" seems to be a citation from Leviticus referring to sexual acts, homosexual acts, not already covered by the use of "sexually immoral" previously in this list.

It is sometimes argued that the Bible does not speak much about homosexuality, therefore, homosexuality is okay. First, the Bible does have a theology of sexuality, and it is clearly heterosexual. This alone would strongly call into question the wisdom of homosexuality. Second, the Bible does clearly reject homosexuality in seven passages: Genesis 19, Leviticus 18:22 and 20:23, Judges 19, Romans 1:18-32, I Corinthians 6:9-10, and I Timothy 1:10. That is actually quite a lot. There are fewer references to burning your baby in a fire in offering to Molech. Is that to be thought acceptable? There are fewer references to having sex with animals. Is that to be thought acceptable? It does not often say, "Love your neighbor as yourself," yet we find that to be authoritative. One passage could well be enough to establish a matter unless there were some other passages of scripture to counter it in some way. Third, the Bible does make clear its abiding concern for sexual morality in numerous ways, including frequent reference to verses connecting the Old to the New. We see this in Matthew 5:33 to Leviticus 19:12; Romans 10:5 and Galatians 3:12 to Leviticus 18:5; Romans 13:8-10 and Galatians 5:14 to Leviticus 19:18; II Corinthians 6:14 to Leviticus 19:19; and I Peter 1:14-16 to Leviticus 19:2, 11:44 and 29:7.

It is sometimes argued that Jesus didn't say anything about homosexuality, therefore, it is okay. To us Christians, Jesus is "the image of the invisible God" (Colossians 1:15). However, for us, the whole Bible is authoritative. As Paul wrote to

Timothy, "All scripture is God-breathed and is useful for teaching, rebuking, correcting and training in righteousness, so that the man of God may be thoroughly equipped for every good work" (II Timothy 3:16-17). "All scripture," said Paul, therefore, even things that are not recorded as being said by Jesus may be authoritative. Jesus is not recorded as saying that people should not have sex with animals, but most Christians would assume that the words about it in the Old Testament were sufficient.

Jesus spoke almost exclusively to a Jewish community, and in the Jewish community to which He spoke, this matter was settled. Homosexuality was not allowed. There was no need to address an issue so clearly settled. So, the lack of direct reference to homosexuality by Jesus is not a sign of approval but a sign that it was so clearly beyond the pale, that it was not necessary to speak explicitly against it. It was Paul who particularly went into the non-Jewish world, a world in which homosexuality had been practiced, and thus it was Paul who needed to address this issue head on, which he did in Romans 1:18-32, I Corinthians 6:9-10, and I Timothy 1:10. Similarly, it was the Jewish writer Philo, roughly contemporary with Paul, who, because he lived in pagan Alexandria, also spoke about homosexuality, and not approvingly.

And then, of course, Jesus did speak against homosexuality! In Matthew 15:1-20, there is a recorded a time when the Pharisees chided Jesus for allowing his disciples to eat without ceremonially washing their hands. Jesus used their rebuke as an occasion to teach about what was really clean and unclean. The hand washings weren't so important, he said, because a little dirt would just pass on through anyway. What was important was what came out of your heart, and among the things of lasting importance that came out of the heart was "sexual immorality." In view of the history of this word in Greek, and in view of the understanding of sexual morality of the community to which Jesus spoke, and in view of what the Bible, both Old and New Testaments say elsewhere about homosexuality, it is inconceivable that the sexual immorality which Jesus condemned would not have included homosexual acts. And Jesus did speak against sexual immorality more than once.

Jesus taught explicitly that the only acceptable alternative of heterosexual marriage was abstinence in Matthew 19:11-12.

Jesus said that he came to "fulfill the law" (Matthew 5:17). I take this to mean, in part, that He came to make it possible for us to actually do what we were supposed to, to enable us to fulfill the law. Now Jesus did that by fulfilling it himself, but this gets to be a more arcane, Christian discussion. Clearly, Jesus did not come simply to do away with what the law was about, and He made clear that He thought sexual morality was a matter of abiding importance. He certainly did things that expanded the law! See Matthew 5:21-48. Jesus did focus on the attitude of the heart, but again there is nothing here to lend approval to homosexuality.

Jesus did teach us a different sort of response to the wrongdoer. Regarding this emphasis on change and redemption, see the story of the woman caught in adultery in John 7:53 to 8:11. Jesus did *not* prescribe a punishment for her, though the law of Moses took adultery to be a serious offense (Exodus 20:4, Leviticus 18:20, Deuteronomy 5:18), nor did He say "Stone her," which the law of Moses sometimes required (Deuteronomy 22:22-24, Ezekiel 18:10-13), and which her accusers were apparently eager to do (John 8:7). But He most certainly did not say, "Hey baby, do your own thing." He said, "Let him who is without sin cast the first stone," and, after the others had all left, He said to her, "Go thou, and sin no more." Jesus upheld both truth and grace, as I believe that all persons should. However, realize the setting. This was not a circumstance in which there was a harlots pride parade and someone was asking Jesus why He was so mean as to think that whoring was not a really good thing. The graciousness of His response is appropriate, and we will consider that further in the section dealing with responses to homosexuality.

Perhaps by implication only, but by clear implication, Jesus did affirm opposition to homosexual conduct.

In these last chapters, we have dealt with those passages giving specific prohibitions on homosexuality in the Bible. Previously I argued that the Bible had a theology of sexuality and that it was heterosexual. Now I have argued that there are seven clear statements reflecting strong disapproval of homosexuality in the Bible. These seven passages are in Genesis 19, Leviticus 18:22 and 20:13, Judges 19, Romans 1:18-32, I Corinthians 6:9-10, and I Timothy 1:10. We have considered a number of pro-gay arguments attempting to overthrow traditional interpretations of these passages. I think we have seen that their arguments are generally inadequate, and sometimes dreadfully so. Thus, I take it as established that the passages do indeed speak ill of homosexuality. We have glanced at a few other passages that seem also to speak against homosexuality, though less clearly, or less directly. Next, we shall look at the general concern of God, as expressed by statements in the Bible, for and about sexual morality in general, and see what, if any, relation that might have to the subject of homosexuality. Recall again, in this section we are merely asking the question: Does Christianity, as expressed by the Bible, approve or disapprove of homosexuality?

Whether or not you think the opinion of the Christian faith valuable is another question, one with which we have dealt a little in our opening chapters. Whether or not you think the Bible is a good sourcebook for an understanding of the Christian faith is a separate issue, with which we have dealt elsewhere. Whether or not there is evidence confirming that the Bible is wise, is another question. I'll give you a preview: I think there is. How to respond to "homosexuality," and here the word is inadequate to express the range of concerns, is an entirely different set of questions, to some of which we will attempt some answers later still.

Chapter 14:

Is There a Pattern of Concern for Sexual Morality that Also Argues Against the Approval of Homosexuality?

She was in her sixties when she first came to me. She had been in church for years, but had not felt led to deal with her real concerns. Not many months after I came to the church, she felt like she could talk with me. There were two instances of sexual molestation that she recalled somewhat, but they were not even the most critical ones. Eventually, she recalled that an uncle had come in to her room when she was four, and made her do things she didn't want to do. He told her that she kissed her toy dolly, and so she should "kiss his dolly." She washed and washed after that. She just never could get clean. After the memory first came back to her, she said, "I never knew why I always hated him." Later she realized that she did tell her mother, that her mother had told the uncle never to set foot in the house again, and that he didn't, but that mother didn't dare to tell her father for fear, a reasonable one, that he would kill the uncle. So, mother did do something to help, but nothing was ever said to her as a little girl, and she felt the parents must think she was dirty too – for more than sixty years.

It had consequences in her life. Many. And big. There were other problems at home. She married the first guy who asked her. He was handsome, but trouble. There were other factors in her life history, but that there is one element that was prominent in her history is clearly relevant to our considerations here: Sex has consequences. Sexual acts have consequences. I would go further: There *is no such thing* as casual sex. This woman's life was much healed. She was freer. She was more confident. A sister of hers who lived in a city two hours away started coming to our church to see what was going on, because she knew something was going on for her sister. There was much healing, where there had been great, great hurt. It had already affected two generations before the healing began.

Another woman, in her forties, had seen psychiatrists and psychologists across the years, with no beneficial results. There had been a time when she had let trash pile up in her apartment, mounds of it and bags of it. Those who knew her knew there was a problem, but apparently they thought the problem was that she just didn't take out her trash. Figuratively, that was true, but in a way no one knew.

She began to recall images that suggested she might have been molested, but it was not immediately clear. We do many things to be sure that we can differentiate between symbolic image sequences and memories, and we do not rush. It was not her father, and it was not a completed act of molestation. It was the brother of a girlfriend in high school, and the incident only came close to being something more. But that was the beginning of the remembering of many things. It was, perhaps, the one which was just barely safe enough to deal with at first. After that more memories came. Oh yes, she had been molested, badly and often, and by, and with the approval of, people in whom she should have been able to have great trust.

She had been physically ill for her entire life: cold, after flu, after bronchitis – always something. No more. For some years, she has had no more than one cold in winter, or none. Her dress has become more feminine. She has found a freedom to do things she never could before. It was not always quick. It certainly was not easy. It is not over. But there is good and great change. While there are many lessons one could learn from her history, here is one I lift up now: sex is not casual.

A young man was nineteen when he came to my office. I had met him once before. He had come unexpectedly and with an acquaintance. We spoke an hour before I found out what he wanted, and then he had only a half an hour before he had to leave to catch a plane. When he was born, his father had wanted a girl. His father had been disgusted with him for being a boy. I don't know what the father's problem was, but he sure passed a curse on to his son. The boy was dressed strangely and treated strangely by his father, but he tried to make his father happy, yet at considerable cost to himself. I do not recall now if he had been molested, but he had taken a turn in homosexuality, and he wanted out. He had been in and out of homosexuality for a while by the age of nineteen, and that means he must have started earlier still. He wanted to marry a girl in another city, and he wanted to be secure in his masculine identity. We prayed. He reported feeling much better. He reported that he experienced five specific signs of benefit: incipient asthma attacks gone, two pains in his body gone, headache gone, and feeling that something had left him. He left, he went to catch a plane for another city, and I have not seen him since. I wish him well. I hope that all has worked out well. I will not assume anything but good. There is much I do not know for sure about this young man, but here is one thing I do know: Sexual identity is not casual. It is not without consequences. It is not trivial; it is not trifling. Sex is not casual.

Another man was in his late twenties when he first came to see me. He was witty, but it was a bitter wit. He expected rejection, and he prepared for it by rejecting the other person first. I do not recall how long it took before he was willing to talk freely, but it came fairly quickly. One time he wanted to confess some things. He came. He asked. I agreed to hear him and pray with him. He had been introduced to sex by other boys when he was just a boy, and then he "returned the favor." He introduced several other boys and young men to homosexuality himself. He wanted out. So far as I know he is out, but I do not claim to know for sure in his case for I have not seen him for some years. Here, however, is one thing I see again: Contrary to the widespread belief of our age, sex is not casual. Actions have consequences. Like tends to beget like, even when the person does not like the spirit so begotten.

Another young woman had what I suppose to be a normal upbringing. But one time a young man from a visiting youth group stayed at her folks house. He raped her. Later on, she decided that she could more easily be intimate with women than men. She worked in a gay bar and worked on the gay pride parade. She wore leathers and took drugs. She came to church high on drugs. She was welcomed. She was loved. She was prayed for. She dropped the drugs. She dropped the homosexuality. For several years, she lived as one who was consciously ex-gay. She thought, for a season, that she would like to counsel others coming out of homosexuality. But she declined to get counseling for herself, she declined to read books about her condition, and then she had a disappointment with a young man who simply didn't fall in love with her as she had with him. Finally, she got counseling, but with a counselor who had a gay child and felt compelled to approve homosexuality in order to assuage his own sense of guilt. She decided that gay was okay after all. She decided to go to a church where there would be no reminder about morality that was not comfortable for her. I don't know that the rape was all there was to her story, but I know this: that rape had consequences. Sex is not casual.

Another lady who came for healing was molested by her father. When the time came to be courted, she turned down the good young men and married one who was a little rougher. She told herself that he needed her more. That's what she thought consciously, but I think what was really going on was that she thought he was what she was worth. Both of them got much healing, she before him, but neither until well into their sixties, and he only shortly before death. Two other generations had already been damaged. Sex has consequences. Sex is not casual.

I could take many more pages giving you case histories, but these should suffice to illustrate my point here. Some of those noted above did not have homosexual involvement. Some did. My point is more general: Sex is not casual. I know, I know. I was once young, too, and in the '60's. We were taught that casual sex is okay. "The only bad sex is sex you haven't had." "If it feels good, do it." "Go for the gusto." We were taught that casual sex has no consequences. But that was wrong then, and it still is now.

God is concerned with things that matter. The Bible spends a great deal of time on money. Why? Because money, and the pursuit if it, and the use of it, is important. The use of money is a reflection of the heart of the person. The manner of its acquisition is a reflection of the heart of the person. And the manner of its use has consequences for others. The Bible spends a great deal of time on honesty, speaking truth, honest weights and measures, keeping your word, and not bearing false witness. Why? Because it matters. Lying damages relationships. Lying can kill. Lying is a reflection of a heart not at peace with God, not secure in Him. The one who is secure in the knowledge that God loves him does not have to lie. The Bible spends a great deal of time on sex. Why? Because sex matters. It is important. It has consequences. Conduct, sexual conduct, is a reflection of the heart and thus it is important as a sign of the peace or disorder of the person. And conduct has consequences. Disordered sex is a consequence of disorder, and it has consequences itself. For the other. And for the self. That is why the Bible gives a lot of time to it.

Consider the costs of sexually transmitted disease, for treatment, for lost work, and other related costs. Consider the costs of adultery, for crime, for divorce, for the children, for the courts, and for lost time. Consider the costs of sexual misconduct for children, including lost time, lost innocence, lost hope, lost confidence, poorer work in school, poorer work in life, damaged relationships, weakened marriages, disease, drugs, and crime. If the costs could be factored, the costs of our society's sexual misconduct is probably in the hundreds of billions of dollars (Muir, 1998). Now, not all of this is related to our current specific theme, homosexuality, but my point at the moment is that sex has consequences, and that is the reason why God gives it attention. Contrary to the established notion among our contemporary intelligentsia, sex is not casual, an appropriate plaything, or inconsequential. That fact, not some excessive prudishness is the reason for the concern for sexual morality expressed in the Bible. God wants good for us, and He tells us to do those things which are a reflection of good and which will cause life to be good for us and for others.

There is hardly a book of the Bible that does not deal with sexual misconduct at some point. The Bible is a very earthy book. It tells of a drunken king who dismisses the queen because she doesn't want to be paraded before his cronies, and this leads to an international beauty pageant that leads to a Jewish girl saving her whole nation. It tells of a woman of easy virtue whose life was touched by a passing teacher whom she came to understand was the Messiah. It tells of a woman who played a harlot with her father-in-law to get justice from him, and of his recognition of her righteousness! The Bible tells of a prostitute saving spies and her and her family being saved as a consequence. It tells of a powerful ruler's adultery, his attempt to hide this adultery, and his murder of his paramour's husband to try to cover up his sin, and of the prophet who confronted this all-powerful middle-eastern potentate with his sin, and of the potentate's repentance and remorse. In some ways, it is a soap opera! Why? Because life is often a soap opera. It speaks of sin to show us that sin does not work. Yes, it even speaks of when the evil-doers win. Among the evil of which it speaks there is considerable notice given to things sexual. However there is not much notice given to things homosexual ... because the matter was so decisively dealt with when it was dealt with. No Jew and no Christian could have a question about that matter. Consider the following:

1. There are numerous specific references speaking against adultery, coveting another's wife, rape, incest, bestiality and homosexuality.

2. There are numerous stories that illustrate the damage wrought by sexual immorality.

3. The concern for sexual purity is revealed in almost every book of the Bible, on hundreds of different occasions.

4. The prohibitions against homosexuality are quite clear in both Old and New Testaments.

5. The prohibitions against homosexuality are consistent with the creation of human beings as male and female.

6. The prohibitions against homosexuality are consistent with the apparent fulfillment of Adam in Eve.

7. The prohibitions against homosexuality are consistent with the unbroken expression of opposition throughout the Bible.

8. The prohibitions against homosexuality are consistent with the words of Jesus in Matthew 15:1-20 where He points out that sexual immorality is one of the things which reflects a man's heart and is of abiding importance.

In light of these considerations, I submit the general concern for sexual morality that the Bible expresses throughout itself does further support the rejection of homosexuality. The supposition that it was just not really thought about by folks in the New Testament, and, therefore, the prohibition would have been overturned if they had gotten around to it, is without foundation. The idea that it was only a strange concern of Paul's, but Jesus wouldn't really have agreed with him, is without foundation, and, in the context of Jesus' words about sexuality immorality in general and the tradition of clear rejection of homosexuality of those to whom he spoke, it is untenable. I ask the reader to reflect upon what he or she may know of biblical expressions of concern for sexual morality in general, and see if the reader can sense that such a concern would be consistent with the acceptance of a little buggery. If the reader is honest, I think not.

Chapter 15:

If God Is a God of Order, Is There Something in the Order of Creation which Speaks Against Homosexuality?
Yes.

"In the beginning, God created the heavens and the earth"
– Genesis 1:1

"So God created man in his own image, in the image of God he created him; ma*le and female he created them."*
– Genesis 1:27

"Then God saw everything that He had made, and indeed it was very good."
- Genesis 1:31

"When I consider Your hea*vens, the work of Your fingers,* The moon and the stars, which You have ordained…"
- Psalm 8:3

"The heavens declare the glory of God;
And the firmament shows His handiwork.
Day unto day utters speech,
And night unto night reveals knowledge."
- Psalm 19:1-2

"He did not leave Himself without witness"
- Acts 14:17

"God, who made the world and everything in it,
since He is Lord of heaven and earth."
- Acts 17:24

"What may be known of God is manifest in them,
for God has shown it to them.

For since the creation of the world
His invisible attributes are clearly seen,
being understood by the things that are made,
even His eternal power and Godhead."
- Romans 1:19-20

It has long been a Christian notion that God has created this world. We understand it to be "fallen," broken, altered, or messed up, but it was created by God and His presence and purpose can be seen in the created order. Is there anything in the creation of men and women which tends to suggest that homosexuality is not a part of God's perfect plan? Yes.

A professor once brought a sheet into his class. This was a long time ago, before designer colors were so common and most sheets were white. He brought in a white sheet. He had it held up in front of the class. (The story as I heard it was that he held it up by himself, but whoever heard of a professor standing in front of a class holding up anything for very long? So I think he had two students hold it up.) There was a small black dot in one corner of the sheet, about which he said nothing. He asked the students to come forward and examine the sheet, and then to report what they saw. The students all went forward to examine the sheet carefully. After a considerable length of time, they were ready to report their findings. They all reported the black dot in the corner of the sheet. No one, not one student, reported seeing the white sheet.

Sometimes the obvious is overlooked.

1. Boys and girls have different plumbing. That is not insignificant. That is not a joke to snicker at. It is a physiological fact of some considerable importance. The reproductive systems of males and females very strongly suggest that males were intended to be in relationship with females in ways that they were not so intended to be with males, or females with females. It takes only a few sentences to say it, but that does not mean that it is a point of less importance than one that takes a lot of words to communicate. If you believe in a God of order, then the

differences in the reproductive systems very strongly imply that homosexuality was *not* God's intention. It is beside the point, at best, or, perhaps worse, a perversion. There are *many* physiological differences between the male and female reproductive systems. Each item might be listed as a point, but I merely list the systems in general.

2. There is reason to believe that the rectum is designed to serve a different purpose than the vagina. The one seems to have a function in the evacuation of waste matter that the other does not. Also, there are key physiological differences between the two structures.

3. There are different kinds of cells in the rectum than in the vagina.

4. The lining of the rectum is made to absorb fluids in ways that the lining of the vagina is not; it is more permeable. This has consequences with regards to the transmission of body fluids.

5. The lining of the rectum is more easily torn than the vagina. This is a matter of consequence for sexual penetration in general, but especially in view of some of the sexual practices commonly practiced among homosexuals, such as "fisting."

6. There is a different muscular structure around the orifice of the vagina than there is around the orifice of the rectum. Damage to the sphincter muscles of the rectal area is a fairly common result of actions common among many male homosexuals. This can lead to a difficulty in retaining fecal matter.

7. There are many other discernible differences, such as a larger amygdala for the male, commonly a different psychology, often differing interests, different secondary sex characteristics, and more.

None of the possible consequences are the issue here. The issue here is design. Are there differences between the reproductive systems of males and females? Are there differences between the physical structures of the vagina and the rectum, and also the mouth for that matter, which we did not list?

If you accept the premise that there is a God of order, and creation, though "fallen," or imperfect, yet it does reflect God's intent in some rough manner, do these differences imply that homosexuality is *not* a part of God's plan? I think the answer is yes.

There are ways you might counter this argument. One, you might say that there is no God. Very well, but then do your homework and think through the consequences of the brave new world you want to create.

Two, you might say there is no order. Very well, but could you really live in such a world? Do you really mean it? Do you know what that then legitimizes? Everything.

Three, you might say that since homosexuality exists, it must also be a part of God's order and is therefore fine. Not so quick now. Many things exist. Christianity has never said that they were all of God. Man has been given free will and has often chosen to misuse it. That is what chapter 3 of Genesis is about, oh, and most of the rest of the book, too, in a way. If you say the above, then the general principle of which that is an instance is this: Whatever is, is good. Are you happy with that? Then gay is good, but so is gay bashing, since, after all, it exists too. War is good, hate, rape and revolution, *etcetera*. No, my argument is not just that the differences in these structures exist, but that they seem to reflect a discernible pattern, the intent of God.

I have argued that it is reasonable and useful to consider the Christian view of homosexuality because Christianity has done much to produce many things that you acknowledge are good for the world: less slavery, better treatment of women and all persons less physically able to fend for themselves, some transcendence of ethnic barriers, the scientific method, industry, and representative government, among them. Thus, since it has produced good in the past, it might be prudent to consider its position on a given matter before rejecting it.

1. In arguing what I have called the Christian position, I have said four things:

2. The Bible has a theology of sexuality and it is clearly heterosexual.

3. The Bible has several specific and clear passages that reject homosexuality.

4. The general concern of the Bible for sexual morality is consistent with the rejection of homosexuality, and not with its acceptance.

5. The ordered intention of God is revealed in the physical structures of the body, strongly implying an approval of heterosexuality and a disapproval of homosexuality.

Now then, if God does disapprove of something, I would expect that one could find reasons why He would do so: generally, perhaps not always readily or easily. Are there reasons that tend to confirm this biblical rejection of homosexuality as wise? Yes. Quite a number. To them we shall turn in the next section of this book.

Part III: Is Homosexuality Healthy?

The condition of homosexuality is commonly associated with:

- *A significantly decreased likelihood of establishing or preserving a successful marriage*
- *A twenty-five to thirty-year decrease of life expectancy*
- *Chronic, potentially fatal, liver disease – infectious hepatitis, which increases the risk of liver cancer*
- *Inevitably fatal immune disease including associated cancers**
- *Frequently fatal rectal cancer*
- *Multiple bowel and other infectious diseases*
- *A much higher than usual incidence of suicide*
- *A very low likelihood that its adverse effects can be eliminated unless the condition itself is*
- *Dr. Jeffrey Satinover in Homosexuality and the Politics of Truth, p. 51*

*No longer quite so fatal, though still debilitating and requiring much, expensive, and regular treatment

Chapter 16:

Introduction to Health and Homosexuality
What are the questions?

**The purpose of this section is to try to answer the question:
Is there evidence** that can help to answer this question: Is
homosexuality healthy? Yes, quite a lot of it. Some evidence is
fairly well known; much is not well known. Some can be clearly
established by re-examining the data of others. The meaning of
some data can be determined by correlating it with data drawn
from different sources. Altogether, I think there will be established
an overwhelming case showing that there are many signs of
disorder in life associated with homosexuality, and great physical
harm.

Those who are proponents of homosexuality would argue
against the conclusions I might draw from this kind of data in
several ways. Some would argue that the data is not sufficiently
clear. Some would argue that the disparity between averages of
various indices for heterosexuals and homosexuals is not all that
great. Some would argue that since not all homosexuals could be
included in any given indication of difficulty, then it follows that
there is no clear relationship to homosexuality. Some would grant
that there are clear evidences of damage or difficulty but that all
such deleterious consequences are consequences *not* of anything
related to homosexuality itself, but rather all such consequences
are the result of societal rejection, and thus it would follow that the
appropriate "answer" to any "homosexual problem" is not more
rejection, but more approval, affirmation, and perhaps, in the
context of full approval, some modest counsel to moderation.
There are reasons why these arguments are argued. They are not
altogether without merit, at least merit sufficient to warrant
examination. I do find that each argument fails, and to each of
these arguments, I will respond in due course. First, it must be our

task to see what, if any, evidence of disorder or dis-ease related to homosexuality there might be for which to attempt to account.

We will consider data relating to physical health, such as rates of STD's among homosexuals and heterosexuals, diseases basically specific to the gay population, physically inimical sexual practices which are largely unique to the homosexual population, and probable life span. We will consider data that might be thought to reflect upon emotional and social health, such as promiscuity, infidelity within couples, anonymity in sexual relations, the use of prostitutes, and the use of under-aged persons in sexual relations. Interestingly, much of the data here will actually come from the studies of gay and pro-gay researchers attempting to establish the normalcy of homosexuality. We will consider some of the comments of traditionalist psychiatrists and revisionist, pro-gay psychiatrists. We will, of course, attempt to consider the pro-gay replies to the traditionalist critique of homosexuality.

In order to gauge the meaning of some of the data available, we will need to have a working estimate of the number of persons who might be said to be "homosexual" in the United States. For much of the data this is not necessary. Such data comes from studies that take the element of the relative involvement of homosexual and heterosexual populations into account. But there is a lot of data available from various studies which bear upon our subject, but the meaning of which cannot be ascertained without reference to data not considered in the studies themselves. Not infrequently, the authors of various studies in recent years casually toss off comments about the "average-ness" of the homosexual population *that their data does not support.* For example, David Finkelhor in *Child Sexual Abuse* (Finkelhor) suggests an abhorrence of child sexual abuse among homosexuals equal to that of heterosexuals, but his data indicates a vastly higher *rate* of same-sex child abuse than average. Similarly, Robin Lloyd casually assumes disapproval of child sexual abuse by homosexuals, but if you compare his data with that of Gail Sheehy (Sheehy) regarding female prostitution in the same time frame, you find a vastly higher *rate* of same-sex child sexual abuse. Be aware also, that in some cases, the "data" is probably not more than a given expert's best educated guess. As we come to such cases as this, we will attempt to see how, if at all, we can still use the data. In order to be able to make use of more of the available data and to be able to deal with these kinds of questions, we will first need to get a working estimate of the size of the "homosexual population" at any given point in time. And that will be our first digression.

By now it should be common knowledge that Kinsey was wrong about many things, certainly including his estimation of the percentage of males who had engaged in homosexual acts. Some proponents of homosexuality ignore the more recent data, and simply refer to Kinsey's "historic" status as a pioneer and as a social "scientist." Other proponents of homosexuality try to have it both ways and acknowledge briefly that he has been superseded, and then return to a hagiographic excursus on Kinsey's virtues. Certainly it has been known for decades that Kinsey's sample relied far too heavily on college students, prisoners, sex offenders and prostitutes, and for that reason alone was of questionable value (Muir, 1998, p. 27). We know that Kinsey and his colleagues "cultivated warm relationships with homosexual groups. His death in 1956 was mourned as a great loss" [by these groups] (Bayer, 1981, p. 45-46). Bergler said of Kinsey: He was a "medical layman" who "undertook the impossible and fantastic feat of attempting to equate heterosexuality and homosexuality. Totally lacking in psychiatric knowledge, this biologist used a simple yardstick for recognizing normality .... When people do certain things, and animals ditto, we know what's what" (Bergler, 1962, p. 177). Bergler notes that Kinsey equated several acts that could lead to orgasm as morally and psychologically equal. See if you agree. Here are the acts with equal value and meaning: "masturbation, spontaneous nocturnal emissions, petting, heterosexual intercourse, homosexual contacts and animal contact" (Bergler, 1962, p. 178). Kinsey has also been sharply criticized for bad science and for probable illegal and immoral conduct by Reisman and Eichel (Resiman, 1990). While I think their critique raises concerns with which the current sexological and psychological establishment ought to deal, my primary concern here is to establish the probable percentage of homosexuals in the United States population.

First, let us deal with the ten percent claim. It is not true. I repeat that. It is not true. AND, Kinsey never said it! The proponents of homosexuality have made the claim for years that Kinsey said that roughly 10% of the US population was gay. Indeed, some gay advocacy groups have occasionally put out literature saying 10 to 15% of the US population is gay, trusting, I suppose that no one would call them a liar for padding it a little bit when, they assumed, the 10% number was authoritatively established. My own guess is that it has only been after the relative success of the civil rights movement for African Americans that the homosexual advocates began to push the 10% figure. The percentage was suggested by the percentage of the US population that blacks once constituted, and of course, the idea being that if so many persons are gay, then it must be okay, or at least really just too awkward to disapprove of. Still, the number is wrong.

Kinsey never said it. At one point he did say (Kinsey, 1948, p. 651) that 10% of the males, in his study, between certain ages, were in one of two categories, which categories were exclusively gay or more or less exclusively gay, for a period of three years or more. There are several qualifications: 1) He is speaking only of males. It has long been established, and even with Kinsey's numbers, that homosexual activity was much less common among females. Thus, 10% of males would not mean 10% of the total population. 2) His study, for this question, studied persons between the ages of 16 and 55. One third or more of the total population was younger or older than the segment studied. Thus, this number would not be reflective of the population as a whole. 3) He speaks of persons in two categories. Frankly, I think this is the least significant qualification to note, since each category did include homosexual activity as at least predominate. 4) It was *only for a period of three years, at some point in their lives,* of which he was speaking here. That does not mean that they remained "gay," or 5) even that they were "gay" at the time of their interview, or had gay self- identity. Elsewhere, his data indicates that many left homosexuality behind. 6) Of course, this still does not factor out youths who may have had one experimental homosexual contact, and then simply did not have any sexual intercourse again for three years, or persons in jail who may have had one or more homosexual contacts while they had no access to a heterosexual outlet and no desire to continue with the homosexual ones once they did. No careful reading of Kinsey's data would lead to the claim that 10% of America was gay, but that was the claim for many years, widely accepted by news media, proclaimed as a given by journalist and public school teacher alike. It was not true. It has been proven untrue by major recent studies. And it is *still* believed, assumed, and propagated by many persons who ought to know better – and doubtless, some do. One pro-gay activist with a scholarly reputation wrote of Kinsey's studies in 1996, "They hold their own against subsequent studies" (Mondimore, 1996, 82). This is simply untrue.

In the 1988, the National Opinion Research Center at The University of Chicago did substantial research on sexual behavior. They discovered that only 1.5% of the persons studied had had *one* or more homosexual contacts within the preceding twelve month period. (*The Universal Almanac 1992*, p. 219) Let us look at this number again. It was not 1.5% of the total group; it was 1.5% of the sexually active persons within the total group. About 20% had been sexually abstinent for the preceding year. That would reduce the number to about 1.2%. It was not 1.2% of the total population of the nation, but 1.2% of the population studied, which was between the ages of 18 and 60. At least one third of the nation's population is above or beyond that cut-off point. Since most persons younger are sexually abstinent, and many older persons are sexually abstinent and fewer homosexual persons live to old age, the number must be reduced still further as a reflection of the entire population. So, we have evidence for *one* or more homosexual acts within a year's time only for about .8-.9%, less than one percent, of the population. Among that .8-.9%, there must be some "experimenters" who, having been taught by their schools and the media that gay is good and think they must try it, and others who have no great commitment to homosexuality nor inclination to try it again. Based upon these considerations, I think it reasonable to suppose that perhaps 1% of the total population or 2% of the sexually active adult population could be said to be "homosexual" at any given point in time.

Better known and more recent is the study by Michael, Gagnon, *et al*, *Sex in America: A Definitive Survey* (Michael, 1994, pp. 169-183). They obtained roughly the same results as did the NORC study. They reported a smaller percentage of abstinent persons. They also reported a marginally larger percentage of persons who had engaged in a homosexual act, but we are speaking of a small fraction of a percent here. Therefore, I would say that the notion that 1% of the total population and 2% of the sexually active adult population is probably still a sound working estimate. That would mean that something like 3 million American adults thought themselves to be "homosexual" at any point in time, a large number, but vastly less than 10%.

Various newspapers have reported after recent elections that the "gay" vote was up to 4%. How can that be if their numbers are only 1% of the total and 2% of the sexually active adults? First, children don't vote. Therefore, it is reasonable to suppose that they constitute nearly 2% of the potential voters. Second, those who see themselves as homosexual have been powerfully activated in the last three decades, and it is reasonable to expect a higher percentage of actual voting among them. Since never more than about half of the potential voters actually vote, that could double their 2% potential to 4% actual. This higher motivation is probably the major reason for the reported disproportionate representation in the vote. Third, when dealing with so small a percentage of any given sample, and of a population that is widely reported to be unevenly distributed (Michael, 1994, pp. 169-183), it is not inconceivable that the reported 4% gay turnout is inflated by the preferences of the analysts presenting it.

It needs to be noted that there are various ways of attempting to define "homosexual." The preceding discussion has assumed that homosexual conduct is a fair way to get some sense of the size of the population. Others might argue for "identity," that the number should be determined by those who "identify" themselves as homosexuals. Perhaps, but that would not affect the percentages much. The Michael *et al* study gives a nearly equal number for self-identity as for one-year conduct. Some who do not act out would be included, and some who have had homosexual acts would be excluded, but that suggests a rough parity between the two measures, and thus perhaps a useful guideline.

Schmidt, citing Remafedi, notes one study in which "only 27.1 percent of students with homosexual experience identified themselves as homosexual or bisexual. This suggests that activity *exceeds* identity. Another implication is also that most adolescents who try it do not like it (Schmidt, 1995, p. 197). Another inference is that self-identification might be *lower* rather than higher than the percentage of persons who try homosexual activity.

Others would argue that sexual fantasies are the real determinant. They might argue that due to societal pressure against homosexuality, some who would like to engage in homosexual acts do not, and some are intimidated from identifying themselves as homosexuals *even to themselves*. Depending on how one evaluates the fantasies of others, such a scheme could easily lend itself to an inappropriate enlargement of the supposed number of "true" homosexuals. Such a scheme is also unwieldy, and still would not greatly affect the working conclusions offered above, of 1% and 2%. I have a bias towards using conduct as a barometer for several reasons: 1) It is more easily measured; 2) It has been more often measured and thus it may provide more means to make meaningful comparisons in different time frames; 3) Since I do not approve of homosexual conduct, and I hold it as a principle not to think ill of someone gratuitously, I prefer not to assume that someone is a homosexual unless they have acted so. I think there is a useful distinction between temptation and sin; and 4) Since I do not find that homosexuality is innate for anyone, I think there is a difference between considering and completing, and that one should not be "consigned" by others to something to which he has not yet consigned himself.

There are reports, after the 2000 census, that there are 600,000 gay "couples" living together. First, the manner by which that number has been concluded is not altogether trouble free. Alas, the past record of the proponents of homosexuality who are doing the figuring also tend to call into question their conclusions. Second, that number is still roughly within the parameters of the total population which I estimate to be sound, based on the various considerations noted above, but most especially on the NORC and the Michael *et al* studies previously cited.

It may be of interest to note that similar percentages have been found in studies of homosexual conduct in various other western nations. In France, exclusive lifetime homosexuality was .7% for men and .6% for women. Lifetime of any experience of homosexuality was 4.1% for men and 2.6% for women. In Britain, 1.4% of men had claimed any homosexual contact within five years; and 6.1% of men in their whole lifetime had had any such contact. In Canada, a study of first year college students under 25 found 98% heterosexual, 1% bisexual, and 1% homosexual. In Norway, .9% of males and females, aged 16-60, reported any homosexual contact within 3 years; and 3.5% of males and 3.0% of females had ever had any homosexual experience. In Denmark, a study found that 2.7% of sexually experienced males had had any homosexual contact (Muir, 1998, pp. 30-31).

So then, I think it is a reasonable conclusion that about 1% of the total population of the United States and 2% of the sexually active adult population might be said to be homosexual at any given point in time. Since these numbers would include persons who might better be called "experimenters," influenced by the pro-gay stance of current media and educational institutions, and others with no current heterosexual outlet, these numbers may well be a bit "generous" in their estimation of the homosexual population, but I think they will suffice for our purposes.

Let me offer a word about the literature by which the reader might more fully study the subject of health and homosexuality. *Health Implications Associated with Homosexuality* is a monograph prepared by The Medical Institute for Sexual Health. It is excellent, and scholarly (Medical Institute, 1999). More easily available and also very helpful is *Homosexuality and the Politics of Truth* by Jeffrey Satinover, a medical doctor, who deals with many issues, but devotes substantial space to health issues (Satinover, 1996). Thomas Schmidt in *Straight and Narrow? Compassion and Clairity in the Homosexual Debate* (Schmidt, 1995) has much data regarding matters reflecting on health. The Satinover, Schmidt and Medical Institute books will also be a source of more scholarly physical health references for those who wish to pursue them. *Reparative Therapy of Male Homosexuality* by Joseph Nicolosi gives some of the data on behavior, with regards to promiscuity, infidelity and anonymity, as well as other data (Nicolosi, 1991). Less scholarly and more polemical, but also with excellent information is *Answers to the Gay Deception* by Marlin Maddoux and Christopher Corbett (Maddoux, 1994).

It may be of interest to note who talks about what. The pro-gay writers seem to touch upon these issues very little. Bell and Weinberg do slightly (Bell, 1978, 1981), and so do McWhirter and Mattison (McWhirter, 1984), in an attempt to blunt some of the sense of disorder in the homosexual life which the data, even theirs, seems to present. They do so with regards to self-report in a limited number of concerns only. The gay activist psychologists that I have seen say even less, speaking in generalities and, in so far as they refer to such kinds of information, attempt to lay blame for whatever is amiss at the feet of those who make the homosexual uncomfortable by disapproving of his conduct (Issay, 1989, and Mondimore, 1996). Christian writers deal with this data, as do the medical doctors. The traditionalist psychiatrists deal with issues like promiscuity and infidelity. The ex-gays do not deal with this kind of data very much. I think that it is uncomfortable for them. They will not deny it. Some will very clearly affirm elements of the normal gay lifestyle. Yet, it seems to me, they do not talk very much about health related issues. Why?

The ones who deal with it do so because it is relevant. The ones who avoid it do so because it is unpleasant, uncomfortable. It is uncomfortable for the proponents of homosexuality because they have no real answers for the data. Their best hope being to blame someone else, and their most common tactic being to ignore the issues. Why do the ex-gays tend to ignore it? In part, because much of their work is confessional, and in their confessions they are certainly honest, but there is more. Their work is largely directed to helping the homosexual struggler. They are speaking to those who want out, and they tell them how it can happen. They are not so much, usually, speaking to "the general public," and thus their concern is not for every related issue. Fair enough, but that is not all. The ex-gays themselves have also felt rejection from the "straights" and from "Christians." They have heard this kind of data used not with sorrow, but with almost a sound of rejoicing at the pain of the homosexuals by those who were using it, and they do not want to add any pain to those whom they know from experience are already experiencing quite enough, thank you. Good, we need to know that.

Again, the matter of response is one I intend to deal with in the last section. Now I will deal with matters reflecting upon the health or wisdom or virtue of homosexuality in general. However, even now we must point out that the proper goal for the depiction of any problem is not a rejoicing in it, nor is it for a rejoicing in the suffering of those who suffer in it, but for the resolution of it. The problem is to be pointed out so that it becomes known that there is a problem and so that the problem may be dealt with. Dear reader, I do not ask you to agree that there is a problem, just to consider the evidence that shall now follow.

Chapter 17:

The Evidence Concerning the Healthfulness of Homosexuality

Persons who engage in homosexual sex experience *vastly* **higher rates of** sexually transmitted disease than persons who do not. Eighty percent of all sexually transmitted disease is experienced by the 2% of the sexually active adults who are homosexual in their activity (Maddoux, 1994, p. 56; Feder, 1992, p. 14). Since 80% of STD's are experienced by homosexuals, this means that 20% is experienced by heterosexuals. Since 2% constitute one fiftieth of the total, and that $1/50^{th}$ have 4/5ths of the disease, this means that homosexuals as a group, on average, experience sexually transmitted disease at a rate *200 times* that of heterosexuals. If one were to put that in percentage terms, it means that a practicing homosexual has a 20,000% greater likelihood of getting a sexually transmitted disease than does a heterosexual. That is an extraordinary disparity.

About a decade ago, there was an article in the *L. A. Times* reporting that a recent study had shown a 50% greater likelihood of getting leukemia if one smoked cigarettes than if one did not. The likelihood was still small, but it was 50% greater with smoking. This was front page news. Perhaps we may take that as an indication of what variation is significant. If a troubling matter of 50% more is likely under condition X, then it is front page news, so to speak. Now then, the data shows that homosexuals are not 50% more likely to get a sexually transmitted disease (an STD), not 100%, not 200%, not 500%, not 1,000%, not 5,000%, but approximately 20,000% more likely. We are not speaking of a modest variation here, nor will we be speaking of only a modest difference in other matters we consider. Bear that in mind. It may be significant.

Prior to the emergence of AIDS in the 1980's, studies suggested that perhaps 78% of all homosexuals had experienced a sexually transmitted disease (Medical Institute, 1999, p. 35). With regards to the entire US population, 18% of women and 16% of men had ever had one of nine STD's included in the Michael study (Michael, 1994, p. 187). This data does not reflect the frequency per person, but it does reflect a great disparity in the experience of any STD by gay and straight populations. Among heterosexuals, about one in six have ever had any venereal disease; among homosexuals, only one in six have *not* had a venereal disease.

Other studies have indicated similar things: youths engaging in homosexual behavior are 23 times more likely to contract a sexually transmitted disease; lesbians are 19 times more likely than heterosexual women to have had syphilis, twice as likely to suffer from genital warts, and four times as likely to suffer with scabies. Male homosexuals are 14 times more likely to have syphilis than male heterosexuals. They are thousands of times more likely to have AIDS (Maddoux, 1994, p. 56). Satinover calculates the likelihood of the homosexual male getting AIDS as only 430 times greater, which would be a 43,000% greater likelihood (Satinover, 1996, p. 57).

One strong advocate of homosexuality notes that at one venereal disease clinic in San Francisco, in the year 1984, 65% of the men visiting the clinic tested positive for HIV (Mondimore, 1994, p. 241). One gay activist who tried to reduce gay bathhouse activity found himself being called a "sex Nazi." "For some gay men, same sex eroticism defined not just their sexual orientation but their identity as individuals. Thus, for them, a gay man who did not have sex whenever, and with whomever, he wanted, was denying his true identity" (Mondimore, 1994, p. 241).

These higher rates of disease are not coincidental. They are related to differences in lifestyle and sexual practices between homosexuals and heterosexuals. Having multiple partners increases the risk of acquiring an STD, and homosexuals have far more partners, as will be discussed below. The lining of the rectum is more permeable than is the lining of the vagina. The lining of the rectum is more easily torn. The environment of the vagina is cleaner than that of the rectum. Engaging in sexual intercourse while already having one STD can, in some cases, make it easier to acquire another. Sexual activity involving oral-anal contact increases the risk of ingesting fecal matter, which has other consequences. It would seem that the health cost to those involved in homosexuality might call into question the wisdom of the conduct.

There are many diseases; some not generally viewed as STD's, which also occur far more commonly among persons who engage in homosexual activities. After a discussion of the reasons for the increased physical risk in anal intercourse, Santinover (Satinover, 1996, pp. 67-68) goes on to say: "As a result, homosexual men are disproportionately vulnerable to a host of serious and sometimes fatal infections caused by entry of feces into the bloodstream. These include hepatitis B and the cluster of otherwise rare conditions, such as shigellosis and Giardia lamblia infection, which together have been known as 'Gay Bowel Syndrome.' A major review article summarizes: 'Because of their larger number of sexual partners and sexual practices such as anilingus and anal intercourse, homosexual men are at particularly high risk of acquiring hepatitis B, giardiasis, amebiasis, shigellosis, campylobacteriosis, and anorectal infections with Neisseria gonorrhoeae, Chlamydia trachomatis, Treponema pallidum, herpes simplex virus, and human papilloma viruses.'

"Another review article classifies the conditions homosexually active men encounter into four general groups:

'Classical sexually transmitted diseases (gonorrhea, infections with Chlamydia trachomatis, syphilis, herpes simplex infections, genital warts, pubic lice, scabies); enteric diseases (infections with Shigella species, Campylobacter jejuni, Entamoeba histolytica, Giardia lamblia, hepatitis A, hepatitis B, hepatitis non-A, hepatitis non-B, and cytomegalovirus); trauma (fecal incontinence, hemorrhoids, anal fissure, foreign bodies, rectosigmoid tears, allergic proctitis, penile edema, chemical sinusistis, inhaled nitrite burns, and sexual assault of the male patient); and the acquired immunodeficiency syndrome (AIDS.)'"

Reviewing studies dealing with health issues similar to those raised above, the Medical Institute (Medical Institute, 1999, pp. 55-56) notes, "the term 'Gay Bowel Syndrome' was first used in the 1970's to describe various gastrointestinal problems commonly seen among homosexual men." While these conditions are not seen exclusively among gay men, they are seen with far greater frequency among gay men. They quote one study that says, "Gay bowel syndrome constitutes a group of conditions that occur among persons who practice unprotected anal intercourse, anilingus or fellatio following intercourse. These same conditions may well occur among women who practice these high risk behaviors." They then go on to list conditions under three headings, caused by various pathogens: proctitis, enteritis, and proctocolitis.

There are also rectal and intestinal injuries that were once extremely rare, but have become fairly common due to homosexual practices. Injuries of this sort include "lacerations, tears, bleeding, perforations of the rectum and/or anal sphincter muscles" (Medical Institute, 1999, p. 57). One study in the early 1990's of more than 2,750 homosexual/bisexual clients of an HIV testing clinic in Mexico City found that one third had experienced rectal bleeding during intercourse. The more common the bleeding, the greater the likelihood that the person would acquire AIDS. "Fisting," inserting the hand or fist into the rectum of one's sex partner, was found to be damaging to the sphincter muscles. Anal receptive intercourse itself was found to stretch the sphincter muscles and decrease the resting pressure of the anal canal, but studies varied as to whether or not this caused fecal incontinence (Medical Institute, 1999, p. 58).

There are some other indices of possible health problems associated with homosexual behavior. Studies suggest that perhaps 10% of the total adult US population are problem drinkers, but 30% of gay men are problem drinkers (Medical Institute, 1999, p. 69). Other studies report that "both male and female homosexuals have far greater percentages of alcoholism than the general population (Saghir *et* al, 1970). In addition, very substantial proportions of homosexuals report that sexual activity occurs under the influence of intoxicating levels of alcohol and many find it a necessary precondition for satisfactory sexual activity" (Fann, 1983, p. 144). The higher rate of problem drinking seems established. The only question is: What accounts for it? Does the rate of problem drinking suggest the presence of unresolved psychological issues?

One comparison study of homosexuals and heterosexuals dealing with rates of tobacco use found that "among adults aged 35 and over, 27.1 percent of men and 22 percent of women reported smoking cigarettes in the past month, compared to 35.4 percent for gay men and 38.1 percent for lesbians" (Medical Institute, 1999, p. 71). Most studies report higher use of drugs by homosexuals than by heterosexuals of the same age group. One startling difference was in a study that found that 1.1 percent of heterosexual men used "poppers," while 57.7 percent of gay men had used this drug (Medical Institute, 1999, p. 71-72). What accounts for the higher rates of these activities generally thought to be unhealthy?

Suicide data seems to vary with the researcher. However, the Bell and Weinberg study found that 20% of homosexual males had actually attempted suicide, and only 4% of their control group of heterosexuals had (Bell, 1978, p. 201). The reader might wish to consider *Health Implications Associated with Homosexuality* (Medical Institute, 1999, pp, 72-74), but consider also "The Gay Youth Suicide Myth" (LaBarbera, 1996, pp. 65-72). While definitions of "intimate partner abuse" vary, and there are problems with reporting incidents, Island and Lettellier believe that "the incidence of domestic violence among gay men is nearly double that in the heterosexual population" (Medical Institute, 1999, p. 80). Again, what accounts for these findings? Is it possible that homosexual ideation and activity is itself a reflection of unresolved issues?

I apologize to the reader. This seems almost too much uncomfortable evidence to ask the reader to bear, but it is a reflection of the reality that simply is to be born by persons who engage in homosexual conduct, and it is only a small fraction of such information that could be presented. Mind you, much of the above applies to males and not necessarily to females. Mind you, theoretically, much of this damage, though never all, could be greatly reduced if persons were more restrained in their conduct than is the custom. But what is, 'is the custom'. The incontrovertible fact seems to remain that, on average, homosexuals experience *vastly* more disease, and that fact may call into question the wisdom of the activity as a whole.

There is evidence that homosexuals experience *greatly* shortened life spans. Surveys in 1991 and 1992 indicated that "the median age of death for a homosexual male, *not having AIDS* was only 42 years, with a mere 9 percent living to old age. Of 106 lesbians surveyed, the median lifespan was only 45 years, with 26% living to old age" (Maddoux, 1994, pp. 56-57). A similar study cites the median age of death for homosexual males, not having AIDS, as 41 years, verses an average of 75.5 for the entire population (Feder, 1992, p. 14). For those who died of AIDS, the median age of death was 39 (Medical Institute, 1999, p. 14). Satinover cites the same phenomenon as "a twenty-five to thirty-year decrease in life expectancy" (Satinover, 1996, p. 51). The first two citations would suggest a decrease in life expectancy of closer to 35 years.

"In April 1993, three researchers presented a paper to the Eastern Psychological Association in which they analyzed the age of death for nearly seven thousand homosexuals and heterosexuals by obituary notices in a large number of gay and a smaller number of large non-gay newspapers. They found that the gay male lifespan, even apart from AIDS and with a long-term partner, is significantly shorter than that of married men in general by more than three decades. AIDS further shortens the lifespan of homosexual men by more than 7 percent.

"Because of the researcher's rough and ready methodology, these findings have to be considered preliminary. Their data for homosexuals and for gay men with AIDS, however, are very close to similar data from other, more reliable and replicated sources." (Satinover, p. 69)

I believe that all of these estimates come from very extensive studies of obituaries, including many gay publications. While they were fairly extensive studies, it is still reasonable to question the accuracy of the findings as a reflection of the entire gay population. It is my guess that Satinover reduced his statement of the number of years the lifestyle costs to try to adjust for any possible misreading to which the data might lead.Other studies, based on a variety of sources, obituaries, survey data, and census data, indicate "an average life span of less than 50 years for both men who have sex with men and lesbian women" (Medical Institute, 1999, p. 14). Using the best information available, there is an absolutely horrific price to be paid in a much reduced lifespan for a life of homosexual activity. Homosexuality, by the best evidence available, is *vastly* more damaging to one's health than is alcoholism (Satinover, 1996, p. 49-51).

The very great sexual promiscuity seen among homosexuals does not seem to be a sign of contentment. Much of the evidence here comes from the Kinsey Institute study *The Male Couple: How Relationships Develop* by McWhiter and Mattison (McWhirter, 1984), everywhere cited. They were sympathetic to the gay position and attempted to establish the normalcy of homosexual relationships. See also *Reparative Therapy of Male Homosexuality* (Nicolosi, 1991), *The Gay Deception* (Maddoux, 1994), *Health Implications Associated with Homosexuality* (Medical Institute, 1999), and *Homosexuality and the Politics of Truth* (Satinover, 1996), with regards to homosexual promiscuity.

The McWhirter and Mattison study found that 28% of male homosexuals had 1,000 different sex partners, or more. Forty-three percent had 500 different sex partners, or more. Seventy-five percent had 100 partners, or more. Less than 10% had 24 partners or less. Only 1% had 1 to 2 partners. The average was about 500 different sexual partners per person (Medical Institute, 1999, p. 18; Nicolosi, 1991, p. 124; Maddoux, 1994, p. 51).

From the NORC surveys, reporting on the entire population, we find: "Over a lifetime, the average American adult will have had 7.14 sex partners since age 18" (*The Universal Almanac 1992*, p. 219).

Since homosexuals were included in these totals for the "average American adult," to ascertain a reasonable comparison, we would need to factor out the contribution to that total by homosexuals, determine the average for gays and for straights, and then make a comparison. Since the average for all adults was 7.14, and, theoretically, an average group of 100 adult Americans should have had a total of 714 partners in their lives to the date of the survey. If we assume that the male homosexual population was only 1% of the total, which may be a little low since we are dealing with the sexually active here, and if we assume that the average homosexual male had only 450 different partners, which is probably a little low, then that 1% would contribute 450 to the total of 714. That would leave 264 to be apportioned among the other 99% of the population. That suggests that heterosexuals, on average, have about 3 different lifetime partners (or less) and that homosexual males have, on average, about 450 different lifetime partners. That means, on average, homosexuals have about 447 *more* lifetime sex partners. Or, that means that homosexuals have about 150 *times* as many sex partners. Or, that means homosexual males, on average, are about 15,000 percent more promiscuous.

These are not exaggerated numbers, nor peculiar to one study. In another study, "homosexual men reported a median of 1,160 lifetime sex partners." In another, the median number of lifetime sexual partners of over 4,000 homosexual respondents was 49.5. Many individuals reported ranges of 300-400, and 272 of them reported over 1,000 different lifetime partners" (Maddoux, 1994, p. 52).

While homosexual women are not as promiscuous as homosexual men, they are considerably more promiscuous than heterosexual women. "One study found that 38 percent of lesbians surveyed had between 11 and 300 partners. Another study revealed that 41 percent of lesbians admitted to having had between 10 and

500 lifetime partners" (Maddoux, 1994, p. 51). While approximately 40% of lesbian women have had 10 or more partners, only 9% of all women in the US have had 10 or more partners (Michael, 1994, p. 102).

My point here is *not* to try to prove that homosexuals are particularly evil, but to raise questions about the healthfulness of homosexuality. Does this degree of promiscuity seem to reflect a spirit of emotional health? Let me offer you two possible readings of this data and ask you to decide which you find most likely. Reading one: It is healthy, it is just good clean fun, and it is a sign of peace and contentment. Reading two: It is a sign of persons desperately seeking something which they are not finding in the activity they are pursuing, and, not having discovered the real need, they seek all the more frantically through an activity which does not, and will not, satisfy. It is not so much passion, nor even pleasure, as it is addiction. Which reading seems best to explain the data?

Cory (Cory, 1951, p. 141) attempts to explain the promiscuity on the basis that: 1) men are just naturally promiscuous, and 2) women are the taming influence in heterosexual relationships, and 3) since women are not involved in male homosexual relationship, then 4) of course, you would expect to see more promiscuity among homosexuals. Not so. First, since homosexual men in a "coupled relationship" are also promiscuous, why couldn't heterosexual men in a marriage be so as well? Second, why are non-married heterosexual men not as wildly promiscuous as homosexual men? (Of course, there are a few public figures that are famous as promiscuous heterosexuals, but we are speaking of information obtained from studies which deal with large numbers and thus, presumably, fairly well reflect significant averages.) Third, the disparity is not a little one, but astronomical. Can that much be accounted for? Fourth, perhaps such promiscuity in some heterosexuals would also indicate instability, and not the universality of male promiscuity. Fifth, why then are homosexual women much more promiscuous than heterosexual women if promiscuity is not a homosexual problem but a male problem?

Also, it is argued by the homosexual Reverend Dr. F. that such promiscuity is all due to the social rejection of homosexual persons. Therefore, it is difficult for them to be able to express their feelings openly and thus harder to develop long term relationships. Again, this is not so. First, the alleged difficulty might very well lead to *fewer* partners, not more. Establishing sufficient relationship to have sexual intercourse with someone five hundred different times might be thought to put one at risk of rejection or exposure or disapproval more often than to do so once or twice or three times. Second, the numbers are simply too high to explain away by such possible rejection. Third, if his theory were so, then one would expect to see more tranquil sex lives in times and places more accepting of homosexuality, but this is not so. So far, times and places offering greater acceptance of homosexual behavior have not led to any visible restraint, but rather the opposite.

I submit that the astronomically higher rate of promiscuity is a sign of an obsessive behavior. It is much like any addiction. The dose must be increased to get the same result, because the activity itself does not intrinsically satisfy the actual need which the person is seeking to have met. The activity is only a means of self-medicating, of numbing the pain, of changing the mood. It serves to give some degree of release for a moment, but since the real need is not met by the activity, the release is very short-lived, and the "dose," or the activity, must be continually increased. Is this not characteristic of addictive behavior? If you do not accept this explanation, splendid; then come up with one that you think can adequately explain the data. Do not simply find some trifling thing that you think might be a flaw in the argument and use that as a smokescreen to hide all else from your view. There is an astronomical disparity. Is there another way to explain it?

There is a *vastly* greater resort to anonymous sex among homosexuals than among heterosexuals. Seventy-nine percent of male homosexuals in "the most ambitious study of homosexuality ever attempted" reported that more than half their sex partners were strangers (Nicolosi, 1991, p. 124). In the NORC study in

1988, only 6% indicated that even *one* or more sex-partners were pick-ups, or strangers. Since at least 1 of those 6 percent must have been homosexual, that would leave not more than 5% as reflective of heterosexual males (*The Universal Almanac 1992*, p. 218-219). One percent of all females reported having had one or more pick-ups.

This means that while only 5% of heterosexual males had *any* pick-ups (one or more), 79% of homosexual males had a *majority* of pick-ups, or sex with persons not known before that sexual encounter. This, again, is a very substantial disparity.

Once more, the explanation is offered by the gay Reverend Dr. F. that this is due to the lack of acceptance of homosexuals by society, that they are compelled to have furtive, anonymous sexual encounters by this lack of acceptance. Again, this does not hold. First, the risk of rejection or disapproval or discovery would seem to be greater by having sex with so many persons unknown. A known person would seem to be a safer risk if disapproval is the issue. Second, this is really quite a lot of anonymity to explain by the possibility of disapproval. Third, there is as yet no indication of a decrease in anonymous sex acts as homosexuality is more accepted. So far, the opposite seems to be the case.

And again, the question is: Is this a sign of health? Of contentment? Of peace? Does this seem to be an expression of healthy social relations? Or does this seem to be an expression of difficulty in establishing meaningful relationships? Does this style of behavior seem likely to lead to stronger lives, better social relations, stronger support networks, more mutual support? Or does this seem to reflect something furtive? Something perhaps which is an embarrassment even to many of those who engage in it themselves? Self-centered? Fleeting? Tending to diminish social relationships rather than build them? You tell me. It is a part of the reality. What does it mean? The current social orthodoxy of America is that "gay is good." This is a part of "gay." Is this good? If not, what does that say?

Infidelity among homosexual men who are in committed relationships is virtually universal. In the McWhirter and Mattison study (McWhirter, 1984), they surveyed 156 gay couples. Two thirds of them had entered into the relationship with the expectation of fidelity. Of these 137 couples beginning their relationship with the expectation of fidelity, only 7 had maintained fidelity. All of these seven couples were together for a relatively short period of time. Not one couple who had been together more than five years had maintained fidelity. Only four couples had maintained fidelity after two years, three after three years, one after four years, and none after five years (McWhirter, 1984, p. 252). They report: "Sexual exclusivity among these couples is infrequent, yet their expectations of fidelity are high" (McWhirter, 1984, p. 252). Typical couples expect "three-way's," "parties," and other affairs on the side (McWhirter, 1984, pp. 249-252).

Note this also: It is *not* the case that homosexuals are simply not troubled by infidelity, as has been argued in some recent court cases. "In fact, more than 85 percent of the [male homosexual] couples report that their greatest relationship problems center on outside relationships, sexual and non-sexual" (McWhirter, 1984, p. 256).

The six most common reasons for having sex outside of the committed relationship are summarized as follows (McWhirter, 1984, pp. 253-254):

1. "All my sexual needs are not met by my partner. Sex together gets boring at times, and I need new material for my fantasies."

2. "My partner is not really my sexual type. I still like to have sex with a certain type of man."

3. "It's fun and adventure. The more variety and number of partners, the more adventure and fun."

4. "I have some kinky sexual interests that my partner doesn't share."

5. "We found that having sex with others often enhances our sex together afterwards."

6. "Sometimes I do it with another guy because I'm so angry at my partner."

Nor is this pattern found only in America or only in times past. In the Netherlands, same-sex marriage and civil unions have been legal for a number of years. Researchers there found, in a long-term study of male homosexual relationships, that "gay men in 'steady partnerships' stay together for an average of 18 months." Also that "gay men with a steady partner' have an average of eight additional sexual partners a year" (Dallas and Heche, p. 368).

Conversely, among the entire population "more than 80 percent of women and 65 to 85 percent of men of every age, report that they had no partners other than their spouse while they were married" (Michael, 1994, p. 105). More than 80% of all adult Americans, aged 18 to 59, had zero to one partner in a year, which reflects the fact that most Americans are married and faithful, and even most who are cohabiting are also faithful (Michael, 1994, p. 106). The average marriage lasts a quarter of a century, and most people report that they do not have additional sexual partners during that quarter century of marriage (Michael, 1994, p. 106). Other studies show that "75% of married men and 85% of married women say that they have never been unfaithful" (Muir, p. 103). The pattern of fidelity among heterosexual men is quite different from that of homosexual men.

Does the degree of infidelity among committed, homosexual male couples bespeak peace? Is it a sign of health? Do you find the Cory thesis that all men are promiscuous and, since there is no taming female influence in a male homosexual relationship, there is naturally more infidelity, intellectually satisfying? It does not fit observed data among heterosexual males. From various studies, not counting those who were abstinent during a year, nor those in other categories, just speaking of *men* who had *only one sex partner in a year*, the following percentages were reported: in the United Kingdom, 73%; in France, 78%; in Finland 78%; and in the United States 67%.

The pro-gay Harry argues, "Non-exclusiveness does not appear to be a problem except when defined as one" (Harry, 1984,

p. 121). This was *not* found to be so by McWhirter and Mattison (McWhirter, 1984, p. 256). Harry also says, "the problem is not that many gay relationships are non-exclusive but that in a number of cases the couples are not able to come to an agreement on the acceptability or unacceptability of non-exclusiveness" (Harry, 1984, p. 144), even though he notes that partner satisfaction in a relationship is heavily dependent upon the other partner's comfort with non-exclusivity (Harry, 1984, p. 117). Does this seem sound to you, or does it sound like special pleading? Is there a virtue in long-term relationship? Is a relationship of intimacy strengthened or weakened by one or each partner having sexual relations outside the committed relationship? Would this seem to be beneficial for child rearing? Beneficial for life-building? I submit that the universality of male homosexual infidelity is not a sign of health.

The evidence is that there is a vastly greater resort to prostitutes by homosexual males. Robin Lloyd (Lloyd, 1976, pp. 226-227) estimated that there were 300,000 to 600,000 under-aged boys used in prostitution. Gail Sheehy (Sheehy, 1973) estimated that there were 200,000 to 225,000 women, of all ages, and mostly of age, used in prostitution. In order to use this data, we will need to make assumptions that surely are imperfect, but probably sufficiently adequate for the task of making some kind of comparison. For the moment, I will assume that the customers for each set of groupings of prostitutes were male, discounting the presence of female customers in each group, which I assume would be small in each case. Then we must bear in mind that only 2% of the sexually active adult population is homosexual (See above). We may increase that to 3% since we are dealing only with the sexually active adult male population. Then, if we take the *average* number for the estimate of boys, 450,000, and the *higher* number for the estimate of women, 225,000, we would find that the 3% of the adult male population that is homosexual, sustains in prostitution *twice* as many boys as the 97% of the male population that is heterosexual, sustains in prostitution of women of all ages. Setting aside other possible variables for the moment, that would indicate that homosexuals, on average, make resort to prostitutes some 64 *times* as often, or, with a frequency 6,400% greater. Incidentally, the number for boys does *not* include male prostitutes who are *of* age as it does for females, therefore, if anything, the disparity in the use by males of under-aged prostitutes who are male is far greater than the number just given would indicate.

Is this an indication of health? Is this social conduct you want to encourage? Do these numbers raise questions about the healthfulness of normal homosexual conduct?

The use of underage children for sex is *vastly* greater by persons who engage in homosexual acts. This point is denied, sometimes even by those whose data proves the point! Please consider the evidence. Robin Lloyd (Lloyd, 1976) made an offhand denial that homosexuals particularly wanted to use boys. However, the data above, even though the data for females includes all ages, indicates a *vast* disparity between the rate of use of children by persons who engage in homosexual sex, and those who engage in heterosexual sex.

Amazingly, A. Nichols Groth seems to deny that *any* child molestation is done by homosexuals, based on his very small study (Burgess, 1978, pp. 4-5). He then goes on to illustrate his argument with summaries of eleven case studies, *five* of which involved homosexual molestation (Burgess, 1978, pp. 7-22). If these case studies are representative, then that would mean that five elevenths, or just less than half of all molestation, was itself a homosexual act. What can explain his apparent claim about the absence of homosexuals among the population he studied? He said, "offenders who selected underage male victims either have always done so exclusively or have regressed from adult heterosexual relationships. There were no homosexual, adult oriented, offenders in our sample who turned to children" (Burgess, 1978, pp. 4-5).

One, if a person who has been heterosexual becomes involved in homosexual acts, the proponents of homosexuality then claim that was who he "really" was, except when it is inconvenient. Two, if these persons who have abused children of the same sex are not to be counted as homosexual, then the percentage of persons who "are homosexual" in the society as a whole would have to be reduced, since they are otherwise counted in the 1.5% of those studied who have had one or more homosexual contacts within a year's time. Three, does that mean that persons who have sex with children of the opposite sex are not *hetero*sexual either? Four, it is a commonplace in the study of childhood molestation that it is a crime of opportunity. Is it possible that persons who are self-identified, practicing homosexuals are less often in family situations and thus have diminished access? Five, how was his sample determined? Six, what did the author want to find? Seven, does being oriented to children of the same sex, but not to adults of the same sex, make one not oriented to persons of the same sex? How? Only by convenient re-definition.

Futher, three of the five males who molested males had been victims of homosexual rape themselves. Virtually all of the perpetrators in his eleven case studies were themselves prior sexual victims in one way or another (Burgess, 1978, pp. 7-22).

David Finkelhor (Finkelhor, 1984) also makes an offhand comment that homosexuals are no more inclined to child molestation than are heterosexuals. At least he is not as sweeping in his claim as Groth. However, his data does not support his claim. He surveys a variety of studies. He estimates both the percentage of reported molestation done by males and by females and the percentage of reported molestation done to males and to females (Finkelhor, 1984, pp. 156 and 173-174). The net result is that the range of same sex molestation is about 30%. Setting aside other variables for the moment, this would indicate that the 2% of the sexually active adult population that is homosexual, has perpetrated approximately 30% of all reported molestation, and the 98% who are not homosexual, perpetrated the remaining 70%. That indicates a rate of same gender molestation that is about 20 *times* greater than the rate of opposite gender molestation.

Now let us note some variables. This reported molestation was from family settings where someone was healthy enough to report something. First, I think it reasonable to assume that heterosexuals have more likely lived in settings of families with children than have homosexuals, thereby increasing the availability of children. Therefore, if the amount of opportunity could be factored in, it is probable that the rate disparity would be greater still. Second, Finkelhor adjusted his data to reduce the amount of female on female sexual abuse. He assumed that many females probably participated in the molestation of their daughters only in submission to their molesting husbands, and therefore reduced his estimate of female on female molestation. This was not a conclusion based on evidence but an assumption based on his personal feelings. It may or may not be sound. Third, Finkelhor (Finkelhor, 1984, p. 156) found that molestation of males is much *less* reported; males do not even want to talk about it for fear of the stigma of homosexuality. However, there was no attempt to take this under reporting into account. Fourth, I would suggest that at least some men also molested females to diminish their shame in molesting males, feeling that it was less shameful to be interested in both girls and boys than to be interested in boys only. Sixty percent of the time, boys were abused with others, usually their sisters, which may have occurred to diminish the homosexual element (Finkelhor, 1984, p. 164). This, too, is only a supposition. Strean finds that men who molest young girls often have strong homosexual feelings and unconsciously identifies with the daughter he victimizes (Strean, 1983, p. 82). However, these reflections suggest that perhaps there was an even higher incidence of homosexual ideation as a factor in the molestation of children than Finkelhor's conclusions suggest.

Now we turn to another body of evidence. Florence Rush (Rush, 1980, p. 165-169) says, "It is estimated that 1.2 million children under 16 are yearly involved in commercial sex, either prostitution, pornography, or both." She says that about 85% of them are males. If this is reasonably accurate, then that means about 1,000,000 boys under age 16 are used in commercial sex every year, with 200,000 girls under 16 so used. If we assume again that the customers are primarily male, that means that 3% adult male homosexuals maintain in commercial sex five times as many boys, one million, as the 97% heterosexual males do girls under 16. This is a rate of use for commercial sex by those who have homosexual interests 160 *times* greater, or 16,000 percent greater.

There is a University of Pennsylvania study released in September of 2001, which estimates the number of U.S. children under 17 used in commercial sex to be 325,000. They estimate that, at any given point in time, 122,000 children under age 17 are runaways who have turned to prostitution or pornography for food or drugs. They estimate that 73,000 are children still at home, who are used in prostitution and pornography by family and friends in exchange for food, drugs, or other enticements. They estimate that 52,000 are "throwaway" children who have been abandoned by their parents or guardians and have turned to prostitution and pornography to survive (Memmott, 2001, p. 1A). "The study found that 47 percent of sexual assaults on children were committed by relatives; 49 percent by acquaintances, such as a teacher, a coach or a neighbor; and 4 percent by strangers" (Hernandez, 2001, A5). They found that 95 percent of the commercial sex that boys engaged in was with men (Hernandez, 2001, A5). About one quarter of those adults who engage in sex with boys were married with children, and three quarters were not (Hernandez, p. A5). These are smaller numbers of under-aged children used in commercial sex than those estimated by Florence Rush, but still quite substantial. Also, this study gives us firm data on the percentage of males who use boys in commercial sex, 95%. It also gives us data to suggest that, while one quarter of those using boys in sex are married, three quarters are not. In *either* case the perpetrators have some sort of homosexual inclination, but in three quarters of the cases, there is no heterosexual relationship to obscure that fact from the observer.

Some may wish to maintain the notion that "real homosexuals" do not desire to have sexual relations with children any more than heterosexuals. However, there are problems with such an argument: 1) This is contrary to the evidence. Curran and Parr (1957) reported 12% of homosexuals seen in practice acknowledged pedophilia, Feldman and MacCulloch (1971) reported 16% of the homosexual seen in their practice acknowledged pedophilia, and Aardweg reported that 10% of the homosexuals seen in his practice acknowledged pedophilia (Aardweg, 1986, p. 157). These reports were offered at times when both the social disapproval and the possible legal consequences were much greater than now, and thus might reflect under reporting more than otherwise; 2) To make this distinction between "real homosexuals" and molesters would require a change in definition of "homosexual" to exclude those who have homosexual acts with children, much reducing their numbers and presenting us with the intellectually untidy question of what that would mean about "heterosexuals" who have relations with children of the opposite sex; 3) If one assumes that homosexuality is generally an unhealthy response to some early childhood event or condition perceived as trauma by the person, then an unhealthy sexual interest in children could fairly easily be explained; 4) While one might have some straws to grab, by which to try to escape the implications of reported, family, same gender abuse (due to the sloppy thinking and pro-gay bias of some researchers), there is nothing that can explain the evidence of the vast use of underage children in commercial sex; 5) And, there has long been an active pedophile element in the gay movement. The best known reflection of this is perhaps NAMBLA, the North American Man Boy Love Association, which has long had as its motto: "Sex by eight or it's too late." One spokesperson for NAMBLA, an admitted pederast, has said, "Scratch the average homosexual and you will find a pedophile" (York, 1999, p. 2); and 6) Indeed, in recent times, there has been "respectable" journals that published articles by "respectable" psychologists declaring that for adults to have "consensual sex" with children is healthy, such as those by Rind, Tromovitch, Baserman, and Baurman. A storm of public protest caused the psychology/psychiatry priesthood to draw back from this claim. Once again, we see this priesthood responding to public pressure, which suggests that the APA may be more a political organization than a scientific one.

"*The Gay Report*, published by homosexual researchers Jay and Young in 1979, revealed that 73% of homosexuals surveyed had at some time had sex with boys 16 to 19 years of age or younger" (York, 1999, p. 8). Homosexuals constitute about a third of all child molesters, but, since they molest more children per molester, "it is estimated that 80 percent of pedophilic victims are boys who have been molested by adult males" (York, 1999, p. 8). A study of pedophiles in Canada notes that 30 percent admitted to engaging in homosexual acts as adults. Ninety-one percent of the molesters of non-familial boys admitted to *no* lifetime sexual contact *other* than homosexual (York, 1999, p. 8). An extensive study of pederasts and pedophiles by Dr. Paul Cameron showed that each homosexual molester on average molested 7.5 *times* as many children as heterosexual molesters over a like period (York, 1999, p. 8).

Many different individuals and organizations have campaigned for the elimination of age of consent laws, to make sex with children legal. While many individual homosexuals would not support this as a goal, it is generally a goal of their organizations. "In 1972, the National Coalition of Gay Organizations adopted a 'Gay Rights Platform' that included the following demand: 'Repeal of all laws governing the age of sexual consent'" (York, 1999, p. 3ff.). In recent times some gay rights organizations have moved to eject NAMBLA from membership, despite its long association with them, perhaps reflecting an awareness that for society as a whole, pederasty is still a bridge too far.

In 1994, the American Psychiatric Association revised its Diagnostic and Statistical Manual IV (DSM IV). They redefined what they call "paraphilias," or sexual perversions. For a person to be diagnosed as having a paraphilia, the person's conduct must "cause clinically significant distress or impairment of social, occupational or other important areas of functioning" (York, 1999, p. 9). Quoting Satinover, York notes that, "a man who routinely and compulsively has sex with children, and does so without pangs of conscience and without impairing his functioning otherwise is not necessarily a pedophile in need of treatment," by this standard (York, 1999, p. 9). This is the same course that the APA's view of homosexuality began to take in 1973. The association of homosexuality with the abuse of children is clearly established by several kinds of inquiry. For more on this theme one might see *Homosexual Activists Work to Lower the Age of Sexual Consent* by York and Knight (York, 1999) and *Kinsey: Crimes and Consequences* by Judith Reisman (Reisman, 1998).

The evidence is substantial that males who are involved in homosexuality *do* use under-aged boys in sexual activity at *vastly greater* rates than do heterosexual persons. Again, the question is: Does this reflect health? Is this a sign of maturity? Is it a sign of healthy social relations? There is much evidence that early introduction to sexual relations is not healthy for those so introduced at an early age, but is the desire to do so a sign of health for the adults so desiring?

We have surveyed considerable data from a variety of sources which clearly indicates that there are numerous evidences of disorder associated with the condition of homosexuality.

1. Persons who engage in homosexual activity experience vastly greater rates of STDs and many other medically harmful conditions.

2. Homosexuals have a greatly shortened lifespan.

3. Homosexuals have vastly higher rates of promiscuity.

4. Homosexuals engage in anonymous sex at vastly higher rates than do heterosexuals.

5. Committed homosexual couples have vastly higher rates of infidelity, with fidelity verging on being non-existent.

6. Homosexuals make vastly greater resort to prostitutes.

7. Homosexuals have vastly higher rates of sexual involvement with under-aged children.

It is not the case that this average is greatly skewed by a few homosexuals who are peculiarly wild in their conduct. The evidence is that 78% have had an STD, 75% of males have had over 100 sex partners, 43% have had sex with over 500 partners, 73% have had sex with a boy, 95% of male couples have not maintained fidelity for even a year, and 79% have had a majority of anonymous sex partners. Are these signs of health? Peace? Contentment? Wisdom? Virtue? Are these things to be encouraged? Promoted? Taught in our schools? Blessed in our churches? Or are these things perhaps signs that homosexuality is not a reflection of health?

Chapter 18:

A Consideration of the Pro-gay Rejoinders to the Preceding Discussion

At the beginning of this section, in Chapter 15, I noted four kinds of arguments that the proponents of the healthfulness of homosexuality might offer in reply to the data I expected to present in chapter 16. I dealt slightly with some of these possible replies in various sections, detailing data about a specific condition or concern that I thought might reflect unfavorably on the healthfulness of homosexuality, but I have largely left these possible rejoinders unanswered. I want to give them fuller attention now. I will begin by reprising those possible, pro-gay rejoinders:

1. The data is not sufficiently clear.

2. Some gays have problems; some straights have problems. There really is no clear disparity between the two groups.

3. Since some homosexuals do not fit in these categories, therefore homosexuals as a group cannot be described as characterized by any of these conditions.

4. Yes, there are some problems among the homosexual population, but these problems are *not* caused by homosexuality *per se*, but rather they are caused by non-homosexuals rejecting homosexuals. Thus, the "cure" is not *dis*approval of the conduct, but *a*pproval of the person.

The data is often extremely clear, and when it is uncertain, the disparity is often so great, that the basic condition remains clear.

The data on the contraction of sexually transmitted disease is really quite clear. The studies derive their data from National Institute of Health sources. The studies are numerous.

The evidence of greatly shortened lifespan is clear, but the quality of the data is not so clear. It is a reasonable supposition from various other data about disease and AIDS. The evidence is clear, but since much of it derives from obituaries, and since it is not established that this is representative, and then the weight of this data is reduced. However, 1) the evidence is substantial, 2) the evidence is consistent with other health related data, and 3) the disparity which it indicates is so great as to mean that some great disparity is most probably here, even if it is somewhat more or less than the data indicates.

The evidence with regards to male homosexual promiscuity is from proponents of homosexuality. If they had any bias, it was to diminish the disparity, not magnify it. The disparity is based upon various extensive and sound studies. The data about promiscuity is clear.

The data about anonymity in sexual contact is again from pro-gay sources, and the comparison data from the best general sexological surveys yet done. Similarly, the data about infidelity among couples is from pro-gay researchers, and the comparison data from the best studies yet done.

With regards to the data about the use of prostitutes and underage children, much of the data are estimates, though some are based on more precise surveys. However, these estimates are by the best experts in the field, and, the disparity is so enormous that it would seem it must reflect some significant reality even if the reality is not as great as the data indicates. And, it is possible that the data *under*estimates the disparity. In any case, 1) it is the best data available, 2) usually from persons who had no ax to grind in our current topic, 3) often from folks who openly tried to minimize the weight of data unfavorable to homosexuals, and 4) it reflects an enormous disparity.

The disparities indicated between the conduct and condition of homosexual and heterosexual persons is often enormous. It has been argued by some proponents of homosexuality, the homosexual Reverend E. for one, that "yes, gays have some problems, and heterosexuals do too," implying, more than stating, that there really isn't that much difference. But there is.

Some years ago, a study was reported in the general media that purported to show that smoking increased the likelihood of a person contracting leukemia by 50%. Please note that number, fifty percent. This was front-page news in the *Los Angeles Times* and the *San Diego Union-Tribune*. The likelihood of getting leukemia was still small, but 50% greater if you smoked. The coverage this study received should mean that any disparity of 50% or more might be a matter that establishes great disparity.

Numerous studies indicate that practicing homosexuality increases one's likelihood of contracting an STD by 20,000%. We are here not speaking of 50%, nor even of twice that, 100%, nor of ten times that, 500%, nor of *one hundred times* that, 5,000%, but of a 20,000% greater likelihood of contracting a venereal disease, not including AIDS. Since most venereal diseases are not as deadly as leukemia, the condition itself, acquiring an STD, is not intrinsically as newsworthy as is acquiring leukemia, but the disparity is astronomical. The increased likelihood of contracting AIDS seems to be about 43,000%. There is evidence to suggest that, on average, a homosexual lifestyle will, on average, decrease one's lifespan by twenty-five to thirty-five years. That is more than a third of one's life taken. If one were to look at the lost years as a percentage of the life span taken after the onset of regular sexual involvement, it might be half, or more. Similarly also, the rates of disparity for promiscuity, anonymity, infidelity, use of prostitutes, and use of children in commercial sex are also enormous. The disparity is enormous.

It is true that not all homosexuals fit any given category, however, the rates of involvement in practices that are not indicative of health are extremely high. It is not the case that "some do, some don't."

1. Over 75% of males had 100 or more partners.

2. McWhirter reports the following percentages of participation in various homosexual acts among males:

a. tongue kissing, 98.7%;

b. performing fellatio, 95.5;

c. being fellated, 95.2%;

d. mutual masturbation, 92.9%;

e. masturbation together, 91.7%;

f. mutual fellatio, 91.7%;

g. being penetrated anally, 71.0%;

h. penetrating anally, 71.0%;

i. performing analingus, 42%;

j. receiving analingus, 42%;

k. other things such as S & M, bondage, and "water sports," 7.1%. (McWhirter, 1984, p. 277)

3. Some 78% of homosexual have had an STD at least once.

4. Ninety-five percent of committed gay couples have affairs within a year of their marital commitment.

5. If there are a million boys or even 300,000 boys under sixteen in commercial sex at any given time, then there must be a large number of persons who are purchasing their wares.

No, once again, the percentage of involvement of persons engaged in homosexuality in acts that might be thought to be unhealthy is really quite large.

Not all smokers are dead. Most smokers you know are alive. Not all persons who have smoked can be seen to have died from smoking. Nevertheless, society has had no difficulty discerning that smoking in general is an unhealthy activity. Not all drinkers are dead. Many former problem drinkers are dead. Most of them that you know are not. Still, there is enough evidence to determine that heavy drinking is unhealthy. The evidence for the un-healthfulness of homosexuality is more extensive and more damning than that for chain smoking or heavy drinking.

Homosexuality can reasonably be characterized by those factors that are characteristic of it.

Now we come to what may be the best argument which the proponents of the healthfulness of homosexuality can muster: The problems associated with homosexuality are not caused by homosexuality, nor inherent in it; rather, the problems seen among persons who engage in homosexuality are caused by their rejection by society, by social disapproval. Society as a whole expresses disapproval in many ways. It is so extensive and pervasive that many gays have internalized this rejection. It is this rejection and disapproval which causes the furtive relationships so often seen, which militates against long-term committed relationships, which leads to the numerous and often anonymous sexual acts that are the real cause of the disease and other evidence of disorder in the lives of homosexual persons.

This is a plausible argument, but it is unsound. Before I move to establish that, however, I would like to point out that rejection *is* damaging. There are many who like to "encourage by discouragement." I have never liked that. Forgive me a Christian reference for a moment, but I do not find that the persons whose lives have been changed by Jesus were usually led to that change by being condemned. "We love, because He first loved us," said John in I John 4:19. I have known persons who were damaged by growing up in a home with verbal and emotional abuse. Even when someone is wrong, and perhaps especially when someone is wrong, a gracious spirit is generally more helpful than a condemning one to allow (enable?) a person to see the wrong. I do not disregard the harm that can be done by scorn or ridicule. Often such abuse serves to shove someone into, or deeper into, the conduct for which he has already being scorned. Still, the pro-gay argument above does not explain the data, and thus cannot be held.

First, there is an awful lot to explain. There is a mountain of self-destructive behavior to explain away on the grounds that somebody else does not like them doing self-destructive things. It is true that we may, in adolescence, do more of the thing we are told not to just as an act of rebellion, but adolescence does not last forever. Adolescence is usually a "disease" that we can grow out of. If one does not, then that in itself suggests some significant lack of appropriate growth. Pick several other things, traits, or activities, things that are unquestionably good to do. Then assume that others were berating one for doing them. What response can you envision? If one pro-gay theory is that criticism for doing what they say is good leads to doing more of it, and that more of it is bad, try out that principle in other settings, and see if you can find results indicating that their theory makes sense.

Second, if it is good, why is more of it bad? Consider that question again: If it is good, why is more of it bad? More cancer is bad, but then so is a little cancer. Much poverty is bad, but then a little poverty is none too good either. Even a little infidelity, promiscuity, anonymity, disease, abuse and such, are not considered good among heterosexuals. Is not the vastly greater prevalence of such things among homosexuals a sign of some discontent?

Third, why does disapproval lead to more of it? Since we have approved of out-of-wedlock births more, have we had fewer or more? More. When we disapproved, did we have less or more? Less. Generally speaking, widespread disapproval has led to less of a given activity, not more. Why then would disapproval lead to greater promiscuity? Is not the risk of rejection greater with more contacts? Either from the persons whose co-operation we seek or from on-lookers in society? It does not necessarily follow that disapproval would lead to the conduct seen.

Fourth, if this theory were sound, then we should expect to see a rise or fall in such activity in inverse relationship to approval: More approval should result in less such activity with its concomitant problems, and less approval should result in more homosexual activity. Is this seen? No. Since homosexuality has been more fully accepted in recent decades, the evidence indicates that homosexual activity has increased, as have related problems. Medical science has meliorated some of the problems. Approval has not. There is evidence that speaks to this theory, and so far, none of it supports this theory.

I submit that there is massive evidence that homosexuality is unhealthy. It commonly involves great promiscuity, great anonymity, great transiency, and great infidelity in relationships. Because of the social practices involved in homosexual life, because of the sexual practices involved in homosexuality, and because of the physiology of the structures involved in homosexual activity, homosexuality leads to vastly higher rates of disease, and a greatly shortened lifespan. There are numerous indications that homosexuality itself is unhealthy. Even if there were not, would not the persistence in an activity with so much consequent damage itself raise questions as to the healthfulness of the impulse underlying it? I submit that it neither leads to health, nor arises from health. But has not psychiatry said that homosexuality is healthy? To that question we turn next.

Chapter 19:

Psychiatry and Homosexuality
Don't the Experts Say It Is Healthy?

No, They Do Not.

For a long time there was a consensus among psychiatrists that homosexuality was pathological. Richard von "Kraft-Ebing maintained through all twelve editions of *Psychopathia Sexualis* that homosexuality was a degenerate and pathological condition" (Mondimore, 1996, p. 32), even though there were gay activists working hard to convince him otherwise. "Like other psychological symptoms Freud understood homosexuality (for males at least) as arising from an aberrant childhood experience, poor resolution of sexual conflict, and the relentless playing out of this conflict in adulthood" (Mondimore, 1996, p. 72).

There has been a movement, mostly by homosexual activists, for the acceptance of homosexuality since the late 1800's. From the beginning of psychology as a field of study, homosexuality was seen as a disorder. The first Diagnostic and Statistical Manual (DSM) of the American Psychiatric Association (APA) in 1952 viewed homosexuality as "sociopathic personality disorder" (Dallas and Heche, p. 165). The pro-gay movement within society increased its influence after WW II. Under political pressure, in 1973, the APA did change its stance on the pathological nature of homosexuality. That the understanding of homosexuality would be changed in the new DSM was not known by the membership of the APA before its meeting at which the new manual was approved. This modification was done as something of a *coup* by the Nomenclature Committee under the leadership of Robert Spitzer, and after much consultation with gay activist groups, which had held disturbing demonstrations at previous APA meetings. This probably did not represent the thinking of the great majority of psychiatrists at that time, nor for some time thereafter, however, this view may well have become the orthodox belief in more recent years. This change was not based upon any new evidence, nor any new study. It was based upon social pressure and a new definition. The definition of health was changed to arrive at a new official opinion about homosexuality. Even with the dominance in society of the gay perspective for some years now, there remain many psychiatrists, psychologists and counselors who still conclude that homosexuality is pathological and work to offer reparative therapy. There are many evidences that the condition is caused, not innate, and that it is pathological, not healthy (See Bayer, and Dallas and Heche).

The definition of mental health was changed so that sub-optimal is now considered healthy. The presence of mental disease was then supposed to be detected in one of two ways: 1) If a condition is perceived by the person who has it as very disturbing, then there may be a lack of mental health, and the lack may be that the condition is misperceived by the person who has it, and not a flaw in the condition itself. 2) If a person is unable to function in society in general, cannot hold a job (?), has no semblance of any even quasi-healthy and transient relationships (???), or perhaps has an endless stream of clearly psychosomatic illnesses (?), then that person might be thought to have a mental disorder – if he reports it as a problem.

Mondimore says, "good science does not prejudge what is normal or abnormal; it merely assembles information logically and postulates how different pieces of information might be related to each other" (Mondimore, 1996, p. xiii), but that is nonsense if one is speaking of medicine. A broken arm is still a broken arm, even if the person with the broken arm says it feels fine. A person with cancerous tumors still has cancerous tumors, even if he denies treatment, saying, "After all, everybody has some problems anyway." Of course, homosexuality is, in objective fact, an "abnormality," in that it is an infrequent condition (one to two percent of the population) that leads to behavior far from the "norm," which means "that which is normal." It is "abnormal." Because Mondimore, and others of his persuasion, seek to "normalize" homosexuality by their treatment of it; their "science" is far from objective. Nor is it good to declare something healthy which is not. The role of medical science might be thought to note that which is unhealthy, that which is associated with unhealthy consequences, that which leads to unhealthy consequences, and that which arises from unhealthy causes. Perhaps it is not surprising that he also disparages the disparagement of "pedophiles, exhibitionists, and other persons with abnormalities of sexual behavior" (Mondimore, 1996, p. 135). Things are quite non-judgmental in current "mental medicine." A person with a sexual perversion does not have a problem unless he "really, really" thinks he has a problem, and then his only problem may be only that he thinks he has one, according to the modern APA. This so-called "non-judgmental" perspective undercuts a primary insight of the whole endeavor of psychology, which is that visible conditions or conduct may have origins in experiences, the meaning of which may not be immediately apparent. I once gave a ride to a youth who had come to the church several times. He had carved his name in his arm. I asked him if he was okay, and he said that he was, but I did not believe him. I tell you that he cut his arm because he felt like the world was carving him up. And I tell you that similar dynamics are behind homosexual ideation and conduct.

Since, it is said, many homosexuals do not claim to find their homosexuality to be intrinsically an unbearable burden, and since many homosexuals are able to function satisfactorily otherwise in society, hold jobs, have friends, etc., then, therefore, homosexuality is not a pathological condition, and if and when persons who engage in homosexuality have pathological conditions, the pathology must not be due to homosexuality since it "is established" that homosexuality itself is not pathological. But this is circular reasoning; its conclusion is dependent upon its premise.

The experts had not said that homosexuality was good, but that you should not call it bad if the homosexual person did not think it so. The psychoanalytical contingent of psychiatrists maintained in 1973, that whatever was sub-optimal was pathological. They never wanted the DSM changed. Those of another orientation maintained that only that which was clearly sub-optimal, or highly undesirable, was pathological (Bayer, 1981, p. 182). Their perspective prevailed. It was put by Peter Sedgwich this way, "mental illness is a social construct" (Bayer, 1981, p. 183). Among the things that Bayer summarized from Robert Spitzer's remarks is this interesting notion: "What distinguished the mental disorders from the physical was the extent of consensus about the undesirability of the latter" (Bayer, 1981, p. 185). Since some have said that homosexuality was not necessarily altogether debilitating, therefore, it should not be called pathological. However, this conclusion requires not only a change of definition, but also a fairly careful avoidance of much evidence.

Ronald Bayer's book *Homosexuality and American Psychiatry: The Politics of Diagnosis* gives perhaps the best overview of the history of psychiatric thought on homosexuality (Bayer, 1981). The standard psychiatric opinion was that homosexuality was an illness, and/or an arresting of development (Bayer, 1981; Mondimore, 1996). "The pathological status of homosexuality [was] a matter of broad professional and lay consensus" (Bayer, 1981, p. 41). As gay psychiatrist Charles Silverstein has put it, when he was growing up in the '50's "there wasn't a book that didn't tell me how depraved I was or that I was doomed to a life of misery and that my only salvation was to seek the services of a good psychoanalyst (at least three times a week) who would help me change my abnormal sexual orientation." "Not a single professional book published before the 1970's contradicted the accepted idea that homosexuality was a serious and obdurate disorder" (Silverstein, 1991, p. 5). There was some variation of opinion on curability, but no doubt that it was not a sign of health. There was the occasional gay activist who tried to assert the normalcy of homosexuality.

In more recent decades, there began to be voices within psychiatry for the perspective of normal variation: Hooker, Marmor. This sentiment was much encouraged by Kinsey's report on the sexual activity of the American male in 1948, which reported such high rates of homosexual involvement that many felt they could not consider something so common, abnormal. We now know Kinsey was wrong as to fact (Michael, 1994) and probably unethical, illegal, and grossly immoral (Resiman, 1990), but his findings had great impact.

Bergler notes "Kinsey has done the homosexual nothing but harm. He has harmfully obscured the only means of coping with the problem: medical treatment" (Bergler, 1956, p. 184). One of his homosexual patients told him, "I know a lot of fellows who turned to homosexuality because Kinsey convinced them" (Bergler, 1956, p. 51). "What's wrong with Kinsey is not the decimal point, but the whole approach. Says who? The psychiatrists of analytic coloring, whose domain Kinsey, as a layman, enters without having the slightest knowledge of the unconscious" (Bergler, 1956, p. 51). Kinsey did much to spur the growth of the homophile movement.

Various homophile organizations were founded, such as the Mattachine Society and the Daughters of Bilitis. These groups worked for the acceptance of homosexuals. At first, being viewed as "sick" was seen as an improvement over being seen as "immoral" and therefore was welcomed. Ken Burns, chairman of the Board of the Mattachine Society, at its Third Annual Convention in 1956, asserted "that homosexuals 'cried out' for assistance in controlling the social and family patterns out of which homosexuality developed," and "he stressed the importance of prevention in the overall effort to solve the problem of homosexuality" (Bayer, 1981, p. 76). Over time, this, too, was seen as confining, and the goal became full acceptance, and the psychiatrists who had once been seen as saviors from the moralists were now seen as the new enforcers of morality, now under a scientific cover. In 1964, "the prestigious New York Academy of Medicine issued a report on homosexuality containing all the views that had become unacceptable to the homophile movement" (Bayer, 1981, p. 80). The pathological nature of homosexuality was still virtually unchallenged within psychiatry. But within the gay movement, from the 1960's on, a new theme began to emerge: "The therapeutic posture itself was morally wrong.... Those who offered assistance to *voluntary* patients who expressed profound distress over their sexual orientation, did so as the agents of society and should be attacked" (Bayer, 1981, p. 65). In 1965, the Mattachine Society of Washington declared that "homosexuality is not a sickness or other pathology in any sense but is merely a preference, orientation or propensity on a par with, and not different in kind from, heterosexuality" (Bayer, 1981, p. 88).

It is interesting to note that one of the factors working in favor of adjusting the DSM to suit the homosexuals was the sense that they were unfairly or inhumanely treated, that the DSM inclusion of homosexuality helped to maintain that treatment, and thus a kind of remedy might be to remove homosexuality from a list which seemed to encourage some to treat homosexuals with a degree of cruelty. The unrighteous pursuit of righteousness is not only unrighteous, but it fails to achieve its stated goal. But then, the self-righteous pursuit of unrighteousness is none too good either.

Nineteen seventy was a time of demonstrations. When the APA met in San Francisco that year, its meetings were interrupted. "Guerilla theater tactics and more straightforward shouting matches characterized" the presence of the gay activist protestors (Bayer, 1981, p. 102). Some meetings were suspended. By 1972, at the APA convention in Dallas, there was "a fully institutionalized gay presence at the annual meeting" of the APA (Bayer, 1981, p. 107). By 1973, the small group in charge of revising the DSM had decided to take homosexuality off the list.

Robert Spitzer, on the Nomenclature Committee, was the real force behind the change. He came up with a new definition of mental disease: To be a mental disorder, a condition 1) must be accompanied by subjective distress, or 2) must result in some "generalized impairment in social effectiveness or functioning." Incidentally, Dr. Spitzer, a strong force for removing homosexuality from the DSM, has since gained notice for his studies finding that many persons can indeed come out of homosexuality (*Time*, May 21, 2001, p. 62).

The matter was not seriously put to the membership of the APA until *after* the change had been made. Traditionalists sought and obtained a referendum. The change was approved by 58%, and opposed by 37% of those who responded. There was substantial support from the leadership, funding from gay organizations, and appeals to the membership to not make the leaders, and by implications their profession, look foolish. Many believe that was the reason for its approval, reporting that many who voted for the change said privately that they disagreed with it (Bayer, 1981, p. 148 and p. 167). Bayer has noted, "In the debate on homosexuality within the American Psychiatric Association, the effort to attain closure was baldly political" (Bayer, 1981, pp. 186-187), and, "Our new wisdom is the result of a collapse of our values" (Bayer, 1981, p. 185).

In 1977, there was a large survey taken of psychiatrists. It found that 69% believed that homosexuality usually represented a pathological adaptation. Only 18%, disagreed with the statement that homosexuality usually represented a pathological adaptation. Sixty percent agreed that homosexual men were "less capable of mature, loving relationships than their heterosexual counterparts." Seventy percent agreed that problems experienced by homosexuals were more often the result of "personal conflicts" than of stigmatization (Bayer, 1981, p. 167).

After the 1970's, "new authors emerged: gay professionals writing on gay themes for a gay audience" (Silverstein, 1991, p. 7). The number of gay therapists grew in the 1980's. The APA approved an official gay division. A lesbian was elected president of the APA (Silverstein, 1991, p. 6).

So then, the best evidence is that by 1973, the official position of the APA was that homosexuality *per se* was not a mental disorder; however, about 70% of psychiatrists actually thought that it was. Since that time, the influence of the pro-gay contingent has grown; however, there remains a strong contingent of psychiatrists, psychologists and counselors who are firmly opposed to the notion of the normalcy of homosexuality and who work from that perspective. One organization that represents this perspective is NARTH, The National Association for Research and Therapy of Homosexuality, which has several thousand members. Their "primary goal is to make effective psychological therapy available to all homosexual men and women who seek change."

What will follow for the next few pages is no longer unchallenged, but I will present to the reader some of what was once simply "the" psychiatric opinion.

Gerard van den Aardweg quotes the well-known homosexual and pedophile writer Andre Gide as saying in his *Journal*, 1906, that he "never was a man, and would remain but a child grown up" (Aardweg, 1986, p. 159).

"Although homosexuality is regarded as a life-style by many professionals and laymen, those who subscribe to a psychosexual perspective on the human being view it as an expression of incomplete maturation" - Herbert Strean (Strean, 1983, p. 29).

It is "a fact that homosexuality is a neurotic disease" – Edmund Bergler (Bergler, 1956, p. 15).

"The psychological and psychiatric nonsense and social recklessness of 'normalization' may well bring social and individual tragedy. There may well be a rise in homosexuality of the nonobligatory type at first, but ultimately profound gender identity disturbances may increase and more true homosexual deviations will result as parents distort the maleness and femaleness of their infants and children" – Charles Socarides (Aardweg, 1986, p. vi).

Homosexuality is "essentially a severe psychosexual disorder" – Charles Socarides (Aardweg, 1986, p. vi).

"A known cause of homosexuality in some adults is unconscious conflict arising from postnatal rearing influences that make heterosexuality unappealing or unattainable" – Warren J. Gadpaille (Lief, 1981, pp. 71-72).

"Profound interpersonal disturbance is unremitting in homosexual father-son relationships. ... In 69 percent of the cases [of homosexual patients] an intimate mother-son dyad characterized by restrictive and binding maternal behavior was found" – Irving Bieber (Bayer, 1981, p. 30-32).

"The homosexual's basic dilemma [is] unconscious masochism" – Edmund Bergler (Bergler, 1962, p. 87).

"Homosexuality is neither a biologically determined destiny nor incomprehensible ill luck. It is an unfavorable *unconscious* solution of a conflict that faces *every* child" – Edmund Bergler (Bergler, 1962, p. 31).

"He [the homosexual] is the unhappy one, who feels condemned to suffering by his fate!" "I have never seen a healthy nor a happy homosexual." "He is an eternal child ... who struggles with the adult" –Wilhelm Stekel (Aardweg, 1986, p. xviii).

The numerous studies on neuroticism and homosexuality indicate a "correlation between the degree of homosexuality and neuroticism." "The more homosexual, the more neurotic" – Gerard Van den Aardweg (Aardweg, 1986, p. 174).

"I think that the constant preoccupation of homosexuals with their homosexuality as well as their attempts at proving that everybody is basically like them reveals their inner insecurity as to their normalcy" – Gerard Van den Aardweg (Aardweg, 1986, p. xii).

"Wherever it has been investigated, an exclusive homosexual orientation has been found to result from deep heterosexual frustration" – Herbert Strean (Strean, 1983, p. 164).

"Over and again, homosexual clients attest to the fact that a total denial of the opposite sex comes out of a background of severe childhood frustration. When a homosexual pair is examined closely, one sees an enormous amount of vulnerability, uncertainty and hatred in both partners" – Herbert Strean (Strean, 1983, p. 162-163).

"In reality, the homosexual condition is a developmental problem – and one that often results from early problems between father and son. Heterosexual development necessitates the support and cooperation of both parents as the boy disidentifies from mother and identifies with father. Failure in relationship with father may result is failure to internalize male gender-identity. A large proportion of men seen in psychotherapy for treatment of homosexuality fit this developmental syndrome" – Joseph Nicolosi (Nicolosi, 1991, p. xvi).

As you might suppose, I could go on with such citations from various persons with expertise in the field of treating homosexuals *ad naseum*. Indeed, some might think I have already done that! In reality, I have given but a small sample of comments from those professionals who think homosexuality is a reflection of harm already done to the person. If this is an accurate reflection of the truth, which the evidence seems to support, then to declare it normal makes one responsible for that damage in much the same way as refusing to shout "Fire" in a burning building simply because a loud noise might offend your neighbor's ear would also make one responsible for resulting harm.

By the way, Edmund Bergler is a very engaging writer, and his case studies are particularly fun to read. While he has certainly characterized homosexuals in ways not very agreeable, please note that he makes it a point to say that this arises from a condition; it is unconscious; they do not do the disagreeable things he sees them do intentionally. As you may know or have guessed, his 1956 book *Homosexuality: Disease or Way of Life* (Bergler, 1962) caused a great outcry among homosexuals. He has a not very attractive list of six primary features of homosexuals (Bergler, 1962, p. 49), but the best-known phrase of his came to be that homosexuals are "injustice collectors" (Bayer, 1981, p. 78), for which homosexual advocates have found him disagreeable. However, his understanding in this matter is shared by many, including some gay activists. Charles Socarides speaks of "a childhood reaction of self-pity" (Aardweg, 1986, p. v). Aardweg speaks of "autopsychodrama," by which he means "infantile self-pity turned autonomous" (Aardweg, 1986, p. 1). The strongly pro-gay Mondimore will speak of homosexuals being "more sensitive" (Mondimore, 1996, p. 163). Is there not a similarity? If this sense of unhealed woundedness is nearly universal, does that suggest that something might be out of order?

(Perhaps we should note also that some suggest that persons who become homosexual are characterized by a greater degree of sensitivity in general. This is viewed, by some, as possibly a partially predisposing genetic condition, partially predisposing, not determining. The sensitivity may be genetic, the homosexual ideation is not, but might more easily arise because of the greater sensitivity to perceived slights or losses. I note this here because it is perhaps of a piece with the prior comments on greater sensitivity to perceived slights. It might also be consistent with the seemingly greater occurrence of homosexual ideation among persons in fields thought to require greater sensitivity.)

Here is something else that Strean says which is interesting: "For clinicians to understand their gay and lesbian clients in depth, they should also recognize that exclusive homosexuality is rarely found among people who have had consistently gratifying love experiences with their parents" (Strean, 1983, p. 162). If healthy family of origin experiences almost always precludes homosexuality, does that not suggest that homosexuality may have some correlation with unhealthy family of origin issues?

Van den Aardweg notes that several studies have found that "homosexual males had a more disturbed relationship with their fathers as compared with control neurotics." He cites Jonas, 1944, West, 1959, Bieber, 1956, and Stephen, 1973 (Aardweg, 1986, p. 99). The strongly pro-gay Bell, Weinberg and Hammersmith also found that "the homosexual male (WHM's) reported less-favorable childhood and adolescent relationships with their father than did their heterosexual counterparts (WHTM)" (Bell, 1981, p. 54).

In an open ended question, far more heterosexuals reported favorable descriptions of their relationship with their father than did homosexuals: Favorable: heterosexuals – 52%, and homosexuals – 23%; Unfavorable: homosexuals – 48%, and heterosexuals – 29%. Twelve percent of heterosexuals disliked or hated their father; 29% of homosexuals did. Fifty-nine percent of homosexuals reported that they did not feel close to their father, while 38% of heterosexuals did. More than twice as many homosexuals felt particularly close to their mothers as did heterosexuals: 47% to 21% (Bell, 1981, p. 44, and pp. 54-55). Heterosexuals reported feeling their fathers were stronger in their families than did homosexuals (Bell, 1981, p. 66). Does this data not tend to confirm that there was regularly some real or perceived difficulty in the pre-homosexual boy's relationship with his father?

Bell, Weinberg, Hammersmith also report 29% of homosexual males had childhood sex play with brothers, compared to only 8% of heterosexual males in his control group (Bell, 1981, p. 72). They also found that the first orgasm of homosexual males occurred during a homosexual encounter for 24% of the group, while among heterosexuals, the first orgasm was in a homosexual encounter only 3%. Do these facts suggest that various early childhood experiences may have an impact upon subsequent orientation?

David Finkelhor states: "Boys victimized by older men are over *four times* more likely to be currently engaged in homosexual activity than were non-victims. Close to half the male respondents who had had a childhood sexual experience with an older man were currently involved in homosexual activity" (Finkelhor, 1984, p. 195). Does this not suggest that early childhood experiences may have something to do with homosexual inclination?

Father McGinnis, a street priest in Houston, and for many years Chaplain of the Harris County Juvenile Probation Department Detention Home, said, "I think one hundred percent of the boys that I have talked to who have become involved in street hustling either had no father because of death, or because the father and mother were divorced. In a few cases, the boy's alienation from his family existed - even if the father was home – because there was no meaningful relationship with the father" (Lloyd, 1976, p. 50). Does this suggest that there may be a relationship between early childhood experience and later behavior? Should that really surprise you?

Two studies cited by Yarhouse (Yarhouse, p. 73), indicates that "those who had a history of childhood sexual abuse were three times more likely to report a homosexual orientation that those who did not report childhood sexual abuse." A later study showed an even higher correlation between childhood sexual abuse and adult homosexual orientation. Does such data indicate that the healthfulness of homosexuality in general may reasonably be called into question?

Herbert Strean notes that there are two prominent theories about homosexuality. "One is the psychoanalytic perspective that men and women become homosexual because they are frightened and sexually frustrated, and have unfulfilling interpersonal relationships in childhood. The other is sociological, and it maintains that homosexuality is simply a socially deviant form of sexual expression. What is important for helping professionals to realize is that no social scientist subscribing to the social deviance theory has offered any explanation of why one person becomes homosexual whereas another does not" (Strean, 1983, p. 163). If one theory can explain the observable data and another cannot, which one is the more "scientific"?

These last few questions lead naturally into the next section, which deals with the mutability of homosexuality. Is it innate? Is it caused? Can it be changed? Has it been done? To which the answers are: No, Yes, Yes, and Yes. But before we go there, I will ask you to take one more digression with me. To try to read the matter fairly, we must look at many academic books, but the matter with which we deal is not academic. It always concerns people.

The gay Reverend Dr. F. has been a friend of mine for more than thirty years. He is very bright, and consistently tries to be honest. I like him, but for several of the years I have known him, he looked like death warmed over. It was not AIDS, his friends said, just other things, a lot of other things. His life-mate of a few years died of AIDS some years ago. The young, gay Reverend Y was a nice enough young man. I worked a retreat he was on shortly before he died. Apparently, he couldn't talk with very many about his homosexuality or his AIDS. Folks knew, you know, but he couldn't talk about it. They say that he was faithful to his partner, but his partner was promiscuous. All I know is he was very sad on a retreat at which many others were very happy, and he couldn't talk, and he was then just over half my age, and now he is dead. The Reverend B is a hero in this region of the church. He died of AIDS. I know, the boy who filed charges against him for sexual misconduct fled; so that doesn't count. His interest in other young persons? Well, I don't know. Now no one says that he wasn't, shall we say, active. He is not now; he is dead. The question in this whole section of the book, is this: Is there evidence which bears on the healthfulness of homosexuality? Is it healthy? Is it?

A young man called me from across town. I don't know how he got my name and number. Somehow he had heard of me. Anyway, he called. I had never met him. He was not a member of my church. He was in a hospital a couple of cities away, and one of them is a pretty big city. But trying to help is what I do, so I went. He had been gay. Was he still? I don't know. People sometimes tell the preacher what they think he wants to hear. He said it was behind him. He was sick. I visited him in the hospital a couple of times, and in some sort of group home later. All I know is, he wasn't well.

I invited Reverend O, a pastor of the local Metropolitan Community Church (gay affirming church) to lunch. He was gay. He was going to picket my church for a conference we planned to hold to offer hope to those who wanted help in changing their same-sex orientation; so, I invited him to lunch. We talked. He was kind enough to share some things about his life with me. I thanked him for that. He thought there might be a connection between the fact that both his parents had a drinking problem and the fact that the first twenty or thirty years (or more?) of his life were pretty thoroughly messed up, but he saw no connection between the disorder of his childhood environment and his subsequent homosexuality.

Many counselors who work from a pro-gay perspective fail to recognize what I would see as clear signs of the troubled origins of homosexuality. Charles Silverstein, Robert Paul Cabaj, Armand Cerlone, Dianne Elise, John C. Gonsioreck, and Marny Hall all speak of homosexual clients. They speak of risks in the relationship with the counselor, well and good. But they all report things that I find glaring indications of a troubled origin of their clients' homosexuality, and yet they never see the homosexuality itself as a problem or a reflection of a problem (Silverstein, 1991): physical abuse by older brother, former therapist initiated client's first homosexual relationship, client confused about sexuality, therapist urged client to explore his same sex feelings (pp. 68-83), client troubled by father's absence on trips, then early death, felt as a "desertion" (pp. 52-67), therapist sees problem as "internalized homophobia," even when the patient does not see it that way, patient's greatest friendship was with a straight married man (p. 42-43), therapist repeatedly missed appointments with one patient and lied to cover it up, strongly wanted to slap a patient, therapist had somewhat erotic fantasies about being a loving, protecting mentor to a young man who came to him for help, "a delicious fantasy" (pp. 11-12), found that "many gay men recall early longings for father or other men, of both affectional and sexual nature" (p 37) (but this did not lead the therapist to suspect that the homosexual impulse was a sexualized need for father's affirmation), and found "masturbation training" groups for women offered at the University of California a fine thing (p. 86).

Wainwright Churchill seems to think it a fine thing that a ten year old boy was introduced to sex by a thirteen year old boy, and sees no problem with the ten year old boy's admiration for the thirteen year old (Churchill, 1967, pp. 179-180). Richard Isay reports on "Eric," a male patient who entered therapy with him at the age of eleven, who had already had "extensive sex play during childhood" with a two-year older brother, including grabbing and fondling genitals. By thirteen, this boy has "horseplay" at camp with a counselor that included fondling his penis, and had probably had sexual activity with his football coach. Yet none of this seems to raise any questions in Isay's mind about the origins of the child's homosexual orientation (Isay, 1996, p. 67). He says, "I believe Eric was homosexual because his history is similar to that described by gay adolescents and adults I have seen over the past fifteen years." (Isay, 1996, p. 69) He describes "Paul's" rage at losing his father's attention after the birth of a younger brother. He was enraged at the father and the younger brother. He "badly" wanted the father to spend time alone with him." He often "returned to the theme of longing for his father" (Isay, 1996, p. 75). Yet none of this apparently suggested to Isay that some unmet need for affirmation from the father, or any unforgiveness of perceived injury on the child's part, might be factors in the origin of the patient's homosexuality.

I do not know if I have ever seen case studies by gay and pro-gay therapists that do not have red flags sticking out all over the place. There are instances of early childhood sexual abuse by counselors or family members, a deep sense of fatherly rejection for a male, or father's physical or emotional absence, or an excessive need of the mother for a young son to fulfill emotional needs not met for her by father, and none of these things suggest themselves as possible sources of disordered development for the gay and pro-gay counselors. I am at a loss to explain it, except that they cannot emotionally afford to see troubling origins for a pattern of thought and behavior they have committed themselves to approve. To see such things would, perhaps, oblige them to revisit issues in their own lives which they have found it too painful to bring to mind, and thus they develop a certain kind of blindness, or so it seems to me.

Another young man called the church. How he called us, I don't know. Maybe he called until someone gave him help. I don't know. He was gay. He had AIDS. He had come out west to be with his sister who had indicated that she would help him before he came. But after he arrived it seemed like she only wanted to beat him over the head with her Bible. He couldn't take it anymore. He was going back east. He had bus fare, but he needed some money to eat during the three-day trip. Could I help him? Well, I had done that before; so I supposed I could.

I invited him to a convenient coffee shop. I was not at all worried to have him come to my office, but if it seemed appropriate, we might get into a serious discussion and I didn't want him to feel like he was "on my turf," so we went to a "neutral" place. We met. I listened to him. I commiserated with him. It's a pretty rotten thing to be dying, and it's not much fun when someone says they will help but then they want to beat up on you emotionally all the time. I could honestly commiserate. Then I gave him the money that I had planned to give; it was enough to eat for three days on the road, and it was my money, not the churches. Then I told him that I had done what I was going to do, that the money was his, that he didn't owe me a thing, but that I did see some things differently than he did, and I asked his permission to share some of my thoughts with him. He gave me permission. I shared a bit. I asked him to think about a couple of things I'd said. I wished him well. I paid the bill for the coffee. We left the coffee shop. I gave him a hug. And we parted. I have never seen him since.

I asked him to see if two conditions I regularly found among homosexuals were consistent with his experience: 1) I told him that virtually all the male homosexuals I knew had had damaged relationships with their fathers. Even when they claimed otherwise, if you let them talk for a while, you hear about the hurt, rejection, or distance; and 2) I told him that nearly all the lesbian women I knew, when I knew them well enough to maybe know, had been raped or molested. I asked him to think over the folks he knew well enough to know. Did that fit them too? Yes, he said, in most cases it did. If that was so, then maybe the homosexuality was not a reflection of health but a reaction to some kind of hurt, and maybe God could deal with that hurt, and maybe we all really needed something like that. You see, my goal is not to cause pain, but to alleviate the very great pain that I think has already been caused, and which lies behind the things we do that are not really good for us. I asked him to think about it. He said he would.

I don't think it was healthy for the sixteen year old boy, twenty years ago, who was standing in the men's room offering to perform fellatio on whoever came in. I know of another boy who, at fifteen, found that he had "gay" feelings, who was told by someone that he must be gay, who had been molested, who had a father who had many problems throughout the boy's childhood, and who likes to look for ways to blame others for what he wants to do. I see a lot of things in his life that I don't think are healthy. He doesn't see any.

I could tell you a dozen other stories, and then another dozen after that. I just want to put a human face on it. I do not rejoice in anybody's suffering; I weep over it. I may have an occasional angry moment, particularly in traffic, but I don't mean it. If homosexuality is a really good thing, if it is God's gift to some folks, then my telling them otherwise is not very helpful. But then, if it is not a healthy thing, then telling folks that *is* a good thing, *is harmful*, because then they will likely do things which will damage their social health, their physical health, their emotional health, and their spiritual health. *And*, if they think something is good which is not, they will leave *untouched* real problems that need to be touched, worked on, dealt with, and healed.

The best evidence available is that homosexuality results in *vastly* more disease. It will probably result in a decrease in lifespan of twenty-five years or more. It seems often to entail the obsessive pursuit of a very large number of strangers for the most intimate acts. It seems to lead consistently to broken relationships, anonymity, and infidelity. There seem to be some commonly recurring activities with youth and children that seem to reflect something unhealthy. Acting out abuse previously received? Vicariously getting even? Trying to imbibe the qualities the other seems to have that one ought to have but does not feel one does? There seems to be so high a correlation with things that are unhealthy that it is difficult not to suspect that homosexuality itself is unhealthy. It is.

Part IV: Can Homosexuality Be Healed?

"The frequent claim by 'gay' activists that it is impossible for homosexuals to change their orientation is categorically untrue. Such claims accuse scores of conscientious, responsible psychiatrists and psychologists of falsifying their data."

- Dr. Ruth Tiffany Barnhouse, in "What Is a Christian View of Homosexuality," Circuit Rider, *(February 1984), p. 12*

"Socarides: You know it is said about so-called cured homosexuals that what they really have done is just suppress their homosexuality and they really would be homosexual but have just learned a way of suppressing it. Do you feel you have suppressed it?

"Paul: No. I don't feel that I've suppressed it. In fact, my thoughts and feelings come out very easily.

"Socarides: About everything?"

"Paul: Yes about everything. I feel very free."

- Charles W. Socarides, M.D. in Homosexuality: Psycho-analytic Therapy, *(Aaronson, Northvale, New Jersey, 1989), p. 502*

Chapter 20:

Can Change Happen?

You know where I'm at by now. At times, I struggle to be punctiliously fair, and at other times I want to strongly impress upon the reader the very great disparity between commonly held current beliefs and the indication of relevant evidence. Let me work on my "punctilious fairness" for a moment. The title of this section of the book implies a perspective. Proponents of homosexuality would deny that there is anything to be "healed" of.

First they argued, for many, many years, that one should not be mean to homosexuals because that's just the way they were, and they could not change. Then they argued that one should not try to change homosexuals because it would not work; whatever the origins, it was fixed, set, and permanent. Since you could not change them, you should accept them. Since you should accept homosexuals, then you should accept homosexuality. Since it was "just how they were," and "could not be changed," then homosexuality itself should be accepted; it's okay; "gay is good." Now, more recently, it having become the established orthodoxy among our intellectual elites that homosexuality is okay, that "gay is good," then it has been argued that since it is good, there is no need to change it, or to justify it. There is not only no need to "heal" it; there is not even any need to change it, because, after all, the established priesthoods of our age have declared that it is good. Therefore, one should not even *ask if* it *can* be changed! Indeed, to seek change or to offer change is to suggest that others should change, and this would cause them discomfort. Therefore, it is *morally wrong* to even offer change, seek change or talk about it! All the "conclusions" in this chain of reasoning are based on assumptions, assumptions which are not in accord with the evidence.

However, for those who want to deal with reality from time to time, I will ask, and try to answer with evidence, these questions: 1) Can homosexuals change their conduct? 2) Can homosexuals change their orientation? That is, their sexual fantasy life, the focus of their sexual interest? 3) Can persons who have been involved in homosexuality find healing for the underlying needs/problems/hurts/misunderstandings that have given rise to their homosexuality? 4) Has it been done? 5) Is there evidence for this? The answer to each of these questions is "Yes!" And the evidence for this is abundant. I will also give some attention to such issues as the origins of homosexuality, and, in these areas, I will also give some attention to the pro-gay evidence that has been offered to support biological origins. Yet, the primary focus of this section is on the possibility of healing, and the evidence for it.

There is a great quantity of psychiatric literature reporting the possibility of change for the person caught up in homosexuality. In the last chapter of Part III, I drew upon many of the authors who have written and worked as psychiatrists from a traditionalist perspective. You might read some of their works: Gerard Van den Aardweg's *On the Origins and Treatment of Homosexuality: A Psychoanalytic Reinterpretation*, Edmund Bergler's *Homosexuality: Disease or Way of Life*, Irving Bieber's *Homosexuality: A Psychoanalytic Study*, Ruth Barnhouse's *Homosexuality: A Symbolic Confusion*, or Charles Socarides' *Homosexuality: Psychoanalytic Therapy*. A more recent study is Joseph Nicolosi's *Reparative Therapy of Male Homosexuality*. For more readily available and perhaps more easily accessible information, I could recommend surveys of many relevant therapeutic theories contained in *Homosexuality and the Christian* by Mark A. Yarhouse and *The Complete Christian Guide to Understanding Homosexuality* by Joe Dallas and Nancy Heche, although these authors, unlike the others, speak from an explicitly Christian point of view, though one very open to contemporary thinking.

There are many testimonies of ex-gays, persons who have come out of homosexuality and have worked thereafter to help others find that which they believe to be their real problems and then to solve them. Most of these that I am aware of speak from an evangelical Christian perspective. Some of them are largely personal stories, others are overviews of homosexuality, which may or may not include significant portions of testimony, and other works are given as overviews and workbooks. I very strongly recommend that anyone who wants help in this area consult three or four of these books. I also strongly recommend that anyone who disagrees with the idea that change is real, read at least three or four of these works. In these categories I recommend: Mario Bergner's *Setting Love in Order*, Darlene Bogle's *Strangers in a Christian Land*, Andy Comiskey's *Pursuing Sexual Wholeness*, Joe Dallas' books *Desires in Conflict* and *A Strong Delusion: Confronting the "Gay Christian" Movement*, Bob Davies and Lori Rentzel's *Coming Out of Homosexuality*, Jeanette Howard's *Out of Egypt: Leaving Lesbianism Behind*, Jeff Konrad's *You Don't Have to Be Gay*, David Kyle Foster's *Sexual Healing: God's Plan for the Sanctification of Broken Lives*, and Frank Worthen's *Steps Out of Homosexuality*.

An organization that is composed mainly of persons who have come out of homosexuality and works to help others come out is one called Homosexuals Anonymous Fellowship Services. As you may have surmised by the name, they use the AA, twelve-step model, changing it to fourteen for their emphases. Their contact information is given in the appendix. I mention them now because I want to give them credit for much information I am going to use that they have compiled. This is from their leaflet "Once Gay, Always Gay???," parts 1, 2, 3, and 4. They give sources for each study they cite. I have spot checked some of their references and have not found them at fault, and thus I treat them as any other published source, and cite them freely. The authors whose works are cited below are a virtual "Who's Who" of psychiatry.

As an aside of uncertain noteworthiness, I will point out that they will cite studies from one or two persons who have been significant in expanding the acceptability of homosexuality, but we are concerned here with their findings about the possibility of change. Some gay writers have claimed that one or two psychiatrists cited had a homosexual proclivity themselves. That may or may not be so; again, at this point, I am concerned with what they found in their work. Also, testimony "contrary to interest" is generally thought to be particularly trustworthy, rather than otherwise.

Let me note also, that I do not endorse every comment made by each author. They were writing at different times, in some cases, when less was known than is now about the causes and cures of homosexuality. Furthermore, most of those cited below write from a position other than that of a Christian, and thus I would expect their results to be less than optimal; but my point here is that dozens of skilled professionals have seen and reported the real and common possibility of change for persons who are in a homosexual lifestyle and who want out.

There are two other themes that run through the writings of the persons noted below. One is that a high motivation is generally required. The other is that the transformation is difficult and will generally require some hard work. Both are true. Neither should surprise anyone. People generally do not act out homosexually unless there has been some serious disturbance. It will require some emotionally difficult work to find the underlying issues and face them, but work with results well worth the effort. There may be a need to change habitual ways of dealing with problems, loneliness, social relations, a sense of self-worth, and more. Such things are not usually easy or quick. *But that is the case with any recovery program.* Difficult problems are difficult. That does not mean that they are not problems, nor that they should not be dealt with. G. K. Chesterton said in *What's Wrong with the World*, "The Christian ideal has not been tried and found wanting; it has been found difficult and left untried." So also is it with many good things.

A few years ago, I was in the living room of a troubled family. The wife loved to run up the credit cards as her way to show anger at her husband. The husband had a drinking problem. Not long before, he had molested his daughter. He said it was just because he was drunk. Of course that's not quite true. He also said that no one ever really quit drinking. He went to AA meetings because the court required him too, but no one really ever quit, he said. That is simply untrue. In one small, young adult group I once met with at church, I had five young men that had quit alcohol and drugs, and I know of none who has since regressed. One was living in the nearby canyons and bushes for about fourteen years, but he came to have a great marriage and job and life. A sixth left behind anger and fights. A seventh left behind anger, regular fights, and being a skinhead, and now he looks like Mr. Rogers, wearing a sweater, when he brings his little girl to church, and he is a sweetheart. Another woman in the church left behind alcohol, cocaine, and some prostitution to support her habits, and after coming to Christ, she worked, she was gracious in speech and manner, and whenever she saw me, she would say, "Remember Jesus loves you and so do I." She has since gone to her eternal reward. I have already told you of some I know who have left behind homosexuality. I'll tell you of more later. The idea that people cannot change is simply untrue. To me it is a lie from hell. Now if people do not *want* to change, ah, well that's a different story. With occasional exceptions, change for the homosexual is not easy. However, it is possible, and it is worth it. Some forty psychiatrists, psychologists and researchers from the works cited below have all published findings that document the fact that change happens. Should the reader's eyes glaze over, feel free to skim, but not until the reader has realized that change is possible. That change can happen. And this is proven because it has happened. Often.

Let me remind the reader that more than 75% of all persons who have ever tried homosexuality have left it behind. Apparently 75% of all persons once "gay" have already changed! And it is most likely that many among those who now think themselves homosexual will subsequently find that they are not, perhaps 75%!

Recall again the declaration of Dr. Barnhouse. Dr. Ruth Tiffany Barnhouse: "The frequent claim by 'gay' activists that it is impossible for homosexuals to change is categorically untrue. Such a claim accuses scores of conscientious, responsible psychiatrists and psychologists of falsifying their data" (HAFS; Barnhouse, 1984, p. 12). "Quite apart from published studies by those who have specialized in the treatment of sexual disorders, many psychiatrists and psychologists with a more general type of practice (and I include myself in this group) have been successful in helping homosexual patients to make a complete and permanent transition to heterosexuality" (HAFS: Barnhouse, 1977, p. 109).

Among the most famous sex researchers of all time are Dr. William H. Masters and Virginia E. Johnson, and they found homosexuality to be treatable much like any other sexual problem they treated. Their failure rate in treating male and female homosexuals who requested conversion or reversion therapy, after a six year follow up, was 28.4%. That means that 70%, after six years, were still successfully living life as heterosexuals. Their failure rate in treating sexual dysfunctions among heterosexuals was 20%, roughly similar. "No longer should the qualified psychotherapist avoid the responsibility of either accepting the homosexual client in treatment or ... referring him or her to an acceptable treatment source" (HAFS; Masters, 1979, pp. 402 and 251). (After the sweeping tide of gay approval among our elites, Virginia Johnson is reported to have had some second thoughts about their findings in this study. Upon what basis, I do not know.)

Dr. Reuben Fine: "It is paradoxical that even though the politically active homosexual group denies the possibility of change, all studies from Schrenk-Notzing on have found positive effects, virtually regardless of the kind of treatment used." "If the patients were motivated, whatever procedure is adopted a large percentage will give up their homosexuality" (HAFS; Diamant, 1987, pp. 84-86).

Dr. Bernard Berkowitz and Mildred Newman: "Analysts once thought they had little chance of changing homosexuals' preferences and had little success in that direction. But some refused to accept that and kept working with them, and we've found that a homosexual who really wants to change has a very good chance of doing so. Now we're hearing all kinds of success stories." (HAFS; Newman, 1971, pp.22-23)

Dr. Anna Freud: In 1950, Anna Freud spoke on advances in the treatment of homosexuals, "stating that many of her patients lost their inversion [an old term for homosexuality] as a result of analysis. This occurred even in those who had proclaimed their wish to remain homosexual when entering treatment, having started only to obtain relief of their homosexual symptoms." (HAFS; Arieti, 1974, p. 308)

Dr. Edmund Bergler: After speaking of hundreds of cases on which he has worked, he says, "On the basis of the experience thus gathered, I make the positive statement that homosexuality has an excellent prognosis in psychiatric-psychoanalytic treatment [of a very extensive nature] – *provided the patient really wishes to change.*" "And 'cure' denotes not bisexuality, but real and unfaked heterosexuality." He also notes that "The color of a person's eyes cannot be changed therapeutically, but homo-sexuality can be changed by psychotherapy." (HAFS; Bergler, 1962, p. 176, p. 279, 166)

Dr. Irving Bieber: "Many homosexuals became exclusively heterosexual in psychoanalytic treatment. Although this change may be more easily accomplished by some than by others, in our judgment a heterosexual shift is a possibility for all homosexuals strongly motivated to change." (HAFS; Bieber, 1988, pp. 318-319, and Bieber, 1979, p. 416)

Dr Samuel Hadden: "Of the thirty-two patients on which this report is based, twelve have progressed to an exclusively heterosexual pattern of adjustment and have shown marked improvement in, or disappearance of, other neurotic traits.... Others still in treatment give every indication of progressing to a reversal of pattern." (HAFS; Hadden, 1966, p. 15)

Dr. Lawrence Hatterer: Reporting in 1970 of his work since the 1950's with hundreds he has seen and worked with, he speaks of a group of whom he had follow-up knowledge. "Of this group, forty-nine patients recovered, nineteen partially recovered, and seventy-six remained homosexual." (HAFS; Hatterer, 1970, p. vii-

viii) "I've heard of hundreds of other men who went from a homosexual to a heterosexual adjustment on their own." (p. 138) "A large undisclosed population has melted into heterosexual society, persons who behaved homosexually in late adolescence and early adulthood, and who, on their own, resolved their conflicts and abandoned such behavior to go on to successful marriages or to bisexual patterns of adaptation" (p. 14). [This last point has already been confirmed by the data in Michael, *et al.* *Far more persons have left homosexuality behind than have remained in it.*]

Dr. Arthur Janov: "I do not believe that there is a basic genetic homosexual tendency in man. If this were true, the cured patient would still have his homosexual needs, which he does not." "I have found that homosexual habits that have persisted for years have faded away in the face of reality." (HAFS; Janov, 1970, pp. 328 and 332)

Dr. Charles Socarides: Reporting on a group of forty-four "overt homosexuals" whom he saw in therapy during a given period, eleven of whom he saw only for a few months, he reported "twenty patients, nearly 50 percent, developed full heterosexual functioning and were able to develop love feelings for their heterosexual partners." (HAFS; Socarides, 1978, pp. 405-406, 418, and 6)

Socarides has also noted that, "Detailed reports of successful resolution of cases of overt homosexuality have been published by Flournoy (1953), Lagache (1953), Poe (1952), Socarides (1969), Vinchon and Nacht (1931), and Wulf (1941)." (Socarides, 1983, p. 49)

Dr. Robert Kronemeyer: "About eighty percent of men and women in Syntonic Therapy have been able to free themselves and achieve a healthy and satisfying heterosexual adjustment." (HAFS; Kronemeyer, 1980, p. 135)

Dr. Gerard van den Aardweg: "Of those who continued treatment ... about two thirds reached at least a satisfactory state of affairs for a long period of time. By this is meant that the homosexual feeling had been reduced to occasional impulses at most while the sexual orientation had turned predominately heterosexual, or that the homosexual feelings were completely absent." (HAFS; Aardweg, 1986, p. 105)

Father Jeffrey Keefe: "Can homosexuals change their orientation? The fact, reported in the literature, proves the possibility. I have seen homosexuals in treatment – and have met more former homosexuals (including those who were exclusively so) – who now respond physically and emotionally as hetero-sexuals in successful marriages." (HAFS; Harvey, 1987, p. 76)

Dr. Judd Marmor: "The myth that homosexuality is untreatable still has wide currency among the public at large and among homosexuals themselves. This view is often linked to the assumption that homosexuality is constitutionally or genetically determined. This conviction of untreatability also serves as ego-defensive purpose for many homosexuals. ... There is little doubt that a genuine shift in preferential sex object choice can and does take place in somewhere between 20 and 50 percent of patients with homosexual behavior who seek psychotherapy with this end in view. (HAFS; Freedman, 1975, p. 1519)

Dr. J. A. Hadfield: "Homosexuality can be 'cured' in the full sense." "By 'cure' I mean that he [the homosexual] loses his propensity to his own sex and has his sexual interests directed towards those of the opposite sex, so that he becomes in all respects a sexually normal person." (HAFS; Hadfield, 1958, pp. 1323 and 1325)

Dr. Daniel J. Cappon: He gave a "distillation of diagnosing and treating some 200 homosexual patients from among a population of 2,000 psychiatric patients who happened to come to me for therapy." He reported: "Bisexual problems: 90 percent cured (i. e., no reversion to homosexual behavior, no conscious-ness of homosexual desire and fantasy) in males who terminated treatment by common consent. Male homosexual patients: 80 percent showed marked improvement (i. e., occasional relapses, release of aggression, increasingly dominant heterosexuality).... 50 percent cured," which means "the loss of all symptoms, cure of

the main problem, and change in sleep dream forms and content."
(HAFS; Cappon, 1965, pp. 265-266)

Dr. Alfred C. Kinsey: Wardell Pomeroy, Kinsey's associate
and co-author of his seminal 1948 work, stated that at an early
stage of his research, Kinsey had discovered "more than eighty
cases of (previously homosexual) men who had made a
satisfactory heterosexual adjustment." (HAFS; Pomeroy, 1972, p.
76)

Dr. Toby Bieber: ""Homosexuality has a 30 to 50 percent
chance of reversing with psychiatric treatment." (HAFS; Bieber,
1971, p. 519) [Of course, I would say that a committed person
with Jesus has about a hundred percent chance of "reversing," but
that is merely a personal estimate.]

Dr. William M. Freeman and Dr. Robert G. Meyer: Reporting
on a group of nine "male homosexual volunteers, ranging in ages
from 19 to 43, each of whom received twenty treatments, at two
per week," which "included the conditioning of heterosexual
stimuli, followed by the electrical reconditioning of homosexual
stimuli." After 18 months, "seven continued their heterosexual
adjustment, but two were living in homosexual unions." One of
those was reintroduced to homosexuality by his employer. (HAFS;
Freeman, 1975, pp. 207-209) Although I am told that the stimuli
are mild, this is not a therapeutic method I would recommend, and
I think is both discarded and discredited today, but the results still
indicate that change can happen.

Dr. William Wilson: "Recently, I have worked with seven
male homosexuals and three lesbians. The outcome of the therapy
of these ten patients has been successful reorientation in their
sexual practices to heterosexuality in seven cases." (HAFS;
Keysor, 1979, p. 164)

Dr. Wilhelm Stekel:"My experience during the last few years
absolutely confirms my belief that homosexuality is a psychic
disease and is curable by psychic treatment.... This belief is
substantiated by the fact that in the last year four of my
homosexual patients have married and are extremely happy."
(HAFS; Stekel, 1930, p. 443)

Dr. Albert Ellis: "Of the 20 patients who came to therapy with a serious desire to overcome their homosexual problems, all made some improvement and 16 (80 per cent) made considerable improvement in their sex-love relations with members of the other sex." "The majority of homosexuals who are seriously concerned about their condition and are willing to work to improve it may ... be distinctly helped to achieve a more satisfactory heterosexual orientation." (HAFS; Ellis, 1956, pp. 193-194)

Dr. Peter Mayerson and Harold I. Lief: "Forty-seven per cent of our patients were found at follow-up to be 'heterosexual.' These patients comprised 22 per cent of those who had been exclusively homosexual, 57 per cent of those who had been mostly homosexual, and 100 per cent of those who had been bisexual at the beginning of therapy." (HAFS; Marmor, 1965, p. 312)

Dr. Frank S. Caprio: "The prognosis ... is a favorable one wherever there exists this genuine wish to be helped." "Many patients of mine, who were formerly lesbians, have communicated long after treatment was terminated, informing me that they are happily married and are convinced that they will never return to a homosexual way of life." (HAFS: Caprio, 1954, p. 301 and 299)

Dr. Charles Williams: "In working with homosexuals, my experience is that they can make a shift in sexual orientation if they are interested and motivated." (HAFS; Williams, 1991, p. 160)

Dr. Benjamin Karpman: "By far the greater number of psychiatrists find the origin [of homosexuality] to be psychogenic; to lie in the family situation." "Every psychotherapist of experience must have in his records at least a few cases of analysis of homosexuality, exhibitionism, transvestism, etc. that he has treated and cured or improved. The presentation of such analyses should convince any unbiased observer that these paraphilias are essentially neuroses and are amenable to treatment as neuroses." (HAFS; Karpman, 1954, pp. 609 and 390)

Dr Edrita Fried: "If attention is directed primarily to the emotional and mental problems of the homosexual and homosexuality is regarded as a symptom that will disappear after the personality has been put on a sounder basis, it is possible to achieve a good percentage of cures. Practicing homosexuals can be helped to achieve a normal and indeed a passionate love relationship with the other sex. They can be helped to build satisfactory marriage relationships and to start a family. This has occurred both with several patients whom I have treated and with those of other therapists." (HAFS: Fried, 1960, p. 99)

Dr. Harvey E. Kaye: Reporting on a study with 24 female homosexual patients and 24 female non-homosexual patients, he said: "This indicates a substantial positive treatment potential in homosexual women.... Apparently at least 50% of them can be significantly helped by psychoanalytic treatment." (HAFS; Kaye, 1967, p. 633)

Dr Stanley E. Willis II: "As a ritualistic compulsion, homosexual behavior is basically no more or less refractory to treatment than any other compulsive ritual not involving homosexual behavior." (HAFS; Willis, 1967, p. 7)

Dr. M. P. Feldman and Dr. M. J. MacCulloch: "Treatment ... was successful in nearly 60% of the cases after a follow-up of at least a year." HAFS: Feldman, 1971, p. 54)

Dr. Earl D. Wilson: "I could not honestly counsel with homosexuals if I did not believe they can change. I believe there is hope and I extend that hope to the counselees." (HAFS; Wilson, 1988, p. 53)

Dr. Jeffrey Satinover reports that committed homosexuals have "an at least 50 percent likelihood of [their orientation] being eliminated through lengthy, often costly, and very time consuming treatment in an otherwise unselected groups group of sufferers (although a very high success rate, in some instances nearing 100 percent, for groups of highly motivated, carefully selected individuals)." (Satinover, p. 51)

Change has occurred even when homosexuality was not treated and/or not treated as a problem. There are therapists who have *not* assumed that homosexuality was a problem and did *not* treat their patients "for homosexuality," but who found that upon gaining improvement is the areas of unresolved conflicts, their patients' homosexual ideation and attraction diminished or disappeared.

Dr. Elaine V. Siegel: Siegel reports on twelve women whom she saw for issues not relating to homosexuality, not treating their homosexuality as an illness, and surprised to find what she did. "As conflicts were resolved and distanced from, anxiety was reduced and life became more joyful and productive for all these analysands. With the attainment of firmer inner structures, interpersonal relationships also solidified and became more permanent. Although I never interpreted homosexuality as an illness, more than half of the women became fully heterosexual." (HAFS; Siegel, 1988, p. xii)

Dr. Elizabeth Mintz: Mintz reports on ten homosexual men whom she treated for anxiety, depression or work blocks. She "tried to make it clear that she would make no attempt to 'cure' the homosexuality." "Five of these men have terminated treatment. Of these, two have accepted themselves as homosexuals, two are enjoying heterosexuality and report freedom from conflict, one is still in conflict and may re-enter treatment. Of the five men still in treatment, one has lost interest in homosexuality and enjoys satisfying heterosexual relationships; one does not intend to change his homosexual adjustment; three appear to be moving toward heterosexuality, but with considerable anxiety and conflict." (HAFS; Mintz, 1966, pp. 193-194)

There are also psychiatric researchers who know that many persons have changed their orientation *without any* resort to psychiatric or psychological treatment. Dr. E. Mansell Pattison: Dr. Pattison studied eleven men between the ages of 21 and 35 who claimed to have changed their sexual orientation from exclusive and active homosexuality to exclusive heterosexuality through involvement in a Pentecostal church. Their study concluded that eight of the eleven "amply demonstrated a 'cure.'" The remaining three had "a major behavioral and intra-psychic shift to heterosexual behavior, but the persistence of homosexual impulses was still significant." (HAFS; Mansell, 1980, p. 1560)

Question: Can change be seen this often if it is not possible?
There are two basic theories offered to explain the existence of
homosexuality. One is that it is innate, immutable, or "natural."
The other is that it is the consequence of some sort of psychic
trauma or disorder. Which one better fits the data that shows that
many, many long-time, practicing, self-identified homosexuals
have, in fact, changed? If it is innate, immutable, or "natural" then
it would not so change, but it does.

Please note this also: Only recently have homosexuals
themselves believed that they were "born that way." "In the
1940s, when sexologist Alfred Kinsey asked homosexuals how
they "got that way," only 9 percent claimed to have been born gay.
In 1970, nearly the same percentage of 979 gays in San Francisco
answered the same way." (Dallas and Heche, p. 181) The notion
of homosexuality being innate is recent, the product of grievously
flawed, polemical and misused studies, a desire to have a
seemingly guilt-free explanation for a condition with which those
who have it and those close to them are uncomfortable, and as an
act of gay advocacy.

Some gay theorists call all of the above cited psychiatrists,
persons who push "dangerous ideas and irresponsible methods"
(Mondimore, 1994, p. 223), with "lame theories." (p. 226). But
whose theories explain the reality of change? There are claims that
"meaningful follow-up cases are nonexistent." (Mondimore, 1994,
p. 226) But that simply is untrue. Only willful ignorance can lead
one to say that at this time.

But doesn't it require a lot of work? Yes, usually. So? So
what? Disorders often require a lot of work to set in order. People
do not do things so clearly contrary to nature easily, readily,
happily, or for no reason. Some matters of consequence have been
put out of order, and homosexuality is the consequence. It will
usually require work to set things in order. Other fetishes require
work to mend as well. Other addictions require work to mend as
well. Other compulsions require work to mend as well. Other
habits require work to change as well. Shedding alcoholism
requires work. Healing from childhood sexual abuse requires

work.   Dealing with the underlying issues of homosexuality requires work, but it can be done, and it is worth the work.

Not everyone gets healed in these reports, do they? No, they don't. So? So what? Not everyone who has a drinking problem gets it dealt with. That does not mean that they should not try, nor that it cannot be done. They should, and it can. Not everyone who goes to the doctor gets healed of cancer, heart disease or arthritis. Shall we shut down the hospitals?   These reports vary in the percentages of cure they report, don't they? Yes, they do. Some of these reports were from earlier days when less was known. Many others report very good cure rates. Kaye reported "at least 50% of them [homosexual women] can be significantly helped." Feldman and MacCulloch reported "treatment ... was successful in nearly 60% of the cases after a follow-up of at least a year." Cappon reported 50 to 90 percent cure rates. Masters and Johnson reported a 70% cure rate, after a six-year follow-up. Kronemeyer reported "about 80 percent of men and women ... have been able to free themselves." Satinover reported nearly 100% in carefully selected and highly motivated groups. All in all, that is really quite good for a number of conditions.   Although perfection is always the goal, the appropriate comparison is not with perfection, but with cure rates for comparable conditions, and in that light, these reports look quite good.

"Last year, NARTH published a study of <u>over 800 people</u> who had made a substantial degree of change in their sexuality. The study was published in a peer-reviewed journal." (Nicolosi, J., 2001, p. 3) There is no lack of evidence. There may be a lack of willingness to consider the evidence.

Furthermore, we are in a culture of affirmation of homosexuality. What might the results be if people were taught the truth about homosexuality and were not so eager to affirm it? We have been railing against smoking in our society for some time. People still smoke. Does that mean that they are just chain smokers by nature? In fact, the percentage of smokers is declining. Does that not suggest that moral suasion may have some effect? Despite preachers' best efforts to discourage it, some people lie.

Shall we affirm them as natural born liars, who are to be praised for their lying? Despite teachers' best efforts to discourage it, the majority of kids cheat in high school, sometimes. Do we proclaim that a new virtue? The persistence of vice does not make it a virtue. The reports cited above are not necessarily those in which I most delight. They are cited because they come from the psychiatric and psychological priesthoods most esteemed by the "general educated public," whose consideration of this evidence I most desire.

There are scores of Christian ministries who report thousands of changed lives of persons who have come out of homosexuality. Satinover reports that some kinds of groups report "a very high success rate, in some instances nearing 100 percent, for groups of highly motivated, carefully selected individuals." (Satinover, 1996, p. 51) He reports on a Desert Stream program called Living Waters. Perhaps 55 persons will be accepted for a given group in a thirty-week cycle. Two thirds of these will typically be dealing with homosexuality and one third with other issues of sexual brokenness. Only one or two drop out of the program in a cycle. Fifty percent receive much benefit. Perhaps a third receive little lasting benefit. Within eight years of completing a program, about twenty-five percent move successfully into marriage. (Satinover, 1996, pp. 203-204) Mario Begner, author of *Setting Love in Order*, leads Redeemed Life Ministries. He reports an 80 percent success rate. (Satinover, 1996, p. 204) These ministries reflect another field of response to homosexuality.

Approximately thirty years ago about two dozen persons who had been involved in Christian ministries to help people come out of homosexuality got together to form an organization to better support and encourage their work. That was the beginning of Exodus International. Their membership rose to about 400 groups nation-wide, fell to about 160, and has recently been dissolved by the leader who led it into its decline. Each year they used to have a weeklong conference offering information, workshops, and training to help folks minister to those who want to come out of homosexuality. At each of these yearly conferences there were hundreds of men and women who have come out of homosexuality. The ministries they represent include thousands of others who have come out of homosexuality. Change is real, it is widespread, it is lasting, it is established, and it is documented.

At the 1999 conference of the American Psychiatric Association, there were former homosexuals demonstrating to show their objection to a proposed APA resolution discouraging therapy to change persons in homosexuality to heterosexuality. Robert Spitzer, the key man in the 1973 APA's decision to remove homosexuality from the DSM, was drawn to their demonstration. It was his belief and assumption that change was not possible. That day he did a rare thing for a pro-gay psychiatrist: he decided to examine the evidence. He did his own study. He developed his own interview. He recruited subjects from persons made available by Exodus International and NARTH. He required that subjects have had a significant shift from homosexual to heterosexual attraction for at least five years. "To the researchers' surprise, good heterosexual functioning was reportedly achieved by 67% of the men who had *rarely* or *never* felt any opposite sex-sex attraction before the change process. Nearly all the subjects said they now feel more masculine (in the case of men) or more feminine (women)." (Nicolosi, L., 2001, p. 28. See also Nicolosi, J., 2001, p. 3, and *Time* May 21, 2001p. 62.)

There is statistical evidence of the reality of change. Many, many persons have left homosexuality on their own. We saw a hint of this fact in a statement by Lawrence Hatterer: "A large undisclosed population has melted into heterosexual society, persons who behaved homosexually in late adolescence and early adulthood, and who, on their own, resolved their conflicts and abandoned such behavior to go on to successful marriages." (HAFS; Hatterer, 1970, p. 14) He also assumes that some went on to bisexual adaptation, which I note to be fair, but that is beside the point at the moment. Many have left homosexuality on their own. There is clear statistical proof that the great majority of persons who have tried homosexuality have abandoned it.

Tommy (all the names in the anecdotes are changed, but all the stories are true) was a little embarrassed by his mother, but he loved her. His parents had divorced, and I never knew all the issues. He was raised by various relatives and friends. He lived with me for a short while. He was also ambiguous in his feelings about homosexuality. He didn't like it, but he didn't want to call it wrong. His mother had lived as a lesbian for several years, and he had some fond memories of both his mother and her long-time lesbian partner. However, by the time he introduced me to her, she was living with a man, as man and wife, and apparently happily so. I was told she was going to a small Pentecostal church, which may or may not have been a factor in her change, but somehow, she changed. No therapy. No organized ministry. But change. Only one case of several of which I know.

Here is some of the statistical evidence: The Michael, Gagnon, *et al*, survey of sexual behavior in America is comprehensive, consistent with other recent and thorough studies, and readily available. They reported that just over 7% of men and women had ever had sex with someone of the same sex since puberty. About 4.5% had ever had sex with someone of the same sex since they were eighteen. But less than 2% had had sex with someone of the same sex in the last year. That means that about 75% of all persons who have ever tried homosexuality have already rejected it, and even then about 60% of all persons who have tried homosexuality since the age of eighteen have already rejected it. (Michael, 1994, p. 175) Since these numbers include the responses of all persons in the survey, aged 18 to 60, it does not show a drop off rate across time; I suspect that more refined data would show more drop off with increasing age, up to a point. In any case, the best data available indicates that the great majority of persons who ever try homosexuality, 75%, reject it. Since I do not believe that there are enough psychiatrists and Christian ministries to account for this quantity of change, I assume that most of these people made this change more or less on their own.

It has been objected that those who left homosexuality were not "true gays." Bear in mind that each of them would have been included in that number of persons who had had a homosexual encounter within a year at some point in time. If they would not then have been "true homosexuals," then it is reasonable to suppose that a majority of those who are currently "gay" are also not "true homosexuals" either. Or, of course, it may mean that there is no such thing as a "true homosexual." In any case, it shows clearly that change is possible. Change happens. Not only is it true to say that people leave homosexuality, it is true to say that *most people* leave homosexuality.

Let me deal with the notion of there being persons who are "true homosexuals" and persons who are *not* "true homosexuals" for a moment. For a brief period in psychiatry there existed the term "dyshomophilia." "Dys" means something like "not," and the idea here was that there were some homosexuals for whom homosexuality was not truly functional, but was really *dys*functional. This term came into the science of psychiatry and went out in the blink of an eye. It had a shorter shelf-life than Nehru jackets at Macy's. As an official paraphilia (sexual disorder), dyshomophila barely lasted until the ink dried on one edition of the DSM. However, another term survived longer. In fact, two terms arose out of the concept suggested by the former term: egosyntonic homosexuality and egodystonic homosexuality. "Ego" means "I" or, in this case, "self." "Syn" means "with," and "dys"means "not with." "Tonic" means anything that produces good muscle tone, or anything that is good for you, or "it's a real tonic for you." So, the "egosyntonic homosexual" is the "true homosexual," or one for whom homosexuality "fits," or at least one who thinks it truly fits them. The "egodystonic homosexual" is one for whom it does not fit. They are not really, really a "true homosexual," or something like that.

There is a range of opinions about the concept of the "true" and "untrue" homosexual one might encounter in various settings: 1) Some would say: Homosexuality is fine; there is no need to justify it in any way; anyone who wants to be gay is and can be and that's that. 2) Others would say: All homosexuals are "true" homosexuals; they are all "egosyntonic;" the notion that some are not is simply a vicious assault upon gentle, peace-loving, law-abiding, healthy, happy homosexuals by mean spirited, ignorant old moralist sourpusses trying to take all the joy away from the homosexual; and what's your problem anyway. 3) Others would say: Well, gosh and golly gee, you know there really are some folks who seem to be truly happy as homosexuals and these folks are "egosyntonic," and we should affirm them in their homosexuality, but others seem to be unhappy in their homosexuality, and these are "egodystonic," and we should be willing to offer help, or somebody should be allowed to offer help, to these folks to change, if they really and truly want to, but we've got to be awfully careful not to offer it too freely and to be sure that we make it clear that gay is really good for those who think so. 4) Others would say: We don't know if there are any homosexuals who are really "egosyntonic," but we don't know everything, besides it's risky to deviate from the official pro-gay orthodoxy of our educated elites anyway, and so we would like to focus on offering help "to those who want it," realizing that it won't do any good anyway if they don't want help, and hoping to help some people out of a really difficult situation. 5) Others would say, look, there is no such thing as an "egosyntonic homosexual." Homosexuality is *always* a sign of maladjustment, of disorder, of dis-ease. Treatment, hope, and healing should be offered. Persons should be treated with respect and dignity individually. Personal rights should be respected in the same manner as the rights of anybody else are respected, but homosexuality should not be encouraged, not with special rights, and not with skewed programs in school to teach that gay is good when it isn't. 6) And, of course, still others would say things far more ungracious, perhaps even vengeful.

I have tried to speak softly, at least some of the time, so I could get you, dear reader, to keep reading, because I think the evidence is terribly clear if only folks will look at the evidence, but by now you must have a fairly clear idea that I am a #5 on the scale given above. I do not think that *any*one is a "true homosexual." If, by egosyntonic, one means that persons are "truly homosexual," then none are "egosyntonic." If, by egosyntonic, one means that some *believe themselves* to be truly homosexual, appropriately adjusted for them, and are generally functional in life and are capable of caring, working, and doing some able, valuable and even noble things, why absolutely, there are indeed such folks in homosexuality! It is ridiculous nonsense, and unfair, and untrue, and either ignorant or mean or both, to deny that. My point is that I do not think that homosexuality is, in fact, the best adjustment for anyone. I think that it is always a sign, a symptom, of some prior problem that has not been adequately dealt with. It almost always, and perhaps always, entails and/or leads to horrific social, emotional and medical problems, and a very high risk of eternal estrangement from God. That is most emphatically *not* my wish for people, not for anyone, and specifically not for persons caught up in homosexuality or other sexual brokenness. It is because I believe that it both *is* and *represents* a problem that I am concerned about it, and desire that fact to be known so that persons can take appropriate action to obtain the healing which is possible. As for the appropriate response, that is a matter for another section, but here I wanted to take up the issue of the possibility of there being "true homosexuals" and persons in homosexuality who are not "true homosexuals," or of the egosyntonic and the egodystonic.

As I have said before, the particular brand of Christianity of which I am a part, The United Methodist Church, is, in my area of the country, very "liberal." Dear hearts and gentle people, terms mean different things to different people and at different times and places. Socially and in worship style, I am more "liberal" than my colleague-adversaries; so try to refrain from jumping to too many conclusions. However, in the current context, "liberal" means, among many other things, pro-gay, pro-abortion, and not too sure about the usefulness of the Bible. Our church elites derive their inspiration in this area perhaps from academe, but not from scripture, tradition, reason or Christian experience. It has been the received orthodoxy for some years among the Bishops, seminary teachers, District Superintendents, and pastors of large churches (after all, the Bishops appoint the last two categories), that "gay is good." Leaders have willfully evaded their responsibilities in order to ordain and retain gay clergy. It has been "known" that homosexuality "is" innate, immutable, "just the way some folks are," and good. Consequently, it was also "known" that any suggestion that folks should change or *could change* was "known" to be wrong, and, since wrong, it must also be mean-spirited and ignorant.

We have had on-going discussions about homosexuality for years. Our Bishops want to be nice, and help those of us whom they see as ignorant bumpkins to come along gently. For which, by the way, I am thankful. In the course of these discussions, gays and gay couples were always sought to be included. At the request of some of us ignorant traditionalists, and as an act of fair play, for which I am also thankful, we were permitted also to invite ex-gays to these discussions, although the thought of inviting ex-gays was initially treated with derision since it is part of gay doctrine that there could not really *be* any such a thing as an ex-gay. For some years, the suggestion that some gays could change was met with derision, anger, and insult. Eventually, after seeing some of these folks who gave their testimony of being in homosexuality and of coming out of homosexuality, some of our pro-gay leaders began to change, a bit. Many concluded that *some* should change, and therefore perhaps that transformation should be offered to some. Let me not underplay this, this was a real growth on their part, at least from my perspective. True, for some, it may have been a bargaining chip: "I'll say some should change if you'll shut up about this transformation thing and say that those who want it should be affirmed in their homosexuality." But still, it was change, and even a measure of grace for some! At this point, a new orthodoxy began to emerge among some, but only among some: Some gays are egodystonic and should be offered change; other gays are egosyntonic and should be given affirmation. What could be fairer? Americans love the middle ground. Compromise is the ticket. Something for everyone, right?

Wrong. If it is not so, it is not so. I don't have any personal animus here. I'd love to go along to get along, but I cannot proclaim as true that which I do not believe to be so. So then, at this point I must defend the position that no one is really and truly gay, or, better put, in psychiatric terms, that homosexuality is not the best adjustment for anyone; in religious terms, homosexuality is not God's perfect plan for anyone. But how can I say that? All the studies show that some people did *not* change. Doesn't that *prove* that that is "who they really are"? No, and I will tell you upon what basis I can say that, but let me clear up one conceptual problem first.

If I accost you on the street and say that I want to beat you to death, and you say no, that I shouldn't beat on you at all, and then I say, well, alright, we'll compromise, I'll only beat you half to death, are you going to say, okay, that is fine and dandy? I think not. And I hope not. Compromise is not necessarily right. Sometimes it is; sometimes it is wise. A degree of humility about our own wisdom should give us a general willingness to compromise, but still, compromise is not always right. If one engineer says that a certain bridge needs X amount of steel and concrete to hold, and another says no, that's wasteful, it only needs ½ of X, and then another engineer, without sorting it out, says, "Okay, we'll compromise. We will give it ¾ X." Would you be happy? Is *that* wise? Or, should whoever is in charge figure out what is going on and get the right amount? Sometimes truth is not fungible. Of course, the virtue of truth itself does not necessarily mean that my answer is the truth. How can I say that *all can* change when only *some* have been able to?

Not all alcoholics change either. From that, we do not usually conclude that some should rejoice in their alcoholism. There is a persistence of many things that are generally agreed to be disagreeable or wrong, but that does not upset the consensus that such ought not to be so. This holds true for any thing that is generally agreed to be a vice. Stealing, cheating, adultery, hatred, and addiction: All these things exist, yet we do not conclude that people who do them should continue to do them. Perhaps the problem is one of will, or of a determination of what is right. Perhaps no evidence is sufficient if one believes that homosexuality is good. The evidence is more than sufficient if one believes that homosexuality is not good. But that is not all.

Confucius said that he told a prospective student the location of three corners of a rectangle, and he was to find the fourth. If he could not find the fourth, then he would not accept him as a student. It is axiomatic that some things are determined from limited evidence. Is there evidence by which we might find the fourth corner? True, not all change. But that is true for many conditions about which we have no doubt that one should change.

Here is a summary of relevant evidence for this issue:

1. There is much change. Therefore, the idea that change is impossible is simply disproved. It is false.

2. *Many* of those who have changed *once* thought that their homosexuality, too, was immutable, innate, unchangeable. Therefore, it is proven that such self-report is not necessarily sound.

3. There is *no* discernible characteristic that marks off some as part of any distinct group, other than changeable conduct. Therefore, it may well be that there *is no* distinct unchangeable group.

4. In virtually *all* examined cases, there are discernible *causes*. That strongly argues that the condition is caused, and not innate.

5. There are massive deleterious consequences of this condition, and that suggests that something extraordinary must have happened to compel persistence in the face of such disadvantage.

Therefore, based upon these five considerations, I take it that the clear preponderance of evidence is that homosexuality is a condition that is caused, has detrimental consequences, and can be changed. Furthermore, I conclude that the clear preponderance of evidence is that, when defined as "natural, healthy and innate," there is really no such thing as an egosyntonic homosexual. The APA licked their finger, stuck it in the air to see which way the wind was blowing, and then made a deadly mistake. The APA is wrong. But then what the APA really did was to change the definition of health. All they really said was that some persons could be homosexual and not be dysfunctional in other areas of their lives, and that such ability to function in other areas showed that they were healthy, and thus that their homosexuality is healthy. A man with a cold may still go to work, but that does not mean he is healthy. A man with cancer may be able to do many things well up until the very last days, but that, again, is not proof of health.

Many experts continue to proclaim what has long been known; homosexuality is pathological. Some "experts" have changed the definition of pathology. They have *not* said that homosexuality was healthy. They have said that some persons could be homosexual and still function in other ways in life. Now then, these last few paragraphs have been a digression to deal with the issue of the possible egosyntonic and the egodystonic homosexual. The general burden of this chapter has been to establish that change is possible. It is. That has been shown in several ways, and we turn to summarize those findings now.

I have presented six bodies of evidence to establish that people can change, can leave homosexuality and become heterosexual in conduct and thought life.

1. There are *scores* of responsible psychiatrists and psychologists, across decades, which have documented their work and reported successful transformation for 30 to 90% of their patients, with the better results seen in more recent years.

2. There are scores of Christian, ex-gay ministries who report thousands of stories of transformation.

3. There are numerous books of individuals chronicling their own personal stories of transformation.

4. There is the NARTH study of 800 persons who made significant change in their orientation.

5. There is the study by Dr. Spitzer, the leading advocate in removing homosexuality from the DSM in 1973, verifying that he who once did *not* believe that change was possible now knows that it is.

6. There is the gross data of all recent surveys of sexual behavior that establishes that the *great majority* of persons who have ever tried homosexuality have left it behind.

The idea that the evidence of change is not there is simply untrue and cannot be maintained by any honest and knowledgeable observer. The idea that this change does not last is simply untrue. The change is real, it lasts, and both facts have been amply documented. The idea that this change is only for a few, is simply untrue. More have left homosexuality than have remained in it.

Can change happen? Yes, of course. Has it happened? Yes, of course. Therefore, is it reasonable to conclude that it can happen for others? Yes, of course. But how can this be if homosexuality is innate, is "natural," is simply "how some people are"? It could not be so if those things were true, but they are not, and in our next chapter we will deal with the issues of the origins of homosexual orientation.

Chapter 21:

The Origins of Homosexual Orientation
Nature or Nurture or What?

Evidence has been given that homosexuality has a number of discernible consequences: disease, death, promiscuity, anonymity, and more. Evidence has been given that homosexual orientation can be changed: published psychiatric studies, numerous personal testimonies, large-scale behavioral data, and more. Since these things are so, does that not mean that it is most probably caused? Yes. Are there those who believe they know something about the causes? Yes. I'll give you excerpts of some theorists, moving from further back in time to more recent works. Eventually, I'll summarize current theories which I have found to fit experience.

Frank Caprio notes a theme you will hear often. Homosexuality is a *symptom* of other, unmet needs. Deal with the underlying needs, and the symptom will diminish or disappear. "Lesbianism is a *symptom* and not a disease entity. It is the result of a deep-seated neurosis which involves narcissistic gratifications and sexual immaturity. It also represents a neurotic defense mechanism for feelings of insecurity – a compromise solution for unresolved conflicts involving one's relationship during childhood and adolescence to one's parents." (HAFS; Caprio, 1954, p. 120)

Peter Mayerson and Harold Lief speak of "partial manifestations" and "underlying disorders.' Hear them: "Many recent investigators ... have considered homosexual fantasies and activities not as separate entities but rather as partial manifestations of more basic underlying adaptational disorders (conflicts dealing with competition, dependency, and power).... Adaptationally oriented investigators have found that the best results are obtained when therapy is directed toward treatment of the patient's problems as a whole; overemphasis on the homosexual aspects of his adaptive defects usually leads to therapeutic failure." (HAFS; Mayerson, 1965, p. 302-303)

In Edrita Fried's work, hear again the word "symptom" and the idea of underlying problems to be dealt with: "Homosexuality is a human rather than primarily a sexual disorder. It is the outgrowth of failings in human relationships.... If attention is directed primarily to the emotional and mental problems of the homosexual and homosexuality is regarded as a symptom that will disappear after the personality has been put on a sounder basis, it is possible to achieve a good percentage of cures." (HAFS; Fried, 1960, p. 99)

Arthur Janov speaks in a similar vein: "I do not believe that there is a basic genetic homosexual tendency in man. If this were true, the cured patient would still have his homosexual needs, which he does not." "The homosexual act is not a sexual one. It is based on the *denial* of real sexuality and the acting out symbolically through sex of a need for love.... The homosexual has usually eroticized his need so that he appears to be highly sexed. Bereft of his sexual fix, his lover, he is like an addict without his connection; without his lover, he is in the Pain that is always there but which is drained off sexually. But sex is not his goal – love is." (HAFS; Janov, 1970, pp. 328 and 322)

Robert Kronemeyer reports from his work and study: "With rare exceptions, homosexuality is neither inherited nor the result of some glandular disturbance or the scrambling of genes or chromosomes. Homosexuals are made, not born 'that way.' From my 25 years' experience as a clinical psychologist, I firmly believe that homosexuality is a *learned* response to early painful experiences and that it can be *unlearned*." (HAFS; Kronemeyer, 1980, p. 7)

Dr. Elizabeth Moberly is one who has done a great deal of work with the concept of gender identity deficit. Here is some of what she has said: "From amidst a welter of details, one constant underlying principle suggests itself: the homosexual – whether man or woman – has suffered from deficit in relationship with the parent *of the same sex*.... In speaking of a deficit, it must be stressed that this does not always imply willful maltreatment by the parent in question, as distinct from unintentional or accidental hurt.... The causation of homosexuality is not a simple matter.... It is not a question of one particular cause leading of necessity to one particular effect. Any incident that happens to place a particular strain on the relationship between the child and the parent of the same sex is potentially causative." (Moberly, 1983, pp. 2-3)

Follow with Dr. Moberly again: "Homosexuality is a same-sex relational deficit, not an opposite-sex one.... The barrier in the homosexual is the defensive detachment vis-à-vis the same sex. Only the resolution of this barrier, and the fulfillment of unmet same-sex needs, may justifiably be regarded as the answer to the homosexual question.... If same-sex needs were to be fully and truly met the erstwhile homosexual would have attained the psychological basis for sexual fulfillment in a heterosexual relationship." (Moberly, 1983, pp. 38-39)

Also working in this vein is Dr. Joseph Nicolosi. Here is a little of what he has said: "In reality, the homosexual condition is a developmental problem – and one that often results from early problems between father and son. Heterosexual development necessitates the support and cooperation of both parents as the boy disidentifies from mother and identifies with father. Failure in relationship with father may result in failure to internalize male gender-identity. A large proportion of men seen in psychotherapy for treatment of homosexuality fit this developmental syndrome." (Nicolosi, 1991, p. xvi)

I will speak now of some homosexuals I know who have retained a homosexual identity. Reverend F. is gay. His father may have been a pretty decent fellow, but he was at least emotionally absent. Apparently, Reverend F. still doesn't see it. Reverend E. had gay feelings. He got married. He decided that he was really gay, but wouldn't leave his family, because, he said with considerable passion, "I said I'd never do to my family what my father did to me." He still doesn't know that he is filled with unhealed anger at his father. Reverend J. is gay. He knows that his family was horrifically dysfunctional, but doesn't see that his reaction to it may have something to do with his homosexuality. Mr. S. is gay. He found out at some point that he was adopted. When that happened, he decided that his whole life was a lie. He was mad at his birth parents and his adoptive father. He spoke to me twenty-five years later, and he was still mad about his adoption when I spoke with him ten years ago. Mr. X, knowing that it might be an issue, proclaimed that he had an excellent relationship with his father, but a few minutes later he spoke with pain and anger of his relationship with his father throughout his life. What he apparently meant when he said before that he had an excellent relationship with his father was that they were now on speaking terms. Miss H. was raped. There may be more, but that much I know of. She thinks that gals are safer than guys, and she wants to be safe. She did leave homosexuality for several years, but she went back after one boy didn't fall in love with her as she did for him. Mr. J. is still a young man. He was molested. His dad was emotionally unstable and that for most of his life. The young man has hinted to some folks that there is more disorder of which to speak, but that seemingly makes no difference to him. He is sure that he was "made" gay. Yes, sort of, but not by God. Remember the young gay man with AIDS who wanted food money for his trip back east? He acknowledged that the two traumas I spoke of fit nearly every gay person, male or female, that he knew, including himself. These are brief notes on some I know who have not come out of homosexuality. In each case, there are things disordered, and they have not yet dealt with them.

I could give you a dozen stories of folks who have come out of homosexuality. The difference would not be in the lack of trauma, some greater than that noted above, some not, but in having come to face and deal with the underlying issues. Homosexuality is impossible to deal with only so long as you don't deal with it, and the underlying problems. Homosexuality so often leads to wildly self-destructive behavior because the homosexual ideation and activity that is engaged in is done to try to solve problems that the activity and ideation does not solve. For many it does become like an addict's fix, ever more desperately seeking in the same place for an answer that cannot be found in that place. As the song says, it is one more instance of, "looking for love in all the wrong places."

Even when homosexuality is not looked upon as a problem, even when the homosexuality is not treated as a problem, it is often found that the result of dealing with underlying problems is that the homosexual attraction fades or disappears. How could the homosexuality fade or disappear, even when the homosexuality is not viewed as a problem or treated in any way, if it were a reflection of the "true self," or of who the person "really was?" I do not suppose this invariably happens, but it has been recorded often enough to provide confirmation of the theory I advance here that homosexuality is a maladjustment, not a given. It is more nurture than nature, though that is not all it is. It is a response to unmet needs. It is an illegitimate attempt to get legitimate needs met, or a mistaken effort to meet a real need.

It has appeared a number of times in published findings that even when counselors agree to begin with the assumption that homosexuality is *not* a problem, and believe it is not, they find that as the counselees get help in other areas, the homosexual orientation consistently diminishes or disappears. That is another strong indication that homosexuality itself is a *symptom* of other problems. A few of such reports are noted below.

Dr. Elizabeth Mintz wrote of a group of homosexual men whom she saw in treatment over an eight-year period. They were all self-referred. They were all able to function in society. None were sociopathic or psychotic, although they had problems they wanted to deal with. All engaged in homosexuality as a way of life. They obtained social as well as sexual satisfaction from their homosexuality. They did not seek treatment for their homosexuality, but for such things as anxiety, depression or work blocks. In accepting these patients, Dr. Mintz made it clear that "she would make no attempt to 'cure' the homosexuality as such," although she would not promise that the treatment might not affect their enjoyment of homosexuality, which promise two men had sought. As of the writing of her article, "five of these men have terminated treatment. Of these, two have accepted themselves as homosexuals, two are enjoying heterosexuality and report freedom from conflicts, one is still in conflict and may reenter treatment. Of the five men still in treatment, one has lost interest in homosexuality and enjoys satisfying heterosexual relationships; one does not intend to change his homosexual adjustment; three appear to be moving toward heterosexuality, but with considerable anxiety and conflict." (HAFS; Mintz, 1966, 193-194) Although she never treated the homosexuality as a disease, simply by dealing with their real, or underlying, problems, three of ten left homosexuality, three were moving out of it, one was uncertain, and three had, so far, decided to remain in homosexuality. This is a remarkable result for 1) not treating something, 2) something that is not a problem, 3) something that is not a symptom of a problem, and 4) something that cannot be changed anyway.

Dr. E. Manell Pattison and Myrna Loy Pattison have published a study of "11 men between the ages of 21 and 35 who claimed to have changed their sexual orientation from exclusive and active homosexuality to exclusive heterosexuality through participation in a Pentecostal church fellowship." The church gave them "a welcome reception as homosexuals. No attempt was made to make them change their homosexuality. (Sadly, this is a grace with which troubled persons in churches are *not* always treated, but it was apparently so in this case.) Rather, they were presented with the invitation to commit their life to Christ and the church. All subjects had an explicit Christian conversion or rededication. They were then invited into small church fellowship groups where they studied the Bible and learned expected Biblical patterns of mature lifestyles. This included an expectation to engage in loving, nonerotic relationships with both men and women in the fellowship groups." The outcome of his study of these men was that 8 of the 11 "amply demonstrated a 'cure.' The remaining 3 subjects had a major behavioral and intra-psychic shift to heterosexual behavior, but the persistence of homosexual impulses was still significant" (HAFS; Pattison, 1980, pp. 1558-1560). This is a marginal example since, although it is claimed that "no attempt was made to make them change their homosexuality," it is clear that that was expected. Still, it was not directly sought, and yet not only a change in conduct occurred, but also in orientation.

Dr. Elaine V. Siegel was surprised by what she found. It was contrary to her expectations. She reported, "As with any other patient, I did not set out to 'cure' them or to dissuade them from their lifestyle. Rather, I prepared myself to listen and to be emotionally available." Eventually, she said, "I was struck by their common need to idealize homosexuality as better than heterosexuality and by the volatility of their suffering." "I came to understand their difficulties as developmental arrests that precluded heterosexual object choices. But that was after I knew them well and had concluded some of the analyses." "To be a liberal and liberated woman and yet to view homosexuality as a result of untoward development seemed at times a betrayal of all I then believed." "As conflicts were resolved and distanced from, anxiety was reduced and life became more joyful and productive for all the analysends. With the attainment of firmer inner structures, interpersonal relationships also solidified and became more permanent. Although I never interpreted homosexuality as an illness, more than half the women became fully heterosexual. This was taken by the referral source as a 'betrayal of the sisters.' The homosexual community and networks to which ... my patients belonged reacted very much like the families of disturbed children when the child, as a result of treatment, is no longer forced to express conflict for them. Even those women who at the end of their analyses remained homosexually inclined were viewed with suspicion by their former peers." (HAFS; Siegel, 1988, pp. xi – xiv) This doctor had been properly indoctrinated in the current pro-gay orthodoxy. She not only did not treat homosexuality as an illness, she did not believe it was – to begin with. She never treated the homosexuality *per se* as an illness, but the end result of dealing with the problems uncovered was the abandonment of homosexuality by most of the women – even in the face of opposition from their current peer groups and support networks. That opposition is worth noting too. It reflects the importance of maintaining denial to many who are caught up in homosexual ideation.

After a significant review of the relevant psychiatric and psychological literature, Dr. Ruth Tiffany Barnhouse, also found that homosexuality disappeared in many cases after homosexuals had received psychological help, *for any reason*! She states: "Many reports have appeared in the professional literature and a number of books on the subject have been published. These have dealt not only with the psychodynamics, but also, and at great and encouraging length, with treatment. What has been learned from this work? Approximately thirty percent of male homosexuals who come to psychotherapy for *any reason* (not just for help with their sexual preference) can be converted to the heterosexual adaptation." (HAFS; Barnhouse, 1977, p. 97)

How can an innate, natural, inborn, healthy predilection be changed, *when its change is not sought*? How can an innate, natural, inborn and healthy orientation be changed without dealing with that orientation, but *only by dealing with theoretically unrelated problems*? It could not be. It is not so. The problems are *not* unrelated. Homosexuality is a symptom of a dis-ease of the spirit. Treating it otherwise, helps no one.

But didn't studies by LeVay and Bailey and Pillard prove that homosexuality is the result of a physiological difference? No. They did not prove that. They did *suggest* that there might be a correlation between homosexuality and physiology or genetics of some kind, and the generally pro-gay and unreflective media did *imply that it proved* that homosexuality was biologically determined, and they surely did want that impression to be conveyed even though they were more cautious in their published studies, but no such thing was proven, not even close. The underlying rationale is, of course, that if a thing, such as a homosexual orientation, were shown to be innate, simply a result of biology, then it would probably be agreed that one could not ask people not to feel that way, and furthermore, that it would be "un-nice" to ask people not to act on how they "naturally" felt, and therefore, everyone should accept homosexuality. To obtain that kind of sympathy is doubtless the impetus for the study. There are horrific flaws in these studies. I shall deal with them in turn, but first let us again clear up a conceptual problem, a matter of how we think.

Does innate necessarily mean good? No. Even if we were to assume that a particular condition were innate, or a given at birth, that does not necessarily mean that it is good and desirable, or should be acted upon.

First, *even if* a condition were shown to be genetically linked that would *not* necessarily mean that it was good. Speaking theologically for a minute, Christians know that this is a "fallen" world. That means that this world, while created good, is now imperfect. Therefore, from a biblical standpoint, merely the fact that a condition now exists does not necessarily mean that it is a reflection of God's perfect will. From whatever standpoint the reader approaches such issues, the reader also agrees with this principle. For example, there are wars, hatred, famine, and disease, among many other disagreeable things; they do exist. Yet their existence does not mean that they are of God, nor intrinsically good or desirable. Some babies are born with an extra hole in their heart, but we do not rejoice in the gift of their being extra "hole-ly." Instead, we do surgery, and fix the hole, when we can. There are many physical defects with which persons are sometimes born, and our response may be sympathy, but will also be surgery, when possible, and not affirmation of the defect. There have been studies suggesting that there may be some genetic component to alcoholism, but that does not mean that we have all concluded, therefore, that alcoholism is good.

Secondly, we do not always believe that we should act upon "what we feel like," even if we think there may be some genetic link. Of course there are many things we all "feel like doing" that we know we should not. If we had tanks, many of us might drive over others once in a while during times of irritation in traffic; yet we know that we should not do such a thing. Perhaps that is why SUV's have more accidents per vehicle. There are many married persons who feel sexually attracted to someone to whom they are not married. This is a daily occurrence for some. Yet the great majority of married persons do not act upon such a sense of desire, knowing that the damage to their marriages and families would far outweigh the "benefit" of adultery. Many of us (most? nearly all?) have felt some impulse to steal something at one time, but most of us have not acted upon that impulse, believing it is wrong. There have been studies suggesting that some criminality is genetically linked, which, by the way, may or may not have any validity, but even if it did, we do not conclude that we are brutish and mean spirited to ask criminals not to commit crimes. All these remarks point out is that "feeling like doing something" does not necessarily mean that we *must* or *should* do it. One final example: There have been studies suggesting that alcoholism has a genetic component, setting aside their validity for a moment, even if they were sound, our response is not generally to give someone a case of Jack Daniels and say, "Hey, God gave you the gift of alcoholism. Go for it. Drink up. After all, that's just who you are, and we want you to be true to yourself. So, drink up, miss work, beat up your wife, disappoint your kids, and generally drink yourself to death." If that is not necessarily what you would say to an alcoholic, then it is *not* necessarily the case that we should encourage people to act upon an impulse *even if* that impulse *were* shown to be genetically linked, which, by the way, has not been proven for homosexuality.

Now then, to the LeVay study. You know, probably, that he is himself gay and a gay activist (LeVay, 1991; Maddoux, 1994, pp. 22-25; Satinover, 1996, pp. 78-81). He has left the scientific institute to promote the acceptance of homosexuality. Motive does not necessarily diminish the objectivity of one's science, but it is something to consider because it may indeed do just that, as, indeed, it seems here it has. There are several problems with his study. He theorized that a certain portion of the brain was larger in homosexuals than in heterosexuals. Many in the media were quick to imply that this proved that homosexuality was biologically determined. This is not so. Some of the factors that lead to that conclusion follow:

1. The motive of the researcher does raise the question of his impartiality.

2. The sample was pitifully small, too small to establish anything by itself.

3. The results have not been replicated by other scientists, and therefore certainly are not "established."

4. The study group was comprised of men who had died of AIDS and thus were presumed to be homosexual. This is a poor way to make a determination of the nature of the study group. It *may* be a roughly fair guess, that might have been adequate for some kinds of study with a very large sample, but one really ought to have knowledge of their homosexuality, and not merely an assumption.

5. The control group of presumed non-homosexuals was determined solely by the fact that they did not have AIDS. This is quite imprecise.

6. It is well known that parts of the brain can be influenced by activity! Rather like a muscle enlarges due to use, so also do different parts of the brain "grow" due to use. Blind persons, for example, experience "growth" in other parts of their brain as they increase use of other senses to compensate for the lack of sight. Thus, difference in the size of some portion of the brain could be either *cause* or *consequence*. So, ...

7. If there is a correlation in the size of the brain structure studied, we do not know if it was a consequence of AIDS, and had nothing to do with homosexuality *per se*. Nor, ..

8. If there is a correlation in the size of the brain structure studied, do we know if it was a *cause* (which is what LeVay implied and the media stated), or if it is a *consequence* of homosexuality (which is equally possible).

9. It is also the case that some of the presumably gay persons' brains had smaller groups of cells in the area studied than did some of the presumably straight persons'

brains. Therefore, this alone would mean that if there were any correlation, it is uncertain and only an influence, and not a determinant.

If this sort of study were ever to become meaningful, one would need to have 1) multiple researchers, 2) finding consistent results, 3) with groups that are clearly identified for both homosexuality and 4) heterosexuality, 5) using samples that can factor out the possible influence of AIDS and other common gay diseases, 6) using a test or samples that can factor out causal or 7) consequential relationships, and 8) adequately dealing with the issue of variance (some larger and some smaller in the same group) in results, and 9) preferably by some scientists who did not have sexual activism possibly influencing their analyses. The LeVay study proved nothing. If one supposes that giving accurate information is an appropriate task of theirs, the media did the public a disservice, again.

In his 1991 study on the "gay gene" in *Science* magazine, Dr. Simon LeVay himself said, "It's important to stress what I didn't find. I did not prove that homosexuality is genetic, or find a genetic cause for being gay. I didn't show that gay men are born that way, the most common mistake people make in interpreting my work. Nor did I locate a gay center in the brain." (PFOX, 2010)

And now to the Bailey-Pillard study: J. Michael Bailey and Richard C Pillard (Bailey, 1991, 1993; Satinover, 1996, pp. 85ff.; Maddoux, 1994, pp. 25-26) studied twins. They found that with identical twins, when one was gay the other was gay 52% of the time, while with non-identical twins, when one was gay, the other was gay only 22% of the time. Since identical twins have the same genetic make-up, and fraternal twins do not, and in light of the higher rate of concordance with identical twins, it was concluded that homosexuality was an inherited, genetically determined trait. To be fair, Bailey and Pillard were more cautious in the statement of their claims than the media, again. However, that is what was concluded by many in the public, that is the impression the media, generally, tried to convey, and that is the result which it is reasonable to suppose that Bailey and Pillard hoped for. Have they not proven the case that homosexuality is genetic? No. There are several reasons why their study is defective, noted below, but the grandest implication of their study is exactly *counter* to what they wanted to prove and the media claimed! That we shall save for last.

1. Their motives are suspect. They did not come to their study to see, but to show. They do have a personal interest in the results that they "found."

2. Their sample was a "convenience" sample. It was not random. It was taken from homosexuals at, for example, gay bars responding to ads for it. Convenience samples are adequate for some purposes, but they are sticky for others. It is particularly troubling if the object of the study was known to the respondents, for they might have volunteered themselves and their answers in part to reflect what they also felt should be shown.

3. Only one twin, one known as homosexual who volunteered for the study, was interviewed. The homosexuality of the non-respondent twin was determined by the report of the respondent one, a less than ideal protocol, which might well lead to false results due to misreport by the respondent for any of several possible reasons.

4. The environment is not factored out. The researchers thought that by comparing them with fraternal twins the element of environment was eliminated, but there is a far greater similarity between twins that greatly increases the probable environmental responses (how their folks and others treated them).

5. Furthermore, there might be something special about "twin-ness" which would affect the results. The special "preciousness" which some see in them might aggravate some factor in the environment. Also, twins more often sleep in the same bed; this might or might not lead to more incest, which is a known factor in homosexuality (Maddoux, 1994, p. 26).

6. I do not know if the sex of the non-respondent-twins was taken into account. Homosexuality is less frequently seen among women. If, with the fraternal twins, this was not factored out, that would significantly skew the results.

7. This is not the first time that such studies have been done, and on other occasions, different results were obtained. A similar thesis was advanced in 1952, but three subsequent researchers found different results (Maddoux, 1994, p. 26). Others have done similar studies since Bailey and Pillard, but they, too, have gotten different results (Satinover, 1996, p. 87).

8. "Furthermore,...in the only available study of mono-zygotic female twins *raised apart* the authors found a concordance rate for homosexuality of 0 percent." (Satinover, 1994, p. 86) This, if representative, is quite significant.

9. King and McDonald got concordance rates half those of Bailey and Pillard, 25% for identical twins and 12% for fraternal twins, but with a similar difference, however, they concluded something quite different from their study. "Discordance for sexual orientation in the monozygotic pairs [identical twins] confirmed that genetic factors are insufficient explanation for the development of sexual orientation." (Satinover, 1994, p. 87; King, 1992, pp. 407-409)

10. Indeed, Bailey and Pillard saw something of this too, for they said, "There must be something in the environment to yield the discordant twins." (Maddoux, 1994, p. 26)

11. Jones and Yarhouse in *The Use of Scientific Research in the Church's Moral Debate* (Jones) question Bailey and Pillard's methodology. It appeared that they counted each fraternal twin reporting a gay sibling as *two* instances rather than as *one* pair, thus explaining the doubling of the percentage.

And with these last notes we get to the real proof of this pudding. Now an identical twin, called monozygotic above, is one where the embryo is split very early on, but both children are the result of the same sperm and the same egg. Fraternal twins are two babies in the womb at the same time, but the result of a different egg and a different sperm. When you have identical twins, if one twin has blue eyes, the other has blue eyes, not 25% of the time, not 50% of the time, but 100% of the time. If homosexuality were genetically *determined*, then researchers should find that one homosexual twin has a twin who is also homosexual virtually one hundred percent of the time. The Bailey-Pillard study did *not* prove that homosexuality is genetically determined, but, for all its flaws, it did prove something: It proved just the opposite, that homosexuality is *not* genetically determined. Something must account for the other sibling *not* being homosexual. This proved that homosexuality is environmentally determined. It raises the possibility that there *may* be a genetic contribution, although it does not even prove that due to the environmental factors not factored out. There may not be *any* genetic contribution, but the determinant *must be* other than genetics for there to exist 50% discordance, or much more in other studies. (See also Satinover, 1996, and the discussion of these and other such arguments in Dallas and Heche and in Yarhouse.)

Once again, realize that the most important facts can sometimes be overlooked in a plethora of lesser facts. "Identical" means "the same." If you have one twin who is African American, and he has an identical twin, he is not going to be Chinese. Although the Bailey and Pillard study find in their sample vastly higher rates of concordance for homosexuality than other researchers find, even in their reported findings, fifty percent of the brothers of the identical twins whom they interviewed were not gay. That, in itself, proves that homosexuality cannot be genetically determined. Some other factor or factors must be the determinants. That means that homosexuality is not innate, but caused.

In July of 1993, Dr. Dean Hammer offered preliminary findings from a study attempting to show a genetic link for homosexuality, passed on through the mother's line. Some scientists were surprised that his preliminary findings were even published, due to the lack of appropriate controls for any scientific study in this field. (Maddoux, 1994, p. 26) Satinover points out that the study was soundly critiqued in the same publication in which it was published a short while later: "The results are not consistent with any genetic model.... Neither of these differences [between homosexuality in maternal versus paternal uncles or cousins] is statistically significant.... Small sample sizes make these data compatible with a range of possible genetic and environmental hypotheses. [After pointing out specific flaws and limitations on the sample, this reviewer went on.] Thus the family data presented [by Hammer *et al*] present no consistent support for the subsequent linkage results. (Satinover, 1996, p. 112, citing Rish *et al*, "Male Sexual Orientation and Genetic Evidence" *Science* (November, 1993). See also Hammer, Dean, *et al* "A Linkage Between DNA Markers on the X-chromosome and Male Sexual Orientation," *Science* 261, no. 5119, pp. 321-27 (July, 1993)

Hammer himself later sought to limit the claims for his study and even then said that it was unclear what significance his findings had. He later declared "complex behavioral traits are the product of multiple genetic and environmental antecedents." (Satinover, 1996, p. 113) Some question the findings of a maternally linked genetic basis for some homosexuals based, in part, on the researcher's motivation (Maddoux, 1994, p. 26). Others question his findings based on very limited sample size and questionable analyses. (Maddoux, 1994, p. 26, and Satinover, 1996, pp. 112-113) Even Hammer greatly downgraded the significance of his findings. The media proclaimed only the first blush of enthusiasm for a non-existent gay gene.

"In a 1993 gay gene study reported in *Science* magazine, researcher Dr. Dean Hammer, a homosexual, formerly of NIH (National Institute of Health), states: 'These genes do not cause people to become homosexuals.'" (PFOX, 2010)

All of the attempts to prove a genetic or a biological or a physiological basis for homosexuality have been proven unsound. Yet homosexuality exists. Since "nature" cannot explain it, what does?

Let's call her Lady L. Her father molested her. For most of her life, she assumed that *all* women were molested. When the time for courting came, many fine young men came to court her. She chose none of them. She chose the one who was a little rougher. She said to herself that he needed her more. But I don't think it was the reason she chose him. I think she chose him because he was what she thought she was worth.

Her idea of the proper Christian housewife was to be a doormat. He chatted up other women in her presence. Once in a while, she woke up in the middle of the night to find him choking her. He said it was due to a flashback from the war (World War II). But when she finally told him in no uncertain terms to knock it off, he quit; he never did it again. I guess his flashbacks just stopped.

One time Lady L. was asking me about divorce. She had had enough. I knew that she loved the church, so I asked her what she would do if her husband came over to the church building and took a sledgehammer to it. She said she would stop him. I told her that she was a temple of the Holy Spirit too, and it was not right for him to treat her badly. She got a different view of her worth that day. She didn't divorce. She didn't do things a whole lot different, but a little different, a significant little. I didn't see her to talk to her for two weeks, but then we spoke. She reported that in those two weeks, her husband had smiled more at her than in all the preceding thirty-five years of their married life together. She saw herself as more valuable; she acted just slightly differently; but it conveyed her new sense of her worth; and he changed his view of her in response. Great, it was a beginning. She got much stronger. He finally got right with God, and, I am told, became a fairly sweet guy. It appears, though, that two more generations were already damaged. I assume damaging patterns continue.

She did not *know* she was choosing him because she felt devalued by her father's actions. She did not make a conscious choice to pick a bad guy. But she picked him.

Somewhere in one of Jim Dobson's videos he tells a fish tale. There were some fish put in a tank. There was a glass partition put in this tank. On the other side of the glass partition another fish was put in. This second fish was the first fish's favorite food in the whole world. Fish number one started licking his chops, he got up a good head of steam and he went after dinner. Wham. He hit the glass. He shook his head a bit, wondering what happened. His nose hurt a little bit, but he wasn't going to let that dampen his appetite. He got up a good head of steam again, and went right for that tasty little fish. Wham. He hit something again. After a while, he slowed down a bit. He rubbed his nose again, and this time he swam a little more carefully. He still couldn't get him. He tried a little bit more, but then he gave up. He just couldn't have that fish anymore. He knew it for a dead certain fact. No doubt about it. Then the human who was in charge of the tank took out the glass partition. That other fish, fish number two, the good-eatin' fish, he swam right around in the whole tank. The big fish did too. The little guy swam right by the big guy. He brushed his gills. But there was nary a nibble. Big fish had learnt that little fish just wasn't available. So he never tried to eat him again. Never. The big fish had *learned* that the smaller fish, his favorite food in the whole world, was not available.

That is a parable, you know. Call it a metaphor if parable sounds too religious. Metaphor is literary. Things happen in life. These things have consequences. It is not surprising. Most of us have seen some of it. A lot of it has been all around us, but we've only seen some of it. Still, we have indeed seen some of it, all of us. Eating off the lunch wagon while working swing shift one time, I got sick from a certain kind of food. I couldn't eat that kind of food for three years. It wasn't *all* bad, I knew that, and I like that food fine now, but for three years, the memory of getting sick was so strong that I had no appetite for that particular food. I didn't think about it. I didn't plan it. I didn't consciously decide not to eat it again. I just couldn't stand the sight of it.

About 1968, living in Venice, CA, I was about to cross the street on foot. I looked north, and there was only a bus stopped at the corner. I looked south, and the traffic was far enough away. I went into the street. What I didn't know was that the bus was stopped to take on passengers, not because of the light. The light was green for folks heading south from the north. One other thing I didn't know was that there was a moving VW heading south as I went into the street. Sound of a horn, I think, a split second flash of the VW hood out of the peripheral vision of my left eye, I think, and then I was up in the air. I landed in the street, after the VW had gone on *under* me. Interesting moment: the traffic to the south had been far enough away when I entered, but I had been planning on continuing to move across the street. I wasn't moving anymore. I wondered if the cars would stop before they got to me. They did. I went to the UCLA Hospital emergency room. Whoever was there went to lunch shortly after I got there. The students (?) they left to baby-sit me while they went to lunch made jokes about my broken glasses. Whoever came back after lunch didn't know what had happened, they thought I looked okay and were going to send me home. I asked if they hadn't wanted to sew up my head, since the guy before lunch had. "Oh yeah," they said, and they did.

I had asked them to call my work, since I wasn't going to make it there. I did not want my mother called until I could call her, thinking that it would be less upsetting if she heard from me that I needed a ride home from the hospital. Work never heard. Mom came after I called. When I got off the table, I was limping, and one (the only one actual?) doctor who was around said in a loud voice, "Why's that man limping?" I guess I didn't look bad enough for them to believe the story the ambulance driver told, and besides he left long ago anyway. I waited for my mother for a couple of hours. They had parking right close by for emergency room patients, so we did not have to walk far to get to the car. By the time I got there, I was blind. Honest, folks, no fooling. A big, blank circle in the middle, and a little fuzzy vision around the edges. But I figured that it must be that my head landed on the pavement (it may actually have been the windshield first) near where the brain stuff relating to vision was, I said let's just wait a minute. The blood returned (I'm guessing here), and so did my vision. I was remarkably un-spooked. We went home. Mom's house, not mine; I had to be looked after for a few days. And now we get to the reason for this whole story being here.

I did not drive for a while after that. When we went out, I rode with my mother. And whenever she got anywhere near another car, nothing really bad, mind you, just a little bit near, nothing that doesn't happen all the time in normal driving, just regular nearness. Well, whenever she got near another car, I got a knot in my stomach. I did *not decide* to get a knot in my stomach. I did not want to get a knot in my stomach. As a matter of fact, I did not enjoy feeling sick, having my stomach twisted, having extra adrenalin dumped into my blood stream and taking a little while (a few seconds, maybe more) to calm down again. It just happened. However, I wasn't born with that. It happened in response to being hit by a car in a situation where I could have been killed. The intense reaction faded, and, after a while (several days or a few weeks), it went away.

That is a very small version of Post-Traumatic Stress Syndrome. It may serve as a metaphor for reactions. Stuff happens. Stuff has consequences. Bad stuff has bad consequences. (An understanding of all these things is in the Bible, but, I don't want to be a Bible-thumper, so I won't talk about it.) Most of the messed-up things that we do, we do in part as a reaction to other messed-up stuff that has happened to us. Child molesters were almost always (maybe without the almost) molested themselves as children. Alcoholic parents tend to produce kids that are messed up somehow, maybe as alcoholics, maybe in some other way, but something is going to be out of whack. Molestation does not always have the same consequences, but it always has consequences. Jan Frank (Frank, 1987) has spoken of the effects of her molestation. She got married, but she was always tough on her husband. One day it dawned on her that she was bringing attitudes into their marriage from something that had happened to her long before she got into relationship with her husband. She had been molested by a man when she was a child, and she made a vow within herself that she would never trust a man again, and her husband was, after all, a man. She got healed; got much more joy, peace, and a much healthier marriage. So, hell does not have to be destiny, but pain leads to pain. That really shouldn't be a difficult concept to grasp.

So how does this relate to homosexuality? I am hopeful that the reader can see that troubling things can have troubled consequences, as a general principle. Therefore, it would follow that if one saw things that seemed to be troubled, then one might consider the possibility that there was some thing or things that either were troubling or seemed to be troubling to the person troubled – on the off chance that the troubling thing or things caused the troubled things. Is there evidence that homosexuality has origins, or, in some sense, causes in prior events of a somewhat troubling nature? Oh, yes. Oh, yes.

[This is an aside. Is it unfair? The Greek word "logos" is the basis for all the words ending in "-ology" that we find in biology, zoology, paleontology, and so forth. That word, "logos," means "word," but in the context of such words as these it means something more like "the organized knowledge about," or "the study of" whatever it is that precedes "ology." For example, "biology" is "the study of life." In the word "psychology" what precedes "-ology" is "psych-", which come from the Greek word "psyche." "Psyche" means "soul." But most of our contemporary psychologists do not believe in the existence of the soul. So, one might say that psychology is the only profession wherein its members spend their entire careers studying something they do not believe exists! Is it unfair to say that? Perhaps, but the foundational insight of the whole field of psychology was that visible thoughts, attitudes, and conduct may well have causes not readily visible. My point at the moment is that many contemporary psychologists seem to have far too little awareness of that.]

Many therapists have studied, discerned and noted the reality of causation in homosexuality:

Strean: "Many dynamically oriented clinicians (Bieber, 1962; Socarides, 1978; Fine, 1981) have consistently demonstrated the profound psychic conflicts in homosexual patients." (Strean, 1983, p. 163)

Bergeler: "The concept of perversion as a direct reflection of inborn drives is untenable. The unclarified problem of biological bisexuality cannot account for homosexuality, simply because of its therapeutic changeability." (Bergler, 1956, p. 177)

Socarides: "It is my belief, following Rado's model (1950), that all disordered behavior [specifically here including homosexuality] begins with an overproduction of fear, rage, guilt and pain, the first clinical manifestations of which are found in early childhood." (Socarides, 1983, p. 39)

"Homosexuality has an etiology, symptomology, and course of development and in most cases responds well to appropriate therapeutic techniques.... Those who advocate declaring homosexuality "normal" betray the fundamental criterion of modern medicine which is devoted to correct diagnosis." (Socarides, 1983, p. 50)

There are extensive discussions of the etiology of homosexuality from a psychoanalytic perspective in Cappon (Cappon, 1965, pp. 67-111), Hatterer (Hatterer, 1970, pp. 34-47), and Strean (Strean, 1983, pp. 11-29).

There is also a great quantity of evidence from other sources and different kinds of sources. Bell, Weinberg and Hammersmith (Bell, 1978, and 1978II) were Kinsey institute researchers, working with a pro-gay position, who did much polling to try to determine certain things about the experiences of homosexuals. Heterosexual males, on average, had clearly warmer and more positive relationships with their fathers than did homosexual males (Bell II, 1978, p. 185). Heterosexual males also perceived their fathers as stronger personages within their marriage than did the homosexual males perceive their fathers (Bell II, 1978, p. 186). Homosexual males experienced their childhoods as tenser and less relaxed, than did heterosexual males (Bell II, 1978, p. 86). Heterosexual males experienced their adolescence as happier. They saw themselves during adolescence as more positive, more adequate, and less uptight than did homosexual males (Bell II, 1978, p. 190 and p. 86).

The average age of a first homosexual encounter for homosexual males was 9.7 years, while for heterosexual males who had had such an encounter; it was 11.6 years (Bell II, 1978, p. 191). Both the greater frequency of such a childhood encounter and the earlier age of it are possible explanatory factors in the later sexual orientation of persons who came to see themselves as homosexual. The use of force or the threat of its use was experienced by 24% of white homosexual males, and 35% of black homosexual males, but by only 11% of white heterosexual males and 14% of black heterosexual males (Bell II, 1978, p. 165). Five percent of white homosexual males had received anal intercourse by the age of 10, 23% by the age of 15, and 42% by the age of 18 (Bell II, 1978, p. 158). White homosexuals experienced being fellated at considerable rates: 10% by age 10, 47% by age 15, and 70% by age of 18. The corresponding rates for the corresponding ages for white heterosexual males in their control group was 2%, 9%, and 12% (Bell II, 1978, p. 157). This is not because they so enjoyed doing such activities, because the reports of white, adult homosexuals as children *performing* fellatio are much lower: 6% by the age of 15 (versus 47% receiving), and 19% by the age of 18 (versus 70% receiving) (Bell II, 1978, p. 156). This data raises the possibility that the early performance of such activity may tend to set the child's sexual sights in a given direction. They reported that 66% of white homosexual males and 50% of black homosexual males had been masturbated by a male by the age of 15, contrasting with 16% and 2% of white and black heterosexual males (Bell II, 1978, p. 155). By the age of 18, 82% of white homosexual males and 77% of black homosexual males reported being masturbated by a male; this contrasts with a total of 19% and 6% for heterosexual white and black males (Bell II, 1978, p. 155). This, too, suggests the possibility that early sexual involvement and early homosexual involvement may tend to lead persons into homosexuality.

Some have suggested that since a given condition is not universal, therefore it must not be a factor, but that is fallacious thinking. First, if anything, both the respondents and the researchers know what the data tends to say, and that it tends to say things about the origins of homosexuality they do not want to hear, and so therefore it may be the case that questions, answers, and analysis might each be affected to diminish the disparity somewhat. Second, and more tellingly, it does not follow that a given action must always have the same effect on different persons. Each person has many different influences upon him or her, and a given action in the lives of two different people might not lead to the same result due to the influence of other factors. Also, contrary to some popular notions, human beings are not automatons. Human beings do have the capability to respond to events differently.

Here is a summary of causal factors that have been observed by many and which I have found to be sound. I think that there are several causal factors that can be influential. I also think that there are other factors that may work to counterbalance a particular causal factor. There is also the element of the individual response to events or factors, both at the time of the events, and subsequently. There are theories that have been largely discarded. There are factors that I find to be more common elements with women or with men. To each of these things I shall give some notice.

Gender identity disorder: The person has not secured his or her identity as male, for the male, or female, for the female (See Moberly, 1983; and Nicolosi, 1991). I have seen this more commonly with males, but it is also offered as an explanatory factor for females. Using the example of the male for the moment: The male does not find his masculinity affirmed. He looks admiringly upon qualities of seeming masculinity in other males. At puberty, this admiring, longing, and coveting becomes sexualized, and the male child then finds himself sexually attracted to other males. The real need here is not sexual union with the other male. The homosexual activity is an attempt to acquire assurance of having those qualities of masculinity that at some level he senses he does not have. The need is to be assured of his masculinity.

Homosexual activity cannot give that, and thus, the activity will never provide the satisfaction which is sought by means of it. Indeed, the homosexual activity itself is a reproach to the individual and only serves to increase his sense of inadequacy as male. The activity increases the discontent. The learned pattern of activity by which to deal with discontent is homosexuality, and this activity cannot meet that need, but increases it. Thus, this may serve to explain why an almost feverish promiscuity may be seen among so many homosexuals.

In one sense, the homosexual impulse is like cannibalism. (See Payne, 1981, and Saia, 1988.) The cannibal desires to acquire the traits he admires in the other whom he consumes. Thus, the homosexual may try to acquire the qualities he feels he does not have by sexually consuming, or possessing, the other male. This might explain the very great premium placed on physical appearance among homosexual males.

This is often caused by a real or perceived father absence. Contrary to the claptrap of recent social theory, children need fathers too. Males especially need to learn from the father what it is to be male. It may be from so simple a thing as the father being busy with two jobs, and not making the extra effort to still have a positive impact on his children's lives, that a child does not find himself affirmed, and is particularly open to inappropriate "affirmation" from another male. As one former homosexual I know has said, "You will drink brackish water when you feel you are dying of thirst." The condition may even arise when the father is not physically absent, but is emotionally absent. I can think of several who would fit this paradigm.

The male child may also reject the father's interpretation of masculinity. If father is clearly abusive or very harsh, one child may find that "men are mean, and I don't want to be mean, so I can't be like a man," or "that men are unsafe, and I want to be with the girls because they are safe." Realize that these responses are rarely verbalized at the time they are made, although it may sometimes be discovered in counseling that a person did indeed make such a specific statement to themselves at a key moment in the past. Realize also, that such responses are incredibly powerful, and absolutely do have life-long consequences.

It was once thought that it was a domineering mother who was a causal factor, but that notion is largely discarded by most recent theorists. There is evidence that more mothers of homosexuals are or are perceived as, on average, more dominant than are the mothers of heterosexuals, but the assumption is that the more important factor is the weakness or emotional absence, real or perceived, of the father. I would suspect that when there is a domineering mother that does make some contribution to a homosexual development, especially for males, and in two ways: 1) by contributing to the weakness of the father, and 2) by contributing to the distaste of the son for the masculine model which he sees lived out.

Elizabeth Moberly finds "gender identity deficit disorder" to be generally true for both men and women. I see it more readily as a factor in male homosexuals. However, I have seen one case of a very highly educated lesbian woman who seems to have found great fault early on with her mother's interpretation of femininity, and I know of another younger lesbian woman about whom I know little, but of whom I have thought this might also be a factor.

When this is a primary factor, then the need is to give the person the sense of worth as male, for men, or as female, for women, that they do not now have. Homosexual activity will never meet the need.

Sexual molestation is often a factor. Sexual molestation is always a damaging experience. (See Allender, 1995; and Frank, 1987.) It does not always, not even usually, lead to homosexuality, but it is damaging and it can be a factor in homosexual orientation. A number of persons whom I have known in ex-gay ministry, male and female, have speculated that 80 to 90% of all lesbians were raped or molested. That certainly accords with my limited experience in helping people in this field. It also accords with the observations of some honest gay activists whom I have asked. While this factor is more often spoken of in relation to women, and while I believe that it is a larger factor with women than with men, my own belief is that this is a much larger factor with male homosexuals than is generally believed.

If a woman is molested, she may say to herself that "men are not safe," or "you can't trust a man," or "you can't be vulnerable with a man, but I need to be able to be tender and vulnerable with someone, so I'll be vulnerable with a woman because they are the only ones it's safe with," or "women get hurt, so I'll have to be a man not to get hurt."

If a man is molested, he may say to himself, "men are brutal, I don't want to be one," or "since I have been penetrated like this, it must mean that I am not really a man, I might as well be a girl."

Early sexualization, either homosexual or heterosexual, can be damaging. By this, I mean the early introduction to sexual activity. I will treat early homosexual activity below separately. Sexual activity of any kind can be troubling to a child. If heterosexual, it may be frightening to the child, and cause him or her to withdraw from normal development. He or she may have internalized a fear of sexual activity and/or of the other sex generally.

Early homosexual imprinting can be a factor. If a child has an early childhood homosexual experience, it may help to establish homosexual orientation in various ways. It will often have the character of molestation and thus carry the freight indicated above, but even if that is not a factor, it has consequences. Our bodies are wired for response. If one has had a physical experience, even if one did not want it, and even if one hated it, and even if one felt repulsed by it and guilty about it, one may still be aroused by it. Thus, a child might find elements of a homosexual experience arousing, even if frightening and hateful. Also, this has now become a conceivable way to obtain sexual gratification, and it is a way that is now known. When the child later goes through puberty, his new sexual interest may have already been steered towards something homosexual and that may be less frightfully new at that time. There was considerable data in the Bell-Weinberg-Hammersmith study (see above) to suggest this kind of correlation.

Many churches have pre-schools, and so have the churches at which I have been pastor. I recall the teachers telling me of one boy who had a tendency to want to touch other children inappropriately, and in wrong places. It was never assumed that that was "just the way he was." It was known that his mom was not too cautious in her boyfriends. It was believed that boy had seen, and may have experienced, things which planted in his mind the doing of the things he did. What the child sees, the child tends to do – for good, or ill.

Let me speak of **defensive detachment** for a moment. This is not a separate causal factor, but a mechanism, a pattern of response, which may be seen at work when one or more of the different kinds of causal factors is involved. Remember the big fish who "lost" his appetite? Perhaps the fish does not have enough analytical ability to speak of himself in these terms, but his conduct is a good illustration of what happens with defensive detachment. Let us stay with the fish metaphor for a moment. The fish tried to go after the desired object. He found he could not get it. He tried again. He still could not get it. He got frustrated. He was hurt and angry that he could not get that little fish. He cried out to God about how unfair it was. He was angry at the ribbing he got from the other big fish in other tanks who got their little fish. He went through all the stages of grief. At last, he resigned himself to the fact that he could not get that little fish. For a while he felt badly about himself. He felt that he must be inadequate as a big fish. But then it became too painful to believe that the fault was his. So he decided that there was no fault. He decided that he just didn't like little fish. He wasn't like those other big, nasty, brutish mean fish who got the little fish. He was the little fish's pal. Someone pointed out to him that there was a glass partition that had hindered him, but he "just couldn't see it," and so he didn't believe it. Since the idea of there being an unseen hindrance threatened to open up the desire for that little fish again, and since that had been so painful a disappointment just a short while before, he even got angry at the one who said there was an unseen barrier. The disappointment had been too great to risk it again. Since it was too disappointing to want, he *detached* himself from his wanting in order to *defend* himself from the pain of disappointment. That is why he still didn't eat the little fish after the glass partition was removed. And that is "defensive detachment."

When for example, a boy finds that he cannot obtain the affirmation he needs from his father as a man, he may "defend" himself from the pain of disappointment by "detaching" himself from a once strong goal. This detachment may not be *from* normal sexual interest; it may be from something else, the desire for approval as a male, for example, which will have as a *consequence* the abandonment of normal sexual interest. The initial goal does not disappear. It only goes underground. There is still a need for that affirmation. That need may now seek fulfillment in the same-sex admiration, then same-sex covetousness, and then same-sex eroticization. This defensive detachment mechanism may also grow and influence one's conscious thoughts in connected areas.

What responsibility, if any, is there for the parents? Do we blame the parents? Is it dad's fault? Is it mom's fault? No, no, and no. As for responsibility, we are all responsible for our actions. If we live out ungracious lives before our children, that will have consequences. We are responsible for our misdeeds. If someone has molested his or her child, he or she is indeed responsible for having done a dreadful thing. It is appropriate for that person to express their remorse, provide the best possible care for the child, get the appropriate healing for their spirit, and do whatever else may be helpful. If, in reviewing one's conduct as a parent, one sees flaws, then by all means seek to correct them and perhaps offer appropriate apology and possibly even amends for your bad conduct. However, do not be too quick to blame yourself for another's actions. You did not force the other person to interpret their experience as they did. At some point, they made their own choices. They are responsible for their choices. You are only responsible for your choices, not for those of another, even your own child. Bear in mind that we are all imperfect. There are no perfect families. There are no perfect parents. You may take appropriate responsibility. Do not take more than that.

The parent may not have done anything wrong. A child may have had an unmet need, but it may not have been possible for the parent to meet that need. The actions of the parent may have been honorable and innocent, yet a given child needed an affirmation that the parents were not able to give. There may have been things unknown to the parents. There may have been an uncle or a neighborhood kid who did something consequential that mom or dad knew nothing about. One child may simply have been particularly needy.

The question of "choice" must be dealt with somehow. Elaine Siegel had as the subtitle of her book "Choice without Volition." There is a clue in that subtitle. I have placed hints about this at several points. It is time to deal with this issue. The most significant causal factors are not the traumatic events themselves but our reactions to them. Again, do not assume too quickly that you know what I am saying here.

I do not believe that we are automatons. Therefore, it easily makes sense to me that our response to events, our reactions to events, or our reading of events would be consequential. However, persons of a more mechanistic frame of mind might arrive at very similar conclusions by speaking of the multiplicity of factors and events that influence our actions.

Another illustration: Two people walk down the street. Both are mugged. One says to him or herself, "Oh, that was terrible. It's not safe to go anywhere any more. They stole all my money. I got a black eye. I'll never leave the house again." While the other person might say to him or herself, "Oh, that was terrible. But fortunately all they got was what I had in my wallet, and I've got more. I've already cancelled the credit cards. I got a black eye, but it sure could have been worse. In fact, I'm thankful that I came out okay. It shows that I am safe. Even when I am attacked, I'll get through it. I may be a little extra careful for a while, but I'm not going to let that so-and-so change my life." Same event, but two different responses are given.

Another true story and this has nothing to do with homosexuality: One woman I know was introduced to all sorts of sexual horrors, and worse. She was badly damaged by it. It caused her decades of emotional pain, physical illnesses, inability to cope well with life in some areas, and diminished social relations, but she never did to others what was done to her. Among the many things she "said" to herself were, "Wow, this hurts. I sure don't want that to happen to anybody else if I can help it. This is really crummy. I want nothing to do with this." As she has discovered what happened and why she was reacting, she has experienced much healing in all of these areas, although there is still more healing to come. Another woman, a relative of hers, was subjected to only a little of what this one was, and yet she joined in the activities. She "said" to herself, "Wow, this hurts. If I join in with them, they won't hurt me so much, and I will get to do it to others and maybe that will feel better too." Same initial event, two different responses. Bear in mind, in each case, each woman was responding to events that began when she was a child, before she had much use of language or analytical reasoning, perhaps some things began even before any words were known. The events were similar. The events were damaging in each case, but the responses were different.

Other illustrations, true ones: A woman I know was molested as a child. She was four years old at the time. She felt dirty all her life. She wasn't, but she felt like she was. She made a decision that she was dirty, and that sexual intimacy was dirty, at the age of four. That affected her life, her choice of mate, her enjoyment of marriage, and much more. She never consciously made a decision, and yet she made unconscious decisions about many important things. A man I know was molested as a child. He made a decision, an unconscious childhood "decision," that sex was evil. He was able to change his mind later, but his head was messed up for many years. Another young man I know learned early on that his dad wanted a girl. He wanted to please his dad. He tried to act girlish. He later learned that it was his dad who was messed up, not him, but it took him a while, fortunately less time than many. A woman I know was told by her father that she was stupid, ugly, incompetent, and not worth much, day after day. She "concluded" that she was not worth much, and that no one cared how she felt, especially that no man cared how she felt. She went through the motions of marriage for years, but it is all messed up for her now. I hope she finds out what happened some day.

Babies react to things in the womb. That's why some folks play Mozart for their babies in the womb, because they know the child is reacting and they hope it will make him or her brighter. We know that if the mother has great turmoil in her life during the pregnancy that can have consequences for the child. (See Seamands, 1985.) Babies do not have linguistic skills but they respond to things. A British literary figure, Lord Macaulay (1800-1859) is reputed to have said nothing until the age of three. At a party for children, some hot cocoa was spilled on him. The hostess rushed to clean him up, and then, at the age of three, he said the first words he ever uttered. According to the story, he said, "Thank you, madam, the agony is abated." Most of us take a bit longer to order our thoughts that well. He was learning things long before he ever put them into words.

All of us are reacting. All of us do, after a fashion, make decisions. Even as children, we make decisions on fashions, on food, on music, on teachers, on school in general, on particular subjects, on friends, and on much more. We like parks, or we like macaroni and cheese, or we are scared of a certain place, or we don't want the lights off in our room at night. We make decisions in college, in high school, in junior high school, in elementary school, in kindergarten, in pre-school, while playing with other toddlers on the block, while still in our cribs. They may or may not be wise decisions. They are probably not well informed decisions. They are certainly not based upon a wide experience of life. We could not articulate our decisions well, perhaps not at all. But we make them. Don't we? That is a serious question. Do we not make decisions as children? As toddlers? Even before that? They may not have been conscious decisions, but they are still decisions of a sort.

If we do, and I do not think that any honest persons even slightly conversant with life can deny the fact, then it should not be surprising to note that in addition to the possibly traumatic events of our lives, another factor is terribly significant, our interpretation of them. By our interpretations of events, we set ourselves on tracks long before we know what on God's green earth we are doing. One person decides that other people are mean, and he goes through life with a chip on his shoulder, bringing about the very rejection he hates! Such decisions have consequences.

I want to talk about choice. Let me say one thing up front, if this can be called "front" after so long an introduction: No one decides to become homosexual. Let me repeat that: No one decides to become homosexual. I suppose there may be some occasional exceptions; after all, there is usually an exception to nearly everything; but basically no one, nobody, decides, consciously, to become homosexual. However, people do make decisions that affect their sexual orientation. As an adolescent, as a child, or even as an infant, a woman may make a decision that it is not safe to trust men, or that it is not safe to be a woman. A man may make a decision that men are too mean or that he isn't really a man or that he can't become one. It is this kind of response to the traumas of life, mostly real, but sometimes only perceived traumas, that lead to homosexual orientation. You might call them "choices," but that would be unfair because we are speaking of things that happen before one is of age to reason very well; we are speaking of things that shape our reasoning itself. I would not call them choices, but responses, or reactions. Elaine Siegel tried to deal with the matter by speaking of "choice without volition." It is something like that.

We all, we all, please hear that, we *all* make some wrong responses or reactions or decisions. Incidentally, many wrong decisions were pretty reasonable based on the evidence available to the one who had to make the call at the time, but if they were wrong, they were still wrong. Each of us in life must re-think and re-examine things as we go, a lot of them. Most of us make some very big changes in what we do in life as we go. That, too, is not surprising. So there is one more word about "choice" I want to offer.

Maybe we didn't have a fair choice before, but maybe we do now. However we got to where we are at, we do not have to stay there. We can move. Persons who find they have a homosexual orientation can make a choice to change it. It will probably not be easy. It may be the hardest thing they have ever done. But it can be done. It rarely happens just by wishing it. As with many other important matters, it does not generally happen just by praying for God to do all the work for you. If you want to acquire knowledge, you generally have to do some reading; it doesn't just happen. If you want to acquire skill, you generally have to do some work; it doesn't just happen. You remember the story about the man who was new to New York and was going to go to a concert at Carnegie Hall, but he had lost his bearings in the city. He met a beatnik on the street and he asked him, "How do you get to Carnegie Hall?" And the beatnik replied, "Practice, man, practice." Even before that, you've got to decide you want to be a musician.

It is amazing to me how many folks I meet who prayed for God to change them, didn't get what they wanted, and decided that God didn't want to change them. As a student in college, would you pray that God give you an A on a test you hadn't studied for, and expect to get it? As one awkward in social skills, would you pray that God just give you a great bunch of friends without ever expecting to have to leave your room to look for them, or ever having to develop any new social skills? As a businessman, would you ask God to have you prosper in business, and expect to prosper without having to open the doors of the shop, put the stock on the shelves, greet the customers and ring up the sales? God is real. Prayer is valuable. But usually you have got to do something too. You see, there are some things that aren't really real if you haven't done something yourself to make it happen. Even if someone else has been driving your car for, oh say, twenty years, if you decide to take over the wheel, you can change course - if you decide to take over the wheel. So long as there is evil in the world, which is likely to be for a long time, there will be a need for those who seek good to do more than just ask for it. But, when you ask, seek, and follow, you will find. It's like a lot of things, first you decide and then you act upon what you decide. If you find you are on road "B," and you do not decide to turn onto road "A," well, then you have "decided" to stay on road "B." You will decide, in one form or another, consciously or unconsciously, anyway. But be sure you know what decisions you have made, and don't blame somebody else for your decisions, or their consequences, not even God.

The burden of this section of the book has been to answer the question: Is healing of homosexuality possible? The answer is yes. We have looked at scores of reports of persons who have come out of homosexuality. We have heard of scores of ministries that have reported that thousands of their participants have come out of homosexuality. We have looked at statistical data that show that the great majority of people who have ever tried homosexuality have left it behind, which clearly implies that many of those already in homosexuality now will also leave it behind. We have seen much evidence of disturbance in the lives of persons who go on to become homosexually oriented. We have tried to look at how some of the disturbing factors might have such an influence on people's lives. We have sometimes looked at similar phenomena in settings other than homosexuality in the hope that it could more easily be seen there, and then be applied in the area of homosexuality. Is healing possible? Oh yes. Yes.

Part V: How Then to Help?

"Come unto me all ye who labor and are heavy laden, and I will give you rest."
> *— Jesus in Matthew 11:28*

"Then neither do I condemn you," Jesus declared, "Go now and leave your life of sin."
> *— Jesus in John 8:11*

"Do not conform any longer to the pattern of this world, but be transformed by the renewing of your mind."
> *— Paul in Romans 12:2*

Chapter 22: The Tale of Mr. G

Mr. G, again the story is true but the names are changed, Mr. G, as a boy, could have used more attention from his father. Father's attention was generally either absent or disparaging and harsh. However, there was an uncle around. He was more than willing to spend time with young Mr. G. He took him on trips, fishing and camping and more. The trips were fun and exciting, and the uncle seemed really to care about young Mr. G. Ah, but it was not long before the uncle wanted something for his efforts. Uncle touched the youth, uncle fondled the youth, and, well, uncle did more. Now, young Mr. G was young, and the uncle told him that he must not tell. His parents would be disappointed in the youth if he told, and he would be shamed, and uncle really did care about him, and so on. I do not recall now, but were there threats of more than shame? Perhaps. Eventually, uncle involved some of his friends who wanted something too. Of course to not go on trips was to make clear that something was amiss, and that could not be acknowledged. So the molestation continued for some years, until the youth felt himself strong enough and secure enough to tell uncle, and uncle's friends, to knock it off.

Mr. G went off on his own. He met a woman. She was his first (and only?) true love. But over time they drifted apart. They each married others. Time passed. Much time.

Mr. G moved to another part of the country. Somewhere along the way, Mr. G made a commitment to Jesus Christ, as we Christians say, as his Lord and Savior. There was something real and good about this new commitment, but all was not resolved overnight by it.

Mr. G got a business going. He met a woman, a different woman from the first. They married. He met a man. For at least ten years this man was also in his life. His relationship with his wife was damaged. Eventually, she could not stand the emotional estrangement. They divorced. The man was still in his life. He continued in church, and, yes, in Christ, but his life was not in order, and he knew it.

About thirty years after he had last seen his first love, he thought about her. He looked her up on Facebook. They communicated. She had married another man, had had children, now grown and gone, and she had divorced. She was now free. Their old love was re-kindled. Many unusual things had to come together for their fast budding plans to come to pass, but they did. She decided to move to where he was and they would get married. They did.

The other man was still in the picture. She had not known about him. She came to know. This was hard for her, very hard. She had not been prepared for this, but she loved him, and she thought God had to have had a hand in this to bring their reunion about.

He had long declined to get counseling. He had long declined to read books about others who had come out of same sex attractions. It is quite common for those with same sex attractions to *not* examine their lives. He always felt something was wrong about it, sort of, but this attraction was just the way it was, he felt. He still had feelings for the man. After all, they had been together for many years. He still did not want to counsel. He was certain that it would do no good. But he loved his wife, and he thought perhaps he should try.

He came for counsel and prayer. Each time he came, he just barely came. Each time, he came convinced that it would do no good, that there was nothing that could do any good. But he was wrong. Things did come out. Past hurts were dealt with. Unclean spiritual influences were uncovered and cast out, although his theology had told him that such things could not be in the life of a Christian. He left relieved, changed, and happy. Yes, there were recurring unwanted attractions, for a season. There were at least three very important sessions, and perhaps it was four or five. Each time he came reluctantly and with little or no expectation of relief. His perseverance required his strong general desire to do right. It may also be the case that if it had not been for the new element of his love for his new wife, he very possibly would never have stuck it out. But he did. Each time he came to counsel and pray there was relief, and then change. Each time he left with a relief and a joy he had not thought possible when he came. After a time, there was no longer need to come for counsel and prayer. The other man is not in his life; his wife is. Their marriage is strong and happy. He has no need for that former friend, nor for any other such a friend. He has been secure enough in his new identity to share the whole story with a small group Bible study of which he has been a part.

He is healed. The man is not only healed enough to be secure and happy in his marriage, but he has even been able to truly forgive his uncaring father, his unseeing mother, and horribly abusive uncle. These are no small things, and these statements are not made lightly. These are things which God can do. I do not know if psychological counseling alone can ever do them, but God can.

It may well be true that in his case he needed the extra impetus of his new marriage to get him through the pain of dealing with what he needed to deal with, but he also needed something else. He needed to know that there was a standard which he was not meeting. He also needed to have the standard upheld, even during the years when he was not able to meet it, and he did not think it could be met. He needed to know that the standard was still there. He also needed to hear that change was possible, even when he could not fully believe that it was. Had these things not been offered, then it seems likely that he would never have found truth, healing, or happiness. It is both untrue and profoundly unhelpful *not* to uphold God's standard, *not* to offer hope, *and not* to offer help.

How then to help? One way to help is to uphold truth, and to offer both hope and help.

Chapter 23:

A Note on Grace, Truth, and Transformation

John the beloved said many magnificent things both in his gospel and in his letters. One I am drawn to at the moment is in John 1:14. In speaking of Jesus he says: "The Word became flesh and made his dwelling among us. We have seen his glory, the glory of the One and Only, who came from the Father, full of grace and truth." I want to call our attention once again to the words "grace and truth." I think we have here not a smorgasbord from which we pick whichever we prefer, but a twofold requirement. Both grace and truth are required. Yes, it may be needful to emphasize one more than the other at times, but both are required, and neither should be lost sight of. I think both grace and truth are required.

I have said previously in these pages that there is no real grace without truth, and that there will surely be no effective truth without grace. Indeed, I am not even sure that the truth is quite true without grace. While I will review our findings in a moment, let me say here that I do not find homosexual ideation and conduct a natural or normal variant. It neither arises from health, nor leads to health. Thus the conduct and the surrounding rationales that support it should, in some manner, be opposed. However, people always need support, not necessarily in what they want to do, but in their persons. The church has earned much of the enmity it has obtained from gay and pro-gay persons in some measure by its common unwillingness to offer anything but condemnation. Ah, but is not the Bible universally condemning, and thus should we not be so as well? No, not quite.

While nearly every New Testament theme can be seen to be foreshadowed in the Old Testament, at least after it has once been made clear in the New, there are clear and important differences of focus. Take another look at the famous example of Jesus dealing with the woman who was apparently caught in the act of adultery and brought to him by a group of "teachers of the law and Pharisees" for judgment. You can read the story in John 8:1-11. Jesus said, "Let him who is without sin cast the first stone." Starting with the oldest, each man concluded that he was not holy enough to stone the woman, and, one by one, they all left. When only the woman and Jesus remained, Jesus asked her, "Does no one condemn you?" The woman replied, "No one, sir." And Jesus said, "Then neither do I. Go, thou, and sin no more."

He did not say what she had done was right. He did say that what she had done was sin. She had done wrong, and she was now told to go and do right. But he did not say, "Stone her to death," either, which He could have by Jewish legal thinking. I think He held up both grace and truth pretty well. But there is something else which is illustrated here. In the New Testament, while there is no loss of concern for holiness, there is shift in focus to redemption, salvation, or transformation. Right is still right, but, unlike the way the Old Testament often feels, the emphasis in the New Testament is not on condemning the wrongdoer, nor only on protecting the community from the example of wrongdoers, but on changing them. This is not a small theme, nor is it seen only here.

When Jesus began his ministry, as recorded in Mark 1:15, He said, "Repent and believe the good news. The kingdom of God is at hand." "Repent," in its Hebrew roots (*shub*, or *shuv*) means "turn around," or "change course." The Latin word underlying our English word and the Greek word here translated mean "re-think," or "re-think your position so thoroughly that you turn around and do what God wants you to do," roughly speaking. The call to repentance presupposes that a person can change course. People can.

Consider the story of the prodigal son in Luke 15:11-32. When the prodigal son got tired of slopping hogs in the far country and thought he might go back home, Jesus spoke of him saying, "when he came to his senses," or "when he came to himself." (v. 17). That presupposes that this image of God in which we are made (See. Genesis 1:27.) is not obliterated, even after mankind had messed up big-time (about which see Genesis 3). Every call to repentance *is* a call to holiness, but it is also a declaration that the change to which we are called is possible. There are a lot of calls to repentance in the Bible. The possibility of answering that call is a major point in the New Testament.

In Romans 12:2, Paul says to no longer be conformed to the patterns we may see around us. Do not do things like everybody else does. A lot of folks do things we don't think are right. So why should we always do what everybody else does? Didn't your mother ever ask you, "If everybody jumped off a cliff, would you do it too?" So, don't do what everybody else does, but rather, be transformed. How? We are transformed by the renewing of our minds through this new life in Christ.

Let me call your attention once more to a passage some who disagree with me may find uncomfortable. It is in I Corinthians 6:9-11. I want us to focus on verse 11 this time. Let's look at the uncomfortable part first: "Do you not know that the wicked will not inherit the kingdom of God? Do not be deceived: Neither the sexually immoral nor idolaters nor adulterers nor male prostitutes nor homosexual offenders nor thieves nor the greedy nor drunkards nor slanderers nor swindlers will inherit the kingdom of God." In light of our theme in this book, note that there are a lot of things on this list and that this list is not said to be exhaustive. God is concerned about many things. But that is not my real point right now. Read one more verse: *"And that is what some of you were.* [emphasis added] But you were washed, you were sanctified, you were justified in the name of the Lord Jesus Christ and by the Spirit of our God." "Some of them *were*" [past tense] various things. Justin Martyr (lived *c.* 100-165 AD) talked about persons coming out of homosexuality in the early church too. People came out of all kinds of stuff in the days of the early church. In many churches, they still do.

My point in this brief chapter is that in the New Testament, I see an emphasis, not just on upholding the right, but on saving people from the wrong, on rescuing people, on showing a way of life (in Jesus' day they sometimes called it, figuratively, a "yoke") that works, on redemption, and on transformation. This note does not answer all our practical concerns, but I thought it might help to communicate it here as we begin to wrestle with a response to the concerns we may think we have found.

Chapter 24:

A Summary of Our Findings Up to Now

We have had four sections prior to this concluding section. Part I was introductory. In that I sought to do three things. I sought to introduce my subject, and to mark out the things I felt I would try to do and should do to "make my case." I also sought to introduce myself a little bit. I have most desired to speak with those who do *not* agree with me. Although there may be some of so strong an opinion that that is impossible, I have assumed that there are many who, if they looked at the evidence at which I have looked, could see things differently than they have heretofore. In order for them to be willing to give me a chance to show them some evidence, I felt I had to introduce myself a little to try to dispel certain assumptions which I felt many readers would bring to their reading. I wanted the reader to know that I once believed much of what you who disagree with me still believe. Thereby, I hoped that you would consider it possible that it is not mere obscurantism, not spite, not ignorance, and not force of habit that have led me to the conclusions which I have drawn. Thus, I hoped that while you might still find me mistaken, you might think me rational enough for you to at least consider my arguments. Furthermore, I hope that the reader might believe that I might have some knowledge of things which the reader finds good or worthy, and thus, that I might not be so out of touch with the reader's concerns that he or she could not give the work a fair reading.

This is what the introductory section was meant to do. One, I sought to mark out the intended work of the book in anticipation of going through it. Two, I sought to establish that, since my conclusions were not ones I had always held, but had only later come to, my conclusions might be the result of reasoned reflection based upon evidence, and not a knee-jerk, traditionalist screed. Three, I sought to make some connections with the reader so that he might find sufficient sense of kinship with me to be willing to take this unwanted and uncomfortable journey with me.

In part two, I tried to answer the question: Is homosexuality holy? I alleged that Christianity is the source of many benefits that nearly everyone is pleased to have received, such as the improvement in the condition of women, reduction of slavery, growth in transcending ethnic barriers, the development of the scientific method with its consequent benefits, the growth of industry with its resulting benefits, and the growth of democracy. Therefore, if this is substantially so, then it might be well to consider the position of Christianity on homosexuality, even if one were not a Christian, on the off chance that Christianity might have something useful to say. Furthermore, I argued that it might be interesting to consider that segment of material to see how the pro-gay arguments in that area ran. Also, I argued that if one chose to deny the validity of Christianity and/or the existence of God, then that person ought to do some serious reflection upon his basis for any decision about right to wrong. I suggested that persons who have cavalierly tossed aside Christian faith have generally not even begun to deal seriously with the basis for any moral order, any declaration that anything is good or not. Alas, this seems to include many clerical leaders.

While I suppose that much of my argument might resonate well with persons of some other faiths, I could speak here only from a Christian perspective. Furthermore, while I would suppose that most of my arguments would be generally accepted by persons of the Catholic and Orthodox traditions, I did but speak as a Protestant. Then I made a brief argument for the appropriateness of using the Bible as the source book for our discussion of "the Christian perspective" on homosexuality. Having laid this groundwork, I spoke of the biblical position on homosexuality.

I pointed out that the Bible has a theology of sexuality and that this theology is clearly heterosexual. I called upon Genesis 1 and 2, and Jesus' words in Mark 10, as well as numerous positive references to heterosexual marriage and the absence of any positive references to homosexual relations as evidence to support this contention. I then looked at passages which more explicitly spoke in a manner rejecting homosexual conduct: Genesis 19, Leviticus 18:22 and 20:13, Judges 19, Romans 1:18-32, I Corinthians 6:9-10, I Timothy 1:10, and, indirectly, Jude, and, less clearly, a few other passages. We took some time to deal with various pro-gay revisionist attempts to discredit traditional interpretations, and why I felt they were far less than sound. We looked briefly at the general concern for sexual morality expressed by the Bible throughout its entirety, considering some of why that emphasis might be there and what that emphasis might suggest about our theme of homosexuality. There was one more argument in this area. I suggested that the Bible argued for a God of order, and that if that is so, then the differences in the physiology of the male and female reproductive systems and the differences in the parts of the body commonly used in sexual acts in homosexual and heterosexual practices strongly argued that God's "real" or "original" intent seems not to have been for homosexuality.

Upon the basis of these considerations, I concluded that the Bible does not approve of homosexuality, and that the Christian faith does not approve of it. I further suggested that some of the pro-gay arguments were so wide of the mark as to undercut the credibility of their analytical efforts in general. Perhaps some factor other than reason had so powerful a hold on them that their reason was affected.

The next section of the book tried to answer the question: Is homosexuality healthy? We considered published data from a number of sources. Based upon such data, it appears to be the case that homosexuals as a group experience *vastly* higher rates of sexually transmitted disease. To be honest, while I will use the word "vastly" more than once in these sentences, the word, if anything, generally *under*states the matters referred to. There seemed to be a much shortened life span for homosexuals, both for male, and, based upon more limited evidence, for females as well. Promiscuity was vastly greater among homosexuals. Anonymous sexual acts were vastly more common among homosexuals. There seemed to be a vastly higher use of prostitutes, and a vastly higher incidence of pederasty and pedophilia among persons with a homosexual orientation. This sort of data was cited *not* to try to establish that homosexuals are intrinsically more evil, but rather to suggest that such disordered behavior is very likely a sign of an internal spiritual or emotional disorder. The homosexual lifestyle does, or, if one prefers, the homosexual lifestyles will, on average, result in vastly more disease, early death, and damaged relationships. But I also argue that this is strong evidence of some internal discontent, and therefore, that the evidence is strong that homosexuality *per se* is not a sign of health, not a healthy condition.

The primary alternative explanation is to try to blame the rejection of homosexuality by others for all the misfortunes experienced by persons in homosexuality. There are other attempts to diminish the weight of the evidence by saying that it is not that different from heterosexuals, but such a position is simply untenable in the face of the evidence. So, we seem to be left with two possible explanations: One, homosexuality is unhealthy and a sign of an unhealthy spirit; or two, homosexuality is healthy, but homosexuals are made unhealthy by their rejection by "society." However, since the unhealthy activity often precedes any rejection of the individual, since the unhealthy activity is astronomical in quantity, and since, thus far, greater acceptance has seemed to lead to greater disorder and not less, I have discounted that pro-gay rejoinder as an adequate explanation for the great quantity of evidence that homosexuality both leads to and arises from things unhealthy.

The fourth section of the book sought to answer the question: Can homosexuality be healed? Here we saw that scores of psychiatrists and psychologists have reported many, many times that homosexuality is psychologically unhealthy. Scores of therapists have reported that their patients have been "cured," that they have been changed not only in conduct but also in orientation, in thought life and sexual desire. Some of the more modern psychiatrists went into therapy with homosexual patients with*out* assuming or believing that their homosexuality was a problem, only to discover that as the underlying problems were dealt with, the homosexuality generally diminished or disappeared. There have been large-scale studies of persons who have changed, such as the 800 person study by NARTH. There was the study by Spitzer, the great change agent of the 1973 APA removal of homosexuality from the DSM, verifying that two-thirds were truly changed and that the other third also experienced great change, even by the standards of a psychiatrist who has been strongly pro-gay. There are also reports from scores of Christian ministries of thousands of persons who have come out of homosexuality through their ministries. There is also the fact that the surveys of sexual behavior establish that the great majority of persons who have ever tried homosexuality have abandoned it. All of this makes it obvious that change can happen. That may yet leave the question of "Should it happen?"

The answer to this question was partially given by the preceding section, a section which clearly established that homosexuality was fraught with horrifically deleterious consequences. I continued to address the question in this section by pointing out evidence, drawn in large part from pro-gay researchers, that homosexuality was the probable result of troubles experienced in early childhood. The allegations of genetic or physiological causation were considered and found to be seriously wanting. There was, and is, a plethora of evidence from multiple sources that homosexuality is a symptom of response to early childhood events, which were perceived by the child as traumatic. Such was the long-held, established view of psychiatry. No study ever overturned that understanding. What the APA changed their mind about was not homosexuality so much as health. For paraphilias, "optimal health" was no longer the standard, but "not-being-entirely-dysfunctional-in-all-areas-of-one's-life" was now the APA standard of health. Scores of psychiatrists have reported finding maladjustments to be the cause, not genetics. Scores of therapists have found that when the mistaken reactions to early childhood events perceived as traumas were properly dealt with, then the condition of homosexuality faded or disappeared. Multiple ministries have found that it was reactions to distorted understandings of self, God and others that were at the root of homosexuality, and that the disorder could indeed be rooted out. Upon the basis of these different kinds of evidence, I conclude that homosexuality is a disorder of the spirit; it is itself the result of grief, it is the cause of grief, it should be ministered to, and it can be healed. Conduct, orientation, and underlying disorders can all be healed.

How then, to try to be healing?

Chapter 24:

There Are Difficulties in Speaking of a Response to Homosexuality.

There is a sense in which every action is a reaction. You cannot understand well some of the statements of a man without knowing his time, his place and his circumstances. Similarly, the speaker does well to know what the experience of the listener has been, what special concerns, what hopes and fears, what given words or phrases mean to him. Surely, any matter can be discussed apart from such considerations, but what is likely to transpire is that the speakers and listeners will still bring their own circumstances to the discussion, simply not knowing consciously what their assumptions are, or that they may be different from those of another. We all do that, but it is helpful to know something of what we bring, and of what the other folks bring to the table. This is not a trifle, nor a pleasantry. It affects the very meaning, or more precisely, our understanding of the meaning of what is said.

Some years ago, my church offered an all day conference entitled "Hope and Healing for the Homosexual." One man came from a church with a strong tradition of antagonism, not just to homosexuality, but to homosexuals. For him, the daring, the risky thing was not to oppose homosexuality, but to suggest that persons in homosexuality should be ministered to, invited to the church, cared for, and spoken of. At the same time, there were persons from gay churches picketing my church. For them, to speak of the possibility of transformation implied that persons in homosexuality should change and they felt that was offensive. One does not "change the truth" for different audiences, but what one needs to speak of will be much affected by to whom one is speaking.

Some have telephoned me at church with great concern about programs in the public schools which assume that homosexuality is innate and is good and which assume that there are "gay children" (among those who have not yet engaged in homosexual acts) who need to be encouraged *in* "their homosexuality." That is a different kind of concern from someone who wants to know how to help his gay child.

One pastor wanted to work with another conference in town for the purpose of training pastors to know a little bit about homosexuality, at least enough not to be horrified and not to chase people away at first sight. He had no interest in dealing with persons in homosexuality themselves, nor in dealing with family members. A word about response would need to be different for him than for another.

Another person is the mother of a gay daughter and she has great concerns for the parents and families, though also for the individual in homosexuality. Another thinks his homosexuality is wrong and is a result of a really messed up family background, but he's pretty skittish about talking about it all nonetheless. Another is a gay reporter from a gay newspaper, and he is looking for the horns and tail on me, tolerably certain that everybody knows I must be evil, and yet he was trying hard, from his perspective, to be honest. Another is a "liberal clergyperson" who knows that they know whatever there is to know since everybody they talk to says the same thing, and thus, they do not need to read or reflect or think. And then there is the conservative who just can't understand how the other guy can be so far off the mark and assume that they must just be evil and there is no dealing with them.

We have spent some time looking at considerable quantities of data and reflecting in some measure on possible understandings of this data. All I really wanted to do when I began was to make the case that homosexuality really was not a good thing! I did not want to go much beyond that for several reasons: One, there is a great morass out there and I did not want to get any more people mad at me than I had to. Two, I hadn't thought a great deal about it all, and I knew that I did not have all the answers. Three, to give very precise answers in various areas of legitimate concern would require research in areas I had not done. Four, I thought that I might get more people to hear my general message about homosexuality if I did not get too specific about responses. Specificity breeds opposition. Five, many times people arrive more fully at a conclusion they arrive at by themselves without a lot of pushing and shoving by someone else, me in this case. I wanted to start their journey, not write out a trip-ticket. And sixth, I am leery of grand theorists. Grand theories tend to achieve their grandeur at the cost of usefulness. I am more comfortable dealing with a specific issue at a given time. If someone comes to me with a problem which he thinks is a problem, great, then we can take care of business. Someone comes to me and wants to talk about something she is not sure of; fine, I can help them think it through; I may plant seeds; I do not have to solve a problem the other is not ready to face. Arising from this mixture of fear and humility, I did not want to go further. But that won't quite do.

My own experience has been that the issue came to me in the setting of the church. Various people were continually pushing acceptance of homosexuality. One man proposed that the church should have gay clergy. Another called because his pastor was trying to hold a series of "homophobia seminars" to "educate" her congregations to the wisdom of accepting homosexuality, and this horrified him. Every year resolutions came to our regional denominational meetings proposing to change the discipline of the church to eliminate any negative reference to homosexuality, to embrace that which previously had been clearly rejected. Good people in the church were upset. Some left the church. People who wanted healing from anything had to go to some other denomination, often, to get any kind of healing, because "our kind" of church did not believe that God could really change anyone's life, in any area. After all, some didn't really seem even to believe in the existence of God! I got involved in the battle a little, and then I was asked to get involved more. And then more. And so on. I have become a fairly "conservative" person in a very "liberal" world, speaking of the small world of The United Methodist Church in my part of the country. Victory here was keeping "the barbarians" from stealing the cross off the altar. We were a small band fighting off Viking raiders in our little monasteries, trying to keep the flock alive in the midst of a Dark Age. Hoping and praying for revival, but not knowing how or when it will come. Many of our "knights" were terribly concerned to keep the dragons happy, often willing to sacrifice some of the villagers so long as the Lords of the church did not humiliate them too openly. (I am mixing my metaphors a little; I hope you can follow my line of thinking.) So, in part, my "training" has been in fighting a rear guard action. I die with Roland fighting the Saracens in the valleys of the Pyrenees, hoping to keep France safe from invasion for a while longer.

My other kind of "training" has been in trying to help persons one on one. I would love to be able to stay in my quiet study, occasionally sipping tea with the ladies' club, laughing over pancakes and bad coffee with the senior men, and tenderly caring for the occasional individual who screwed up his courage enough to actually come for help. But it is not like that anyway. And that won't work. The world is moving. The world *will* move, for good or ill, but it will move, and those who want that movement to be for good must try to influence that movement. People do not seek help because they do not know right from wrong. We have leaders telling people to do that which will cause harm, within the church and without. Our leaders do not draw inspiration from any source common to Christians, but from the common faith sources of *our* age, which is academe and the media. It is there that I must try to go and do battle.

In this wider world, there are many settings, and many assumptions, and many sets of experience brought to bear on the matters of which we speak. People will draw conclusions, even if I don't ask them to, even if I don't want them to and tell them not to. People will assume things mean what they think they ought to mean based upon their own background and experience. If I do not suggest some outlines for understanding, then perhaps I cannot greatly complain of errors I do not put to rest. Besides, in some cases, suppose this discussion does lead some to see something differently. Then they will want to know where to go from here.

So I think that I need to sketch out some elements of response. However, I need to speak of responses, plural. I will also need to speak of possible responses in different settings.

Therefore, I will speak of possible responses based upon the conclusions that seem to follow from the information that we have examined thus far. I will speak in four broad areas: 1) In general, 2) With regards to responding to an individual, 3) With regards to attempting to minister, or respond helpfully to persons in homosexuality, and 4) With regards to possible social policy issues. This will not be comprehensive, only illustrative and suggestive. It is often hard to shed more light than heat.

Chapter 26:

After You've Thought it Through, Then What?

Here are some general observations. My first general suggestion is that honesty is a virtue. Now I grant you that honesty is never the whole truth! I grant you that honesty can be a cover for villainy; after all, any virtue can be a cover for vice. Yet honesty is still a virtue.

It may be irritating to have the gage on your dashboard tell you that you are low on oil, but it is significantly more inconvenient if you burn up your engine because you did not know that you were low on oil, or because you chose to ignore the gage, or because someone disconnected it for you. It may be inconvenient for your thermometer to say that you have a temperature of 102, but it is still more problematic if someone lies to you about what the thermometer says because they did not want to face your irritation, and you did not know you had a fever and you got sicker and died. If someone takes down a road sign to take home for a trophy in his den, and you drive into a deadly accident as a result, you might not find the sign removal amusing. Truth has its place. We cannot function well without accurate information. If the altimeter on the airplane did not work, you might not want to fly. If stop signs gave green lights to all directions at the same time, more would die on the road. If the Thomas Bros. Guide Books or your GPS system had all the streets wrong, your blood pressure would go up, the graciousness of your language down, and your ability to arrive on time might altogether disappear.

It is not always easy. A woman gave me a gift. I did not want to be indebted to her, so I gave her one. In my mind, this was keeping our relationship distant. To her, this proved that I felt about her the way she did about me. By the time I figured out there was a problem and that I needed to address it and did, she got mad, left the church and took two friends with her. I haven't dared to date anyone since. (Well, almost. At least not in church.) It can be painful to someone you care about to tell them the truth, but not telling the truth is worse; at the very least hinting at it and telling as much as you think they can stand to hear at the moment, not doing something like that is worse. So, what does that mean here?

You must deal with the evidence, and speak what the evidence indicates. The evidence indicates that the Christian faith does not approve of homosexuality. If that faith tradition is authoritative for you, then that is something you should follow. If that faith tradition is not authoritative for you, then you need to reflect upon your own faith tradition or upon whatever basis you have for determining right and wrong and see how that speaks to the matter of homosexuality. Be careful about how many fences you try to straddle.

Many say that they are "good Christians" but they just feel like doing things contrary to the Christian faith. However, "just doing what you feel like" was exactly Adam and Eve's problem in the Garden of Eden. You can blame the snake, but you still lose the Garden. Are you quite sure that your transitory feelings are the surest guide? Have you never found it wise to refrain from acting upon your transitory feelings? Even if you think your feelings are the best guide, you will certainly want to acknowledge to yourself that you are not acting upon the basis of Christian faith, nor, perhaps, upon the basis of any other faith you might suppose.

The evidence is massive and multifold, that homosexuality is associated with medical and social consequences that are absolutely horrific: extremely high disease rates, shorter lifespan, promiscuity, anonymity, infidelity, prostitution, and pederasty among them. I do not find that the theory that all this is a result of social disapproval holds water. In the absence of some other explanation, it certainly seems that homosexuality is horrifically damaging. The fact that it has persisted in the face of such massive damage might further suggest that it is the result of some deep psychological or spiritual problem.

The evidence is also massive that persons can come out of homosexual behavior and homosexual ideation, thought–life, or orientation. The evidence for the possibility of change is so extensive and so well documented that no honest and knowledgeable observer could deny that change is common for many. The evidence is also extensive that in virtually all examined cases of homosexuality, there is evidence of underlying disorder to be found. Based upon these kinds of evidence, I think one must conclude that it is most probable that homosexuality is both consequence and cause of damage, and that both it and the underlying causes can be ameliorated and/or healed.

If the reader finds these conclusions sound, then I think the reader must also conclude, in general, that homosexuality should not be encouraged, and, in general, that persons in homosexuality should be made aware of the possibility of transformation. It would be apt to follow, that social policies that tend to encourage homosexuality, to equate it with sexuality, or what is now called heterosexuality, are probably not wise. This general statement does *not* necessarily guide policy on many different matters, some of which I will attempt to speak to in subsequent paragraphs. My own general inclination would be to be personally gracious, but yet some measures proposed in recent times to compel personal graciousness by legal sanction may be unwise. All I am really saying here is that one needs to recognize that homosexuality is not healthy and that it can be changed, although usually only with great difficulty. How one is led to work out that general understanding in personal and community life might vary a great deal.

Based upon my Christian values, I would further say that each person is of sacred worth. The reader must determine what value he or she chooses to bring to bear in such matters. I would say that one should have loving concern even for those with whom one disagrees. I would say that even one whom one finds to be a wrongdoer should be treated with as much compassion as you find the situation to allow. I would be inclined to say that while it is extremely important that we do not encourage evil, it is usually far less important that we use force to stamp out everything that we believe to be evil. I would suggest that there is some useful distinction to be drawn between the person who is caught up in an inappropriate pattern of behavior and the one who promotes it. There remains a useful distinction to be made with regard to children, that they are appropriate objects of special concern.

All of this is general. Yet this is still the place to begin. As you may have noticed, even to say this small amount has required that I make use of principles, or values, which I have drawn from my own experience but which we have not examined in the course of these discussions. Most of my readers would agree with most of these values, but they are not universal, and we have not examined them, and I still want to sharpen the reader's habit of reflecting upon the principles he or she brings into play in each evaluation. Love God, and, as Dr. Laura would say, "Do the right thing." Also love your neighbor, which especially includes those whom you love (an easy thing to do), and includes those who are least able to defend themselves (a harder thing to do), and also includes those whom you see as unrighteous (harder still), and even includes those whom you see as your enemy (still harder yet). Know also that "love" does not necessarily mean "giving in," or "being a doormat," or "doing what the other guy wants," although it may sometimes mean some of that too! Know also that "tough love" is not to be used as an excuse for spite, or as a cover for vengeance. Those, dear friends, are some of the parameters. Now, I'll try to sketch out a few possible applications in our time and place.

How do you respond to an individual? Well, by God, how do you respond to any other individual? That's how. First, I will speak of responding to a person who is himself or herself caught up in homosexuality. It also makes a difference if they are coming to you for help, or coming to you to seek your approval, or coming to you to shock you, or if they do not really know yet what is going on with them and they just want someone to talk with.

Dusty (Not his name, but a true story) tells of going to chapel at a well-known Midwestern Bible college some thirty plus years ago. The day's preacher said that he wanted the students to feel free to come to him and talk about things if they had a problem, any problem, just feel free. Wow, that was great. He had had this thing bothering him for a long time. He felt like he was attracted to boys. He felt real bad about it, and he had never acted on it, but he wanted to get help in changing these feelings. So, with this great invitation, he felt confident that he could go and talk to the chaplain. Wrong! After Dusty told him his problem, the chaplain told him to get out. He, Dusty, could either leave the school now or the chaplain would put it on the official record and kick him out. Great choice. The kid left. This kid had never acted upon his impulses up to that point in time, but after that "warm and loving Christian response," he did. He slipped into and out of hell for nearly twenty years. He got married along the way. His homosexuality ruined his marriage too. He's out. He came out through an HA (Homosexuals Anonymous) group. He has been out of homosexuality for twenty plus years now. His relationships with family members are wonderfully restored. He loves God, has a good job and does fine, now. He also counsels others struggling to overcome their homosexual ideation. But this knucklehead chaplain kicked him when he went to ask for help. Don't do that.

The "gay church" is wrong in its affirmation of "gay-ness," but in many ways it is the product of the conservative Christians who had only condemnation to offer. Condemning persons, Christian or otherwise, can take a great deal of credit for the whole of the gay movement. It has been, in some measure, an effort to offer comfort and support to persons who felt alone, rejected, and despised. That is very much among the things which the church should attempt to do. Furthermore, the gay movement can take some of the credit for the compassion and wisdom now offered by those evangelical churches who have realized that more was needed than had been offered and who have risen to the occasion.

Is not being a jerk really so hard to figure out? When have you responded well to instruction? Was it in response to someone who cared about you, or in response to someone who just beat up on you? Oh I know, we are all different, and some might have got their act together after being verbally beaten, but that is not usually how it works. As a rule of thumb, be nice. I am speaking about an attitude here, not about giving away the store.

To whom do you willingly tell intimate or emotionally risky things? To someone who hates you? To someone who verbally beats the daylights out of you? If not, and I suspect not, then don't do that to any reasonably honest person coming to you to seek your advice, help or response. Make it safe for them. Generally respect confidences. If you are not going to be able to keep a confidence, tell them as soon as you see something confidential coming that you cannot keep confidences. If you don't say that, then keep it. Yes, with kids, it may be different, but then it may, sometimes, not.

Speaking of kids, your kids. It's not about you. Let's repeat that. It's not about you. You can go have your own pity party later. You can feel bad or guilty or angry or hurt or whatever you feel like later. If your underage child comes to you with a problem, it's about him, or it's about her. It's not about you. Separate the two, you and him. How would you deal with your kid if he came and told you that he had a drug problem, or a pornography problem, or some other problem? Assuming your reactions in that situation would be fairly healthy, then that's how you go about responding to your son or daughter.

If you want to begin to know a little about this subject, read three or four of these books. As an introduction to homosexuality, I would recommend *Coming Out of Homosexuality* by Bob Davies and Lori Rentzel, *Desires in Conflcit* by Joe Dallas, *Pursuing Sexual Wholeness* by Andrew Comiskey, *Unwanted Harvest* by Mona Riley and Brad Sargent, *Reparative Therapy of Male Homosexuality* by Joseph Nicolosi, *Homosexuality and the Politics of Truth* by Jeffrey Satinover, and *Straight and Narrow?* by Thomas Schmidt.

If you want help in dealing with your own emotions as you encounter the painful news that someone you love is gay, then read a book with that title, *Someone I Love Is Gay* by Anita Worthen and Bob Davies; you might also read *Where Does a Mother Go to Resign* by Barbara Johnson; or *When Homosexuality Hits Home* By Joe Dallas; or *Loving Homosexuals As Jesus Would* by Chad Thompson.

If you are particularly interested in issues relating to the Christian faith and homosexuality, read *Straight and Narrow?* By Thomas Schmidt, *A Strong Delusion* by Joe Dallas, *Homosexuality* by James B. DeYoung, or *The Complete Christian Guide to Understanding Homosexuality* by Joe Dallas and Nancy Heche, or *Homosexuality and the Christian* by Mark Yarhouse.

If you are predominantly interested in passing on to one who is struggling in this area a book which shares the testimony and triumph of how others have gone before, consider: *Out of Egypt* by Jeanette Howard, *Strangers in a Christian Land* by Darlene Bogle, *You Don't Have to Be Gay* by Jeff Konrad, and *Setting Love in Order* by Mario Bergner.

There are sources of potential help available, some of which are noted in an appendix. PFOX (Parents and Friends of Ex-gays) is one, Desert Stream, an ex-gay ministry is another. HAFS (Homosexuals Anonymous Fellowship Services) is still another. NARTH (National Association for the Research and Therapy of Homosexuality) is an organization which may help you find a therapist who can work from a reparative perspective.

If your concern is dealing not with a person who struggles, but with a person with opinions about the matter, then another set of considerations comes into play. Reading a half a dozen books of those above will help a good deal no matter what particular task you have. If they are hard-nosed opponents of homosexuals (I stated it differently here.), then you may need to help them increase their compassion. You will need to help them make the distinction that Christians try to make by speaking of "loving the sinner but hating the sin." (See also Hill, 2001 and Hill, 2007.) Help them find some other activity of which they do not approve, but wherein they do not hate the persons who do it. You might help them recall an error of their own which they have outgrown or for which they have been forgiven, and thereby help them to see that there may be a place for compassion. Their opposition may have root in some deeply troubling personal experience too. In that case, they may need to deal with that deep seated problem before they will be able to deal with anyone else whose conduct suggests something which was once horrifying to them and which is still unresolved for them.

For many traditionalists, you will simply need to offer education, information, and resources. They may require a little help to get up to speed on understanding, but they will have a reasonable heart and a willing hand.

For the moderately pro-gay you will need the patience of Job. I am not always sure they can be redeemed, but I am always committed to trying. I think you simply explain your point of view. Give evidence. Evidence may not be able to penetrate their presumption, but it has a better chance than anger, imprecation, or table thumping, I think. In a way, this whole book is my attempt to speak to folks in this category. I hope it helps.

For the hard core pro-gay, nothing may work. Your task is not to condemn, but to offer all the hope and light you can. When my church was going to host a conference offering the possibility of change for homosexuals, I got a nasty e-mail from the pastor of the nearby gay church. I wrote him and invited him to lunch. I got another nasty e-mail. I wrote another invite to breakfast or lunch. Finally, he replied that I didn't sound as mean as he first thought I was and he would be willing to meet. (There may have been a third letter of mine in this series; I don't recall now.) He was busy just then, but at a later date, we could get together; he'd get back to me. He didn't get back to me; so, on a Sunday I was off, I went to his church. I had planned to introduce myself to him after the service and press my invitation again. I am afraid I was put off by the notice in his bulletin announcing a planning meeting for those who were going to picket my church during our upcoming conference. But, next day, I tried one more time. We eventually agreed to meet at a downtown restaurant. I bought lunch. We had a nice chat. We did share a bit about ourselves with each other. He still picketed my church, but later he did send me an approving note about an ad I had run. I hope some seeds were planted. I offer no guarantees that kindness converts, but buying lunch didn't kill me.

When we had our conference, we had folks designated to do many things: to handle registration, to make signs for bathrooms and such, to provide transportation for special guest speakers, to arrange for food, to set up tables, *and to take refreshments out to the picketers.* It was not an accident. It was planned. We took out coffee and doughnuts to them. One of the picketers said, "You're not what we thought you'd be." Great. That's a start.

I know several of the gay lay and clergy members who are delegates to the regional meetings for our church, which we call Annual Conferences. I usually make it a point to greet some of them. One fellow and I had a good talk about helping folks with AIDS at the last conference. He may still think I'm nuts. That's okay. That won't kill me either. He even said nice things about me at a plenary session of the Annual Conference one time. Great, I am thankful for that kind word. In the very "liberal" world of my Annual Conference, a kind word from a gay man is very helpful to me. It gives me credibility in the eyes of the "liberals" that I am not totally the mean spirited person they would like to think I am. They still might believe that I am a little slow or a lot ignorant. I like this fellow too, but I still think he is dead wrong about homosexuality, including his own homosexuality.

That is how I have dealt with some of the gay rights activists in my neck of the woods. There were earlier days when I was more roundly criticized. I still said my piece. And, who knows, maybe I said my piece with more of an edge then, maybe. But then, maybe the slow and steady work of getting out information, bringing in folks to give their testimonies of transformation, and continuing to dialogue in as friendly a manner as I could is bearing a little fruit, maybe.

Here are a few thoughts on trying to minister in this area. First, read some of the books that give an overview on homosexuality noted above. Second, contact NARTH and see if they can recommend any counselors who work from reparative perspective in your area, both as a possible resource to gather more information and as a possible resource to refer folks to when counseling is what might be most helpful. Third, contact Desert Stream and find out about their Living Waters program. Fourth, contact Homosexuals Anonymous and get an introductory information packet to see if that might be a useful program for you. Fifth, see if you can attend a conference put on by one of the various local ex-gay ministries.

To begin to equip yourself to offer a bit of insight into healing and/or to pass on recommendations for folks who seek healing to look at themselves, consider: *The Broken Image* by Leanne Payne, *Setting Love in Order* by Mario Bergner, *Homosexual No More* by William Consiglio, *Sexual Healing* by David Kyle Foster, *Counseling the Homosexual* by Michael Saia, *Pursuing Sexual Wholeness* by Andrew Comiskey, *Steps Out of Homosexuality* by Frank Worthen, *Journey Toward Wholeness* by Don Crossland, and *Reparative Therapy of Male Homosexuality* by Joseph Nicolosi. For inner healing in general, not focused on sexual maladjustments, you might read my book *To Be Made Whole: A Handbook for Inner Healing.*

People need community. If you are in a healthy church, you have a community available right there. If not, I don't know what you are going to do. You might look for a healthy church. I know former homosexuals who got healed in churches that knew next to nothing about homosexuality, but they did know about Jesus and they did know how to love. They hugged. They prayed. They baited fishhooks when the guy had never done that before and he still couldn't quite get himself to put the worm on the hook. He never became a great fisherman, but he became a good man. He's married. He's got three fine boys. The church hung in there with him. They did not rebuke. They did not rebuke. They did not rebuke. That is not a typo; I said it three times for a reason. See if you can figure out why. They never told the lie that gay was good, but they did not rub his nose in anything either. They reasonably well knew that we are all messed up (Christians call that being "sinners."), and that we all need God's grace, and that it is that gracious love that enables us to become more the men and women God always intended us to be. They gave out God's love pretty good. Eventually the guy got understanding through books, a small ex-gay ministry, and some counseling, but it was the love of God lived out by the church that made the rest of it possible.

If you want to minister, contact some established ministries and see what they are doing. Import some speakers and see what they have to say. Read a whole bunch of books. Contact local counselors who work from a transformational or reparative perspective. Thereafter, it depends on how much you want to do. You might start a small support group for friends and families of persons in homosexuality. Contact Spatula Ministries about that, or PFOX; Spatula is in the resource appendix. You could call on Desert Stream or HA for possible resources. Know what you are about. Know why you want to minister, to be sure that your motives are in order. Be under authority. Have others to whom you are accountable. Be slow to claim expertise you do have; and be sure not to claim expertise you do not have. Be gentle. Be persevering. If God calls you, He surely can sustain you. But do be sure it's God you are listening to.

Social issues are of great importance to some, but areas in which I have studied less, and on which I have reflected less. Folks who write in this area have a great deal of passion. Two books that raise many of the concerns in this area are *Gay Rights Or Wrongs* edited by Michael Mazzalongo, and *Sex, Politics and the End of Morality* by J. Gordon Muir. These two books speak from a very conservative perspective. I do not know of any books that fit my ideal in this area. With fear and trembling, I offer a few thoughts on a few issues.

Since homosexuality is wrong, it should not be promoted. A few years ago, the Los Angeles Unified School District developed a program called Project 10. It was based upon the assumption, now known to be false, that 10% of the nation was "gay," and on the assumption, also false, that "gayness" was innate, and therefore it was assumed that 10% of the students must be "gay." It was further assumed, and not without some reason, that others were unkind to gays, and that therefore, the school district should offer counselors to encourage them in their homosexuality and develop programs to make the schools more gay friendly. Similar programs have since sprung up throughout the country. Teachers are given sensitivity training to perceived homosexual conduct, teaching them that homosexuality is innate and good, which is untrue. Teachers are taught to squelch any comment that might reflect ill on homosexuality. They are trained to give segments of false teaching that homosexuality is innate and good. Gay clubs have been started on many high school campuses. Counselors are trained to encourage children who report homosexual feelings to feel good about that, and perhaps to "explore" their feelings, which means to "experiment" with various sexual acts.

First of all, 10% of Americans have never been in homosexuality. So the name itself is based upon a falsehood. Second, homosexuality is not innate. Third, it is not the case that a child with homosexual feelings is destined to go on to feel himself or herself confirmed in homosexuality as an adult and therefore teaching him that he is, is not neutral, and it is not helpful. Although its *stated* purpose is not to promote homosexuality but rather to promote an accepting response to persons who "are" homosexuals, it does also serve to promote homosexuality, and to recruit children into it. Fourth, there is much evidence that homosexuality is not really good for people. Therefore, to encourage a child to assume that he is gay is to encourage a life that is fraught with horrific consequences, and thus probably should not be done. Further, to encourage those who do not have a homosexual problem themselves to believe that homosexuality is innate and immutable would also seem to be unhelpful.

Therefore, such training programs should be greatly changed or ended. There certainly is disparagement of kids who act differently. This has been going on since forever. That does not mean it is good. As kids try to figure out who they are, there are powerful forces at work in peer group pressure to help them figure out who they are. This is common. This is partially inevitable. This is partially valuable. This is not always kind. Being picked last for the team has never been fun. Being ridiculed for lack of a prized skill, for your clothes, for your family background, or for just about anything else is no fun. I heartily affirm trying to train children to comport themselves like ladies and gentlemen, which would include being gracious towards persons of whom they disapprove. But that is not what I fear our current crop of gay sensitivity training experiences are about. If my fears are well founded, then it would seem that such programs should be altered to reflect the reality of the gay life and the possibility of change, or they should be ended.

From 1971 to 1991, the Boy Scouts indicated that more than 2,000 boys reported molestations by adult Scout leaders (York, 1991, p. 8). Willie Sutton was asked once why he robbed banks, and he replied, "'Cause that's where the money is." Similarly, persons with a sexual interest in boys will try to access Boy Scout programs "because that's where the boys are." The sexual molestation of children is a real and important concern. The evidence is extensive that a vastly greater proportion of sexual molestation is homosexual. Therefore, it seems a reasonable conclusion that the risk of sexual molestation of boys increases exponentially when homosexual persons are given free access to them, especially in leadership positions. Many homosexuals would not do such a thing, but, on average, a far higher risk exists with homosexuals than with heterosexuals. Kindly review the evidence given previously on this subject. I think it is wisdom on the part of The Boy Scouts of America to keep known homosexual persons out of the Scouts, certainly as leaders, and probably as youth members as well, although how one defines "known" will likely present problems. I regret the apparent recent weakening of the Boy Scouts wise mistrust of persons with homosexual ideation.

I personally was never a Boy Scout. I was in Cub Scouts and in Indian Guides, for whatever that is worth, but never in Boy Scouts. By my Boy Scouting age, I was more of a loner and not any sort of joiner, but I have no need to wreak vengeance on them for the sake of some hidden emotional agenda. So far as I know, the Boy Scouts have been a fine organization. They have done much to help build youth into men. They have excellent reasons for keeping homosexual persons out of their programs. Therefore, it seems to me that the current movement to force them to accept homosexuals and deny them the access to tax-supported facilities to which they have long had access is quite mistaken.

No one denies that they have done good. Furthermore, no one has alleged that they would cease to do good. Therefore, the current cry to expel Scouting from various public facilities seems to exist primarily as a means to increase the acceptance of homosexuality. It seems to exist as a program to coerce all other prominent social institutions to pay homage to the healthfulness of homosexuality. As the foregoing materials in this book have indicated, I do not find that, as a matter of fact, it is healthy, but also I question the wisdom of too quickly rushing to compel all other social institutions to espouse the "party line" or a "politically correct line," even if one were sure of the wisdom of that line, whereas I am rather sure of its folly in this case.

It was long thought to be enshrined in our Constitution that Americans had freedom of religious expression, and that such expression might be exercised in various associations. Our modernist courts have often found ways to limit that expression. It is no longer a politically acceptable position that one may disassociate from homosexuals for religious reasons other than in a church setting itself. Our modern, largely "post-Christian" elites have now concluded that you may have any religious opinion you want, so long as you do not let it affect anything you do – a notion which would once have been seen to be the contradiction in terms that it is.

What protection has been afforded to the Scouts has come from the less clear right of association. Many leaders in local government have sought to impose *their* unfortunately mistaken and unsubstantiated, *religious belief* that homosexuality is good on all associations, including the Boy Scouts of America. Perhaps it is the case that some courts and some local governments are the ones who have been imposing *their religious beliefs on others*.

The Shorter Oxford English Dictionary (SOED, 2002, v. 1, p. 1706) defines marriage as a "legally recognized personal union entered into by a man and a woman usually with the intention of living together and having sexual relations, and entailing property and inheritance rights; the condition of being a husband or wife." It does seem to find that male and female together have something to do with this thing called marriage.

Black's Law Dictionary (Black's, p. 1123) defines marriage as "the civil status, condition, or relation of one man and one woman united in law for life, for the discharge to each other and the community of the duties legally incumbent on those whose association is founded on the distinction of sex." Did the reader notice the phrases "one man and one woman," and "founded on the distinction of sex."

That marriage means some sort of special commitment of a man and a woman to a life together seems to have been the basic pattern for all societies at all times and in all places. It has been explicitly the pattern for western civilization for the last several thousand years, even in ancient societies which tolerated some forms of homosexual practice. The idea that we should toss marriage aside in what is, historically, the blink of an eye is astonishing.

I am afraid that I find that anything properly called a marriage is between a man and a woman. It is true that we are imperfect in our support of marriage. Imperfection does not mean that the institution is not of great worth. It is, and it ought to be protected. I am inclined to believe that there are legitimate state purposes served by the support of marriage, which of course means "heterosexual." I do not believe that there is any serious question that children are, on average, more happily raised with both a father and a mother. Overall, the single greatest determinant of poverty is a fatherless family. Something like 70% of all felons in prison grew up in fatherless families. The evidence is simply overwhelming that a healthy father and mother are far and away the best familial situation for children. There are benefits to society that come from the benefits to the man and the woman in a marriage, in terms of stability, responsibility, and in an increased growth of concern beyond oneself. *Some* of these benefits would probably also accrue through "homosexual marriage" to a society that accepted homosexuality as normative. However, the rub is in the virtue; such a "marriage" would tend also to make homosexuality normative, and that would itself be unfortunate. The evidence is clear that homosexuality is neither cause nor consequence of happiness, and therefore, the more needful course is to uphold an ideal to which people can aspire. Furthermore, such a "marriage" would not provide the diversity of input that a male and female do, nor the best illustration of roles of male and female for the children.

Depending upon the degree to which society wishes to accommodate persons who are caught up in homosexuality, there might be established something like a living will, which secures one person some authority over the affairs of another person to whom that person is not related by blood or marriage. I believe such instruments could now be drawn up by a lawyer. There might be some such device, a mutual, or reciprocal, power of attorney that could be standardized in some fashion, a legal form which would not need to make any reference to homosexuality nor conjugality and which yet could suffice to secure any possibly necessary involvement of one person in the life of another.

It is alleged in recent times that having laws that bar same-sex marriage are "discriminatory." This is quite true and utterly meaningless. *All* laws are discriminatory. The law that says one may not drive faster than 35 miles an hour in a given place discriminates against those who wish to go faster. Laws that say you cannot open a metal workshop in your garage in some residential neighborhoods discriminate against those who wish to do so. Laws that say you cannot marry a fourteen year old girl without parental consent discriminate against those who might wish to do so. And so on. All laws discriminate. That is their intent! And so what?

Once upon a time one might hear it said of someone that "he had discriminating taste." This was a good thing. This meant that the person referred to could better evaluate the qualities of food, or wine, or painting, or music, or literature, or some such thing, than others. To discriminate is to make distinctions. In the 1960's, in America, "discrimination" came to be a short-hand word for inappropriate discrimination of persons based on false assumptions that persons of one ethnicity or another were inherently inferior or superior to another. Gay activists have attempted to draw upon the language, symbols, and understandings from that civil rights era usage in order to gain acceptance for their cause, attempting to claim a similar legitimacy for their conduct. As we have seen previously, 75% of black persons rarely become white later in life, nor do Irish become Chinese, whereas 75% of "gays" do become "straight." So the presumed parallel is a good deal less precise than gay activists claim. A clearer statement of the gay activist professed argument would be that they believe that laws prohibiting same-sex marriage are unwarranted or unwise.

There are two baskets of concerns that might arise at this point. One concerns Constitutional law and the other is a matter of policy. When laws prohibiting various homosexual acts have been passed by every state of the nation and the federal government itself repeatedly throughout our national history, it is pretty well inconceivable that such laws could reasonably be found unconstitutional. They have been so found, but this was not by virtue of any Constitutional mandate, but rather by the imposition of the new religious (paganism is religious too) beliefs of our imperial magistrates. Policy, in our governmental system, is theoretically to be set by legislatures. It is an entirely appropriate thing for legislatures to pass laws with which some may not agree, whether wise or foolish. It is not the purview of the judiciary to legislate from the bench. This they have done, with consequences society has not yet begun to appreciate.

It could be argued, for example, that "gay marriage" might be beneficial as a way to diminish the wild promiscuity seen among homosexuals. However, the actual track record of "married" homosexuals, as noted previously, does not well support that expectation. Furthermore, it is my understanding that most homosexuals are not really interested in marriage. Their primary interest in the passage of same-sex marriage laws has been the sense of social approbation which such legal normalization gives to homosexuality. Since homosexual conduct *per se* is damaging, and since the encouragement of it leads persons to decline to examine underlying issues, then I would argue against the wisdom of "gay marriage." Since presumptuous judges have done much to compel society to accept their alternative religious vision, the road out of our current social folly is likely to be longer and more difficult than it should have needed to be. Still, persons and churches are not yet compelled to support such efforts in general. As for the concerned individual who wishes to be personally supportive of a family member who seeks their involvement in inappropriate ceremonies, I can only say, "May God guide you," for I have no hard and fast rule to offer here.

Once upon a time, in olden times, a man went riding through the woods. He saw a target with an arrow in the bulls-eye. He nodded in appreciation, and went on. Then he saw another, and then another. Soon he was filled with a passionate desire to see this great archer. He began to inquire of him, until he found him. When he came to him, he asked him, "How can you get the arrow in the bulls-eye each time? Do you never miss?" "No," said the archer, "I never miss. It is easy. Here let me show you." Then the archer took an arrow, he shot it casually towards an object, and after it landed, he went to the object, taking a can of paint with him, and he painted a target around his arrow, with the bulls-eye centered on his arrow. It is always tempting to affirm where we are at, but it is not always wise.

The issues are more complicated in areas of housing and employment. Personally, I see no reason in general why persons caught up in homosexuality cannot work in whatever job they can handle and is otherwise appropriate. It is certainly true that some prominent homosexuals have been prominent traitors. This proclivity to betray has, in the past, sometimes been motivated by fear of outing. More recently, it may have been motivated by a perceived sense of injustice. This *may* have been influenced by the "hyper-sensitivity" of homosexual persons noted by many psychologists, but I believe that many persons with homosexual attractions can well and responsibly carry out sensitive duties. The greater acceptance of persons with homosexual orientation should diminish the risk of betrayal under threat of outing. And, there is too little data to draw sweeping conclusions about a too hasty response of personal offense.

Generally, I am also inclined to believe that housing should not be restricted to bar homosexuals. However, it is probably also true that there is no documented need for laws seeking to secure such access as rights. Therefore, it may again be the case that the movement for such laws is primarily for the purpose of coercing social acceptance of homosexuality, and not for the redress of any real and current problem.

We are all "libertarians" when the "liberties" we speak of are the ones we want to enjoy. We are all more readily in favor of state intervention when the "wrong" we see we think can be "corrected" by such intervention. True, I think that we should be slow to assume that our wisdom will enable us to divine every matter correctly. Thus, in general, in the absence of significant evidence of need, I would not readily lean towards imposing legal sanctions. However, I say this not having examined the possible evidence for the need in this case and thus can offer it only as a suggested point to ponder in this area.

Virtually all the goals spoken of in favor of "hate crimes" legislation I would affirm. However, heretofore, it is actions that have been criminalized. Motivation has been taken into account by the judge in sentencing, but the motivation was not the basis for the crime. There is some danger with "hate crimes" legislation that it becomes "thought crimes" legislation. Assault is wrong. Is it necessary to characterize the reason for the assault? Not intrinsically. Then why do so? Perhaps because the real goal is to alter thought patterns, not behavior patterns. If that is so, then I am troubled by the general concept of "hate crimes" legislation. If there are not adequate laws on the books to cover some actions that now seem to be covered only by hate crimes law, then I would be inclined to prefer some way to arrange legislation to deal with those *behaviors*. I am entirely in agreement with most of what most advocates of hate crimes law would offer as the things they oppose. Stalking, harassing, vandalism – all these things can be dealt with as behaviors.

What is the particular need of "hate crimes" law? In some cases there are actions that may have been criminal wherein the laws have not been enforced. In those cases the law should be enforced. There may be other cases in which there are objectionable actions that should have been criminalized but have not been. In those cases, we might need more laws. Many suspect that one "need," or better, *goal* is to coerce, or at least "teach," certain kinds of thinking. While I would probably be whole-heartedly in support of the kinds of thought that advocates would like to inculcate in the area of racial equality and religious tolerance, and would only have some discomfort with the thought that some advocates want to inculcate in the area of homosexuality, and even in the area of homosexuality, I would be uncomfortable with only some of that, still I am uncomfortable with the idea of thought crimes legislation in general. I suspect that this notion arises from the modernist belief that there is no God, and thus we are fully at liberty to play God, and "we" really means whoever has the power at the moment. It is a role for which we humans are not well fitted. I would be inclined to try to achieve worthy goals in this area under some other rubric than "hate crimes," but then, of course, that is how it appears from my set of experiences, maybe not from yours.

Assorted "Human Rights Commissions" seem to be acquiring themselves quite a record of intervention, restriction of speech, coercion, and abuse in Canada and some Scandinavian countries. Since 1735 and the Peter Zenger trial, we have had a fairly robust tradition of freedom of speech here in the United States of America. Heretofore freedom of speech has been acknowledged as a right which was actually in the Constitution, and not a mere figment of judicial imagination. I rather hope this continues.

"Thought crime" laws and "speech crime" laws are dangerous. I hope we are suitably cautious about condemning the truth.

Finally, I do not suppose that you agree with me on everything, even at the end of our journey. I am not so terribly concerned about the things I have addressed in these closing pages accept these admonitions to read, to face the evidence squarely, and to be cautious in our assumptions about our own wisdom. I have argued that Christianity rejects homosexuality, that it is a faith system which has produced much good and that therefore one should not lightly reject its view of homosexuality. I have argued that the evidence is massive and compelling that homosexuality is itself both a cause and a consequence of much that is harmful. I have argued that the evidence is again massive that persons can leave homosexual behavior and orientation, and, indeed, that more people have left it than have remained in it. For these reasons, I would urge the reader to move to reverse the normalization of homosexuality, while offering help to those in homosexuality who want to change, and grace towards those who find they do not want to change; grace towards persons, not acquiescence towards programs. I think my conclusions on applications are far less certain than my conclusions on the main points I have sought to address.

I believe that homosexuality does not bespeak another kind of life, but another kind of death of the spirit. I do not want that, not for anyone. And as I do not respond well to condemnation, so also do I not desire to dishonor those who disagree. It is true that I find homosexuality should be rejected, but I do not wish to reject persons who are caught up in it. So then, while I may fail, I desire for all those concerned neither death nor dishonor. I have endeavored to present truth. I think that truth can be healing. Though the healing can be painful, it is still beneficial, even needful. Ultimately, it is freeing.

I thank the reader for the gift of his attention. I hope that some of the foregoing has been informative. Once again, I exhort the reader to face the evidence and draw his own conclusions based upon it, and then to make his own applications based upon those conclusions. Whether you agree with me or not, may God bless you. Where I am wrong, may He show me. Where the reader may have been mistaken, may He reveal that as well. Peace be with you.

A Resource List

Desert Stream Ministries
706 Main Street
Grandview, MO 64030
(866) 359-0500
Living Waters program
(816) 767-1730
desertstream.org or info@desertstream.org

Homosexuals Anonymous Fellowship Services
c/o Dr. Douglas McIntyre
18147 Dinner Creek Drive
Katy, TX 77449
homosexuals_anonymous.com

National Association for Research & Therapy of Homosexuality (NARTH)
1-(888) 364-4744
info@narth.com

PFOX (Parents and Friends of Ex-Gays & Gays)
P. O. Box 510
Reedville, VA 22539
(848) 453-4737
www.pfox.org

Restored Hope Network
(503) 927-0869
www.restoredhopenetwork.org

Spatula Ministries
Spatula_Ministries@Yhoogroups.com
www.BarbaraSpatulaJohnson.com

Transforming Congregations
A Program of Good News
2412 Second Street
Monroe, WI 53566
(608) 325-5712 or (608) 426-4337

Bibliography

References in the text have been indicated by the last name of the author or first named author of a book. When the same author has two or more entries, a date has also been given to indicate which work is cited. When an author is also a co-author with others, an additional name has been given to indicate which work is being cited. If page numbers have been given then the specific information noted can be found there. If no page numbers have been given then the matter cited was a more general theme of the work cited.

Aardweg, Gerard J. M. van den. *On the Origins and Treatment of Homosexuality: A Psychoanalytic Reinterpretation* (New York: Praeger Publishers, 1986)

Aardweg, Gerard J. N. van den. *Homosexuality and Hope: A Psychologist Talks about Treatment and Change* (Ann Arbor, MI: Servant *Books*, 1986)

Aarons, Leroy. *Prayers for Bobby: A Mother's Coming to Terms with the Suicide of Her Gay Son* (San Francisco: Harper, 1995)

Adam, Barry D. *The Rise of the Gay and Lesbian Movement*

Agnew, J., "Some Anatomical and Physiological Aspects of Anal Sexual Practices," *Journal of Homosexuality* 12 (Fall, 1985), pp. 75-90.

Allen, Jimmy. *Burden of a Secret* (Nashville, TN: Morrings/ Ballantine, 1995)

Allender, Dan. *The Wounded Heart: Hope for Adult Victims of Childhood Sexual Abuse* (Colorado Springs, CO: Navpress, 1995)

Allender, Dan, "When Trust Is Lost," a booklet, (Grand Rapids, MI: Resources for Biblical Communication, 1992)

Arieti, Silvano, and Eugene B. Broady, editors. *American Handbook of Psychiatry*, second edition, vol. 3. (New York: Bacis Books, 1974)

Arterburn, Jerry, with Steve Arterburn. *How Do I Tell My Mother?* (Atlanta, GA: Nelson Books, 1988)

Bahnsen, Greg L. *Homosexuality: A Biblical View* (Grand Rapids, MI: Baker Books House, 1978)

Bailey, Derrick Sherwin. *Homosexuality and the Western Christian Tradition* (New York: Anchor Books, 1955)

Bailey, J. Michael, and Richard C. Pillard, "A Genetic Study of Male Sexual Orientation," *Archives General Psychiatry* 48 (1991) pp. 1089-96.

Bailey, J. Michael, and Richard Pillard, Michael Neale and Yvonne Agyei "Heritable Factors Influence Sexual Orientation in Women" *Archives of General Psychiatry* 50, No. 3 (1993, pp. 217-223)

Ball-Kilbourne, Gary L., editor. *The Church Studies Homosexuality: A Study for United Methodist Groups* (Nashville, TN: Cokesbury, 1994)

Barclay, William. *Introduction to the First Three Gospels: a Revised edition of The First Three Gospels* (Philadelphia: Westminster Press, 1975)

Barna, George. *The Barna Report 1992-1993: Ana Annual Survey of Life-Styles Values and Religious Views* (Ventura, CA: Regal Books, 1992)

Barnhouse, Ruth Tiffany. *Homosexuality: A Symbolic Confusion* (New York: The Seabury Press, 1977)

Barnhouse, Ruth Tiffany, "What Is a Christian View of Homosexuality?", *Circuit Rider* (February, 1984)

Bauer, Walter, translated by William Arndt and Wilbur Gingrich, second edition. *A Greek-English Lexicon of the New Testament and Other Early Christian Literature* (Chicago: The University of Chicago Press, 1979)

Bauerman, M. C. *Sexuality, Violence and Psychological After-Effects: A Longitudinal Study of Cases of Sexual Assault which were reported to the Police* (Wiesbaden: Bundeskriminalamt, 1988)

Bauserman, R. and Rind, B. "Psychological Correlations of male child and adolescent sexual experience with adults," *Archives of Sexual Behavior*, 1997, 26, pp. 105-141

Bayer, Ronald. *Homosexuality and American Psychiatry: The Politics of Diagnosis* (New York: Basic Books, 1981)

Bell, Alan P., and Martin S. Weinberg. *Homosexualities: A Study of Diversity Among Men and Women* (New York: Simon and Schuster, 1978)

Bell, Alan P., and Martin S . Wienberg and Sue Kiefer Hammersmith. *Sexual Preference: Its Development in men and Women* (Bloomington, IN: Indiana University Press, 1981)

Bell, Alan P., and Martin S. Weinberg and Sue Kiefer Hammersmith. *Sexual Preference: Its Development in men and Women: Statistical Index* (Bloomington, Indiana: Indiana University Press, 1981)

Bergler, Edmund. *One Thousand Homosexuals* (New York: Pageant Books, 1959)

Bergler, Edmund. *Homosexuality: Disease or Way of Life* (New York: Collier Books, 1962)

Bergner, Mario. *Setting Love in Order: Hope and Healing for the Homosexual* (Grand Rapids, MI: Baker Books, 1995)

Bettenson, Henry, editor. *Documents of the Christian Church*, second edition. (Oxford: Oxford University Press, 1975)

Bieber, Irving, and Toby B. Bieber, "Male Homosexuality," *Canadian Journal of Psychiatry*, vol 24, No. 5 (August, 1979)

Bieber, Irving. *Homosexuality: A Psychoanalytic Study* (Northvale, NJ: Jason Aronson, 1988)

Bieber, Toby B., "Group Therapy with Homosexuals," *Comprehensive Group Psychotherapy*, edited by Harold I. Kaplan and Benjamin J. Saddock. (Baltimore: The Williams & Wilkins Company, 1971)

Black, Henry Campbell. *Blacks' Law Dictionary* (St. Paul, Minnesota, West Publishing Company, revised fourth edition, 1986

Bloom, Allan. *The Closing of the American Mind: How Higher Education Has Failed Democracy and Impoverished the Souls of Today's Students* (New York: Simon and Schuster, 1987)

Bogle, Darlene. *Strangers in a Christian Land: Reaching Out with Hope and Healing to the Homosexual* (Old Tappan, NJ: Chosen Books, 1990)

Boswell, John. *Christianity, Social Tolerance, and Homosexuality: Gay People in Western Europe from the Beginning of the Christian Era to the Fourteenth Century* (Chicago: The University of Chicago Press, 1980)

Brown, Colin, editor. *Dictionary of New Testament Theology*, in three volumes. (Grand Rapids, MI: Regency, 1975)

Brown, Michael L. *A Queer Thing Happened to America: And what a long, strange trip it's been* (Concord, North Carolina: Equal Time Books, 2011)

Bryson, Bill. *A Short History of Nearly Everything* (New York: Broadway Books, 2003)

Bullough, Vern L. *The History of Prostitution* (Hyde Park, NY: University Books, 1964)

Bullough, Vern L. *Sin, Sickness and Sanity: a history of sexual attitudes* (Garland, 1977)

Bullough, Vern L. *Homosexuality: a history* (New York: New American Library, 1979)

Burgess, Ann Walbert, and A. Nicholas Groth, Lynda Lyttle Homstrom, and Suzanne M. Sgroi. *Sexual Assault of Children and Adolescents* (Lexington, MA: Lexington Books, 1978)

Burns, John, *et al. The Answer to Addiction: The Path to Recovery from Alcohol, Drug, Food and Sexual Dependencies* (New York: Crossroad, 1990)

Burton, Larry. *The Social Significance of Homosexuality: Questions and Answers* (Colorado Springs, CO: Focus on the Family, 1994)

Cappon, Daniel. *Toward and Understanding of Homosexuality* (Englewood Cliffs, NJ: 1965)

Caprio, Frank S. *The Sexually Adequate Male* (New York: The Citadel Press, 1952)

Caprio, Frank S. *Female homosexuality: A Psychodynamic Study of Lesbianism* (New York: The Citadel Press, 1954)

Caprio, Frank S. *Variations in Sexual Behavior: A Psychodynamic Study of Deviations in Various Expressions of Sexual Behavior* (New York: The Citadel Press, 1955)

Carnes, Patrick. *Shaping Your Child's Sexual Identity* (Grand Rapids, Michigan: Baker Books, 1982)

Carnes, Patrick. *Out of the Shadows* (Minneapolis, MN: Compcare Publishers, 1983)

Chesebro, James W., editor. *Gay Speak: Gay Male & Lesbian Communication* (New York: The Pilgrim Press, 1981)

Churchill, Wainwright. *Homosexual behavior Among Males: A Cross-Cultural and Cross-Species Investigation* (New York: Hawthorn Books, 1967)

Cleaver, Richard. *Know My Name: A Gay Liberation Theology* (Louisville, KY: John Knox Press, 1995)

Comiskey, Andrew. *Pursuing Sexual Wholeness: How Jesus Heals the Homosexual* (Lake Mary, Florida: Creation House, 1989)

Comstock, Gary David. *Gay Theology Without Apology* (Cleveland, OH: The Pilgrim Press, 1993)

Consiglio, William. *Homosexual No More: Practical Strategies of Christians Overcoming Homosexuality* (Wheaton, IL: Victor Books, 1991)

Cory, Donald Webster (psedonym). *The Homosexual and His Society: a view from within* (New York: Greenberg, 1951)

Countryman, L. William. *Dirt, Greed, and Sex: Sexual Ethics in the New Testament and Their Implications for Today* ((Philadelphia: Fortress Press, 1988)

Crossland, Don. *A Journey Toward Wholeness: Discover the Healing Power of Christ's Authority Over Sin and Guilt* (Nashville, TN: Starr Song, 1991)

Dalbey, Gordon. *Healing the Masculine Soul* (Waco, TX: Word Books, 1988)

Dallas, Joe. *Desires in Conflict* (Eugene, OR: Harvest House Publishers, 1991)

Dallas. Joe. *A Strong Delusion: Confronting the "Gay Christian" Movement* (Eugene, OR: Harvest House Publishers, 1996)

Dallas, Joe, "Responding to Pro-Gay Theology," in *The Journal of Human Sexuality* (1996) b.

Dallas, Joe. *When Homosexuality Hits Home: What to Do When a Loved One Says They're Gay* (Eugene, Oregon: Harvest House Publishers, 2004)

Dallas, Joe and Heche, Nancy. *The Complete Christian Guide to Understanding Homosexuality* (Eugene Oregon: Harvest House Publishers, 2010)

Dannemeyer, Congressman William. *Shadow in the Land: Homosexuality in America* (San Francisco: Ignatius Press, 1989)

Davies, Bob, and Lori Rentzel. *Coming Out of Homosexuality: New Freedom for Men and Women* (Downer's Grove, IL: InterVarsity Press, 1993)

Dawkins, Richard. *The God Delusion* (Boston: Houghton Mifflin, 2006)

De Koven Stan E. *Journey to Wholeness: The Restoration of the Soul* (Ramona, CA: Vision Publishing, 1993)

DeParrie, Paul. *Romanced to Death: The Sexual Seduction of American Culture* (Brentwood, TN: Wolgemuth & Hyatt Publishers, Inc., 1989)

De Young, James B. *Homosexuality: Contemporary Claims Examined in the Light of the Bible and Other Ancient Literature and Law* (Grand Rapids, MI: Kregel Publications, 2000)

Diamant, Louis, editor. *Male and Female Homosexuality: Psychological Approaches (Washington, D. C.: Hemisphere Publishing Corp., 1987)*

Diamond, M. "Homosexuality and Bisexuality in Different Populations," *Archives of Sexual Behavior* 22, no. 4, 1993, pp. 291-310

Drakeford, John W. *A Christian View of Homosexuality* (Nashville, TN: Broadman Press, 1977)

Dynes, Wayne R., Warren Johansson, and William A. Percy. *Encyclopedia of Homosexuality* (New York: Parland Publishers Inc., 1990) (check publisher)

Edwards, Katherine. *A House Divided* (Grand Rapids, MI: Zondervan Publishing House, 1984)

Ellis, Albert, "The Effectiveness of Psychotherapy with Individuals Who Have Severe Homosexual Problems," *Journal of Consulting Psychology vol. 20, No. 3, (1956)*

Ellis, Albert. *Homosexuality: Its Causes and Cure* (New York: Lyle Stuart, Inc., 1965)

Ellison, Marvin M. *Erotic Justice: A Liberating Ethic of Sexuality* (Louisville, KY: John Knox Press, 1996)

Fadiman, Clifton, editor. *The World Treasury of Children's Literature* (Boston: Little, Brown and Company, 1984)

Fann, William E. and Ismet Karacan, Alex Pokorny, and Robert Williams, editors. *Phenomenology and Treatment of Psychosexual Disorders* (New York: SP Medical and Scientific Books, 1983)

Fairs, Donald L. *Trojan Horse: The Homosexual Ideology and the Christian Church* (Burlington, Ontario: Welch Publishing Co., 1989)

Feder, Don. Article reprinted in *Journal of the American Family Association* October, 1992.

Feldman, M. P., and M. J. MacCulloch. *Homosexual Behavior: Therapy and Assessment* (Oxford: Pergamon Press Ltd., 1971)

Fine, Reuben *The Psychoanalytic Vision* (New York: The Free Press, 1981)

Fine, Reuben. "Psychoanalytic Theory," *Male and Female homosexuality: Psychological Approaches*, Louis Diamant (Washington, D. C.: Hemisphere Publishing Corporation, 1987)

Finkelhor, David. *Child Sexual Abuse: New Theory and Research* (New York: Macmillan, 1984)

Fisher, Kathy, and Bob Fisher and Debbie Bennett. *A Mother's Heart, A Father's Hurt, a Sister's Love* (Baltimore: Regeneration)

Forward, Susan, and Craig Buck. *Betrayal of Innocence: Incest and Its Devastation* (New York: Penguin Books, 1988)

Foster, David Kyle. *Sexual Healing: God's Plan for the Sanctification of Broken Lives* (Hermitage, TN: Mastering Life Ministries, 1997)

Foster, Richard. *The Challenge of the Disciplined Life: Christina Reflections on Money, Sex and Power* (San Francisco: Harper, 1985)

Fowler, Richard A., and H. Wayne House. *Civilization in Crisis: A Christian Response to Homosexuality, Feminism, Euthanasia, and Abortion*, second edition (Grand Rapids, MI: Baker Books, 1998)

Frank, Jan. *A Door of Hope* (San Bernardino, CA: Here's Life Publishers, 1987)

Freeman, William M. and Robert G. Meyer, "A Behavioral Alteration of Sexual Preferences in the Human Male," *Behavior Therapy* (1975)

Fried, Edrita. *The Ego in Love and Sexuality* (New York: Grune & Stratton, 1960)

Gairdner, William D. *The War Against the Family: A Parent Speaks Out* (Toronto: Stoddart Publishing Co., 1992)

Gallagher, Maggie. *Enemies of Eros: How the Sexual Revolution Is Killing Family, Marriage, and Sex and What We Can Do About It* (Chicago: Bonus Books, 1989)

Geisler, Norman L., and Paul K. Hoffman, editors. *Why I Am a Christian: Leading Thinkers Explain Why They Believe* (Grand Rapids, MI: Baker Books, 2001)

Grant, George, and Mark Horne. *Unnatural Affections: The Impuritan Ethic of Homosexuality and the Modern Church* (Franklin, TN: Legacy Press, 1991)

Grant, George, and Mark A. Horne. *Legislating Immorality: The Homosexual Movement Comes Out of the Closet* (Chicago: Moody Press, 1993)

Gribbin, John. *History of Western Science* (Londom: The Folio Society, 2006)

Grief, Judith, and Beth Ann Golden. *AIDS Care at Home: A Guide for Caregivers, Loved Ones, and People with AIDS* (New York: John Wiley & Sons, 1994)

Hadden, Samuel B., "Treatment of Male Homosexuals in Groups," *The International Journal of Group Psychotherapy* XVI, No 1, January, 1966

Hadden, Samuel B., "A Way Out for Homosexuals," *Harper's Magazine* (March, 1967)

Hadfield, J. A., "The Cure of Homosexuality," *British Medical Journal* (June 7, 1958)

Hamer, Dean H. *The Science of Desire: the search for the gay gene and the biology of behavior* (New York: Simon & Schuster, 1994)

Harry, J. *Gay Couples* (New York: Praeger Books, 1984)

Hartman, Keith. *Congregations in Conflict: The Battle over Homosexuality* (New Brunswick, NJ: Rutgers University Press, 1996)

Harvey, John F. *The Homosexual Person: New Thinking in Pastoral Care* (San Francisco: Ignatius Press, 1987)

Hatterer, Lawrence J. *Changing Homosexuality in the Male* (New York: McGraw Hill Book Company, 1970)

Hernandez, Raymond, "Children's Sexual Exploitation Under-estimated, Study Finds," *The New York Times National* (September 10, 2001, p. A18)

Hernandez, Raymond, "Study Details Sex Abuse of Kids," *The San Diego Union-Tribune* (September 10, 2001, p. A5)

Hill, James R. *The Gay Emperor Is Naked: The Confessions of an Ex-pro-gay* (San Diego, CA: James Hill, 1996)

Hill, James R. *Una Breve Consideracion Sobre La Homosexualidad* (San Diego, CA: James Hill, 1999)

Hill, James R., "Love the Sinner: A Pastoral Response to Homosexuality," *Pastoral Care and Counseling in Sexual Diversity* H. Newton Malony, ed., a double issue of the, *American Journal of Pastoral Counseling*, 2001

Hill, James R., "The Reality of Change," in *The Faithful Support: Affirming the Church's Position on Homosexuality*, edited by H. Newton Malony and Maxie Dunam. (Nashville, TN: Abingdon Press, in preparation 2001)

Hill, James R. *To Be Made Whole: A Handbook for Inner Healing* (Ramona, CA: Vision Publishing, 2007)

His Majesty's Media. *Understanding Homosexuality and the Reality of Change* (a video) (Murrieta, CA: Impact Resources)

Hoffman, Martin. *The Gay World; male homosexuality and the social creation of evil*

Howard, Jeanette. *Out of Egypt: Leaving Lesbianism Behind* (Crowborough, UK: Monarch, 1991)

Hybels, Bill. *Christians in a Sex-Crazed Culture* (Wheaton, IL: Victor Books, 1989)

Isay, Richard A. *Being Homosexual: Gay Men and their Development* (New York: Farrar, Strauss & Giroux, 1989)

Janov, Arthur. *The Primal Scream* (New York: Dell Publishing Co., 1970)

Jarvis, Debra. *The Journey Through AIDS: A Guide for Loved Ones and Caregivers* (Batavia, IL: Lion, 1992)

Jay, K. and A. Young. *The Gay Report* (New York: Summit, 1979)

Johnson, Barbara. *Where Does a Mother Go to Resign?* (Minneapolis, MN: Bethany House, 1994)

Johnson, Phillip E. *Darwin on Trial* (Downers Grove, IL: InterVarsity Press, 1993)

Johnson, Phillip E. *Reason in the Balance: The Case Against Naturalism in Science, Law & Education*

Jones, Stanton L. and Yarhouse, Mark A. *Homosexuality: The Use of Scientific Research in the Church's Moral Debate* (Downer's Grave, Illinois, InterVarsity Press, 2000)

Joy, Donald. *Becoming a Man* (Ventura, CA: Regal Books, 1990)

Judson, F. N., "Sexually Transmitted Viral Hepatitis and Enteric Pathogens," *Urology Clinics of North America* (11, no. 1, February, 1984)

Karlen, Arno. *Sexuality and Homosexuality: A New View* (New York: W. W. Norton & Co., 1971)

Karpman, Benjamin. *The Sexual Offender and His Offenses: Etiology, Pathology, Psychodynamics and Treatment* (New York: The Julian Press, 1954)

Katchadourian, Herant A., ed. *Human Sexuality: a Comparative and Developmental Perspective* (Berkley, CA, University of California Press, 1979)

Katz, Jonathan. *The Invention of Homosexuality*

Katz, Jonathan. *Gay American History: Lesbians and Gay Men in the USA: A Documentary* (New York: Crowell, 1976)

Kaye, Harvey J, *et al*, "Homosexuality in Women," *Archives of General Psychiatry* (November, 1967)

Keller, Werner. *The Bible as History*, second revised edition. (New York: William Morrow and Company, 1981)

Keysor, Charles W., editor. *What You Should Know About Homosexuality* (Grand Rapids, MI: The Zondervan Corp., 1981)

King, Michael, and Elizabeth McDonald, "Homosexuals who Are Twins: A Study of 46 Probands" *British Journal of Psychiatry* 160 (1992) pp. 407-9

Kinsey, Alfred C., Wardell B. Pomeroy and C. E. Martin. *Sexual Behavior in the Human Male* (Philadelphia: Saunders, 1948)

Konrad, Jeff. *You Don't Have T Be Gay: Hope and Freedom for Males Struggling with Homosexuality or For Those who Know of Someone Who Is* (Hilo, HA: Pacific Publishing House, 1992)

Kronemeyer, Robert. *Overcoming Homosexuality* (New York: Macmillan Publishing Company, 1980)

Kubetin, Cynthia A., and James Mallory. *Beyond the Darkness: Healing for Victims of Sexual Abuse* (Houston, TX: Rapha Publishing, 1992)

Kuyper, Robert L. *Crisis in Ministry: A Wesleyan Response to the Gay Rights Movement* (Anderson, IN: Bristol House, 1999)

LaBarbera, Peter. "The Gay Youth Suicide Myth," in *The Journal of Human Sexuality* George A. Rekers, editor. (1996, pp. 65-72)

Latourette, Kenneth Scott. *A History of Christianity* revised edition (New York: Harper & Row Publishers, 1975)

Laumann, E. O., *et al*. *The Social Organization of Sexuality* (Chicago: University of Chicago Press, 1994)

LeVay, Simon, "A Difference in Hypothalmic Structure between Heterosexual and Homosexual Men," *Science* 253 (1991)

Lewes, Kenneth. *The Psychoanalytic Theory of Male Homosexuality* (city: publisher, date) (check all info)

Lewis, C. S. *Miracles* (New York: Macmillan Publishing Co., 1952)

Lewis, C. S. *Mere Christianity* (New York: Macmillan Publishing Co., 1952)

Licata, Salvatore J., and Robert P. Petersen, ed., *Historical Perspectives on Homosexuality* Vol. 6, Nos. 1 and 2, Fall/Winter, 1980/1981 (New York: The Haworth Press and Stein and Day, 1981)

Liddell, Henry George, and Robert Scott, revised and augmented by Sir Henry Stuart Jones, *et al*. *A Greek-English Lexicon* (Oxford: The Clarendon Press, 1968)

Lief, Harold I. editor in chief. *Sexual Problems in Medical Practice* (Monroe, WI: American Medical Association, 1981)

Linn, L., *et al*, "Recent Sexual Behaviors Among Homosexual Men Seeking Primary Medical Care,) *Archives of Internal Medicine* 149 (December 1989), p. 2685-2690.

Little, Paul E. *Know Why You Believe* (Wheaton, IL: Victor Books, 1984)

Lively, Scott, "Homosexuality and the Nazi Party," in *The Journal of Human Sexuality* (1996)

Lloyd, Robin. *For Money of Love: Boy Prostitution in America* (New York: Vanguard Press, 1976)

London, Louis S., and Frank S. Caprio. *Sexual Deviations: A Psychodynamic Approach* (Washington, D. C.: The Linacre Press, 1950)

Maddoux, Marlin and Christopher Corbett. *Answers to the Gay Deception* (Dallas: International Christian Media, 1994)

Magnuson, Roger J. *Are Gay Rights Right? Making Sense of the Controversy* (Portland, OR: Multnomah, 1990)

Marco, Anton N., "Gay 'Marriage'?" in *The Journal of Human Sexuality* (1996)

Marmor, Judd, "Homosexuality and Sexual Orientation Disturbances," *Comprehensive Textbook of Psychiatry II*, second edition, edited by Alfred M. Freedman, *et al*, (Baltimore: The Williams and Wilkins Company, 1975)

Marmor, Judd, ed., *Homosexual Behavior: A Modern Reappraisal* (New York: Basic Books, 1980)

Masters, William and Virginia E. Johnson. *Homosexuality in Perspective* (Boston: Little Brown and Company, 1979)

Mayerson, Peter, and Harold I. Lief, "Psychotherapy of Homosexuals: A Follow-up Study of Nineteen Cases," *Sexual Inversion: The Multiple Roots of Homosexuality*, Judd Marmor, editor. (New York: Basic Books, 1965)

Mazzalongo, Michael, ed. *Gay Rights Or Wrongs: A Christian's Guide to Homosexual Issues and Ministry* (Joplin, MO: College Press Publishing, 1995)

McConaghy, Nathaniel. *Sexual Behavior: Problems and Management* (New York: Plenum Press, 1993)

McDowell, Josh. *Evidence That Demands a Verdict* (San Bernardino, CA: Here's Life Publishers, 1981)

McDowell, Josh. *Evidence That Demands a Verdict, Vol. II* (San Bernardino, CA: Here's Life Publishers, 1981)

McDowell, Josh. *The Myths of Sex Education* (San Bernardino, CA: Here's Life Publishers, 1990)

Mc Dowell, Josh, and Don Stewart. *Answers to Tough Questions: What Skeptics Are Asking About the Christian Faith* (Nashville, TN: Thomas Nelson Publishers, 1993)

McGrath, Alister and McGrath, Joanna Collicutt. *The Dawkins Delusion: Atheist Fundamentalism and the Denial of the Divine*

McGeady, Sister Rose Mary. *Are You Out There, God?* (Covenant House, 1996)

McNeill, John J. *The Church and the Homosexual*, third edition (Boston: Beacon Press, 1988)

McWhirter, D., and A. Mattison. *The Male Couple: How Relationships Develop* (Englewood Cliffs: NJ: Prentice Hall, 1984)

Medical Institute for Sexual Health, The. *Health Implications Associated with Homosexuality* (Austin: The Medical Institute, 1999

Meeks, Wayne A. *The Origins of Christian Morality: The First Two Centuries* (New Haven, CN: Yale University Press, 1993)

Memmott, Mark, "Sex Trade May Lure 325,000 U. S. Kids: Report: Abused Children, runaways typical victims," *USA Today* (September 10, 2001, p. 1A)

Michael, Robert T., and John H. Gagnon, Edward O. Laumann and Gina Kolata. *Sex in America: A Definitive Survey* (Boston: Little Brown & Co., 1994)

Mintz, Elizabeth, "Overt Male Homosexuals in Combined Group and Individual Treatment," *Journal of Consulting Psychology*, (1966, vol. 30, No. 3)

Mitchell, Marcia. *Surviving the Prodigal Years* (Lynnwood, WA: Emerald Books, 1995)

Moberly, Elizabeth. *Homosexuality: A New Christian Ethic* (Cambridge, UK: James Clarke & Co., 1983)

Mondimore, Francis Mark. *A Natural History of Homosexuality* (Baltimore: Johns Hopkins University Press, 1996)

Monteith, Stanley. "AIDS: The Unnecessary Epidemic"

Muir, J. Gordon. *Sex, Politics and the End of Morality* (Raleigh, NC: Pentland Press, 1998)

Narramore, Clyde M. *The Compact Encyclopedia of Psychological Problems* (Grand Rapids, MI: Zondervan, 1984)

NARTH Bulletin (August , 2001) vol. 10, no. 2)

Newman, Mildred, Bernard Berkowitz, and Jean Owen. *How to Be Your Own Best Friend* (New York: Lark Publishing Co., 1971)

Nicolosi, Joseph. *Reparative Therapy of Male Homosexuality* (London: Aronson, 1991)

Nicolosi, Joseph. *Healing Homosexuality: Case Studies of Reparative Therapy* (North Vale, NJ: Joseph Aronson, 1993)

Nicolosi, Joseph, "Firsthand: My Experience Attending the American Psychiatric Association Panel Discussion," *NARTH Bulletin* (August 2001) vol. 10, no. 2, pp. 3-27

Nicolosi, Linda Ames, "Historic Gay Advocate Now Believes Change Is Possible" *NARTH Bulletin* (August, 2001) vol. 10, no. 2, p. 1 and 28

Nissinen, Martti. *Homoeroticism in the biblical World: A Historical Perspective* (Minneapolis: Fortress Press, 1998) (check city and/or pub)

OED. *Oxford English Dictionary* (Oxford: Clarendon Press. 1989)

Owen, William F., Jr., "Sexually Transmitted Diseases and Traumatic Problems in Homosexual Men," *Annals on Internal Medicine* (vol. 92, 1980)

Oxford Latin Dictionary (Oxford: Clarendon Press, 1982)

Pakenham, Thomas. *The Scramble for Africa: The White Man's Conquest of the Dark Continent from 1876 to 1912* (New York: Random House, 1991)

Pattison, E. Mansell, and Myrna Loy Pattison, "Ex-Gays: Religious Mediated Change in Homosexuals," *American Journal of Psychiatry* (December, 1980)

Paulk, John and Anne, "The Other Way Out" in *The Journal of Human Sexuality* (1996)

Payne, Leanne. *The Broken Image: Restoring Personal Wholeness through Healing Prayer* (Westchester, IL: Crossway Books, 1981)

Penner, Clifford, and Joyce Penner. *The Gift of Sex: A Christian Guide to Sexual Fulfillment* (Waco, TX: Word Books, 1981)

Petronius, translated by William Arrowsmith. *The Satyricon* (New York: New American Library, 1959)

Petronius, translated by John Sullivan. *The Satyricon and the Fragments* (Harmondsworth, UK: Penguin Books, 1965)

PFOX (Parents and Friends of Ex-Gays and Gays). "Can Sexual Orientation Change?" (Reedville, VA, 2010)

Pomeroy, Wardell B. *Dr. Kinsey and the Institute for Sex Research (New York: Harper & Row Publishers, 1972)*

Prince, Derek. *Husbands and Fathers: Rediscover the Creator's Purpose for Men* (Grand Rapids, MI: Chosen Books, 2000)

Rector, Frank. *The Nazi Extermination of Homosexuals*

Rekers, George, "Gender Identity Disorder," in *The Journal of Human Sexuality* (1996)

Reisman, Judith A., and Edward W. Eichel. *Kinsey, Sex and Fraud: The Indoctrination of a People* (Lafayette, LA: Huntington House, 1990)

Reisman, Judith, "Kinsey and the Homosexual Revolution," in *The Journal of Human Sexuality* (1996)

Reisman, Judith. *Kinsey: Crimes and Consequences* (Arlington, VA: The Institute for Media Education, 1998)

Remafedi, G., "Demography of Sexual Orientation in Adolescents," *Pediatrics* 89, no. 4, pt. 2 (April, 1992), pp. 714-721

Rench, Janice E. *Understanding Sexual Identity: a book for gay and lesbian teens and their families*

Richter, Alan. *The Language of Sexuality* (Jefferson, NC: McFarland & Co., 1987)

Riley, Mona and Brad Sargent. *Unwanted Harvest? (Nashville, TN: Broadman & Holman Publishers, 1995)*

Rossiter, Richard T. *Out with a Passion: A United Methodist Pastor's Quest for Authenticity* (Takique, MN: Alamo Square Press, 1999)

Rueda, E. T. *The Homosexual Network: Private Lives and Pubic Policy* (Old Greeenwich, CN: Devin Adair Co., 1982)

Rush, Florence. *The Best Kept Secret: Sexual Abuse of Children* (Englewood Cliffs, NJ: Prentice Hall, 1980)

Saia, Michael. *Counseling the Homosexual* (Minneapolis, MN: Bethany House Publishers, 1988)

Saghir, Marcel T. *The Same Sex: an appraisal of homosexuality* (New York: Pilgrim Press, 1969) (check city)

Saghir, Marcel T., and E. Robbins. *Male and Female Homosexuality: a comprehensive investigation* (Baltimore: Williams & Wilkins, 1973)

Sample, Tex, and Amy DeLong. *The Loyal Opposition: Struggling with the Church on Homosexuality* (Nashville, TN: Abingdon Press, 2000)

Satinover, Jeffrey. *Homosexuality and the Politics of Truth* (Grand Rapids, MI: Baker Books, 1996)

Satinover, Jeffrey B., "The Gay Gene?" in *The Journal of Human Sexuality* (1996) b.

Scanzoni, Letha, and Virginia Ramey Mollenkott. *Is the Homosexual My Neighbor: Another Christian View* (San Francisco: Harper and Row, 1980)

Schaumburg, Harry W. *False Intimacy: Understanding the Struggle of Sexual Addiction* (Colorado Springs, CO: Navpress, 1992)

Schmidt, Thomas E. *Straight and Narrow? Compassion and Clarity in the Homosexual Debate* (Downers Grove, IL: InterVarsity Press, 1995)

Scroggs, Robin. *The New Testament and Homosexuality* (Phila-delphia: Fortress Press, 1983)

Seamands, David. *Healing of Memories* (Wheaton, IL: Victor Books, 1985)

Seamands, David. *Healing Your Heart of Painful Emotions* (New York: Inspiration Press, 1993)

Sheehy, Gail. *Hustling: Prostitution in Our Wide-Open Society* (New York: Delacorte Press, 1973

Shilts, Randy. *And the Band Played On: Politics, People and the AIDS Epidemic* (New York: St. Martin's Press, 1987)

Shorter Oxford English Dictionary. (New York, Oxford University Press, 2002)

Siegel, Elaine V. *Female Homosexuality: Choice Without Volition – A Psychoanalytic Study*, (volume 9 of the Psychoanalytic Inquiry Book Series, (Hilldale, NJ: The Analytic Press, 1988)

Silverstein, Charles. *Gays, Lesbians, and Their Therapists* (New York: W. W. Norton & Co., 1991)

Simpson, D. P. *Cassell's New Latin Dictionary* (New York: Funk & Wagnalls, 1968)

Socarides, Charles W. *The Overt Homosexual* (New York: Grune & Stratton, 1968)

Socarides, Charles W. *Homosexuality: Psychoanalytic Therapy* (New York: Jason Aronson, 1989)

Socarides, Charles W., "Homosexuality and the Medical Model," *Phenomenology and Treatment of Psychosexual Disorders*, William E. Fann, editor, (New York: SP Medical and Scientific Books, 1983)

Socarides, Charles W., in *The Journal of Human Sexuality* (1996)

Stekel, Wilhelm, "Is Homosexuality Curable?" *The Psychoanalytic Review* (1930, vol. XVII)

Stekel, Wilhelm. *The Homosexual Neurosis*, translated by James S. Van Teslarr (New York: Emerson Books, 1950)

Stott, John. *Decisive Issues Facing Christians Today* (Grand Rapids, MI: Fleming H. Revell, 1995)

Strean, Herbert S. *The Sexual Dimension: A Guide for the Helping Professional* (New York: The Free Press, 1983)

Strobel, Lee. *The Case for Christ: A Journalist's Personal Investigation of the Evidence for Jesus* (Grand Rapids, MI: Zondervan, 1998)

Strobel, Lee. *The Case for Faith: A Journalist Investigates the Toughest Objections to Christianity* (Grand Rapids, MI: Zondervan, 2000)

Switzer, David K., and Shirely Switzer. *Parents of Homosexuals* (Phiadelphia: Westminster Press, 1980)

Tawney, R. H. *Religion and the Rise of Capitalism* (New York: Mentor Books, 1954)

The Universal Almanac 1992, John W. Wright, ed., (Kansas City: Andrews and MacNeil, 1991)

Thompson, Chad W. *Loving the Homosexual as Jesus Would: A fresh Christian Approach* (Grand Rapids, MI: Brazos Press, 2004)

Thorndyke, Dame Sybil, "Introduction," in *Nicholas Nickelby*, in The Oxford Illustrated Dickens series. (Oxford: Oxford University Press, 1987)

Time (May 21, 2001, p. 62)

Veith, Gene Edward, Jr. *Postmodern Times: A Christian Guide to Contemporary Thought and Culture* (Wheaton, IL: Crossway Books, 1984)

Weaver, Richard. *Ideas Have Consequences*

Weber, Max. *The Protestant Ethic and the Spirit of Capitalism* (New York: Charles Scribner's Sons, 1958)

Weber, Max. *The Sociology of Religion*, translated by Ephraim Fischoff. (Boston: Beacon Press, 1964)

Webster, Noah. *Webster's New Twentieth Century Dictionary of the English Language*, unabridged, second edition. (Cleveland, OH: The World Publishing Company, 1967)

West, D. J. *Homosexuality Re-examined* (Minneapolis: University of Minnesota Press, 1977)

White, John. *Eros Defiled: The Christian & Sexual Sin* (Downers Grove, IL: InterVarsity Press, 1977)

White, John. *Parents in Pain* (Downers Grove, IL: InterVarsity Press, 1979)

White, John. *Eros Redeemed* (Downers Grove, IL: InterVarsity Press, 1993)

Whitehead, Alfred North. *Science and the Modern World* (New York: The Free Press, 1953)

Wilkins, Michael J., and J. P. Moreland, editors. *Jesus Under Fire: Modern Scholarship Reinvents the Historical Jesus* (Grand Rapids, MI: Zondervan Publishing House, 1995)

Williams, D. Charles. *Forever a Father, Always a Son* (Wheaton, IL: Victor Books, 1991)

Willis, Stanley E., II, *Understanding and Counseling the Male Homosexual* (Boston: Little Brown and Co., 1967)

Wilson, Earl D. *Counseling the Homosexual* (Waco, TX: Word Books, 1988)

Wilson, William P., "Biology, Psychology and Homosexuality," *What You Should Know About Homosexuality*, edited by Charles Keysor. (Grand Rapids, MI: Zondervan, 1979)

Wood, Robert W. *Christ and the Homosexual* (New York: Vantage Press, 1960)

Wooding, Dan. *He Intends Victory: Real-life Stories of Christians Living with AIDS* (Orange, CA: Promise Publishing, 1994)

Worthen, Anita, and Bob Davies. *Someone I Love Is Gay: How Family and Friends Can Respond* (Downers Grove, IL: InterVarsity Press, 1996)

Worthen, Anita and Bob Davies, "When a Friend Says, 'I'm Gay'" in *The Journal of Human Sexuality* (1996) b

Worthen, Frank. *Steps Out of Homosexuality* (San Rafael, CA: Love in Action, 1984)

Worthen, Frank. *Leadership* (San Rafael, CA: Love in Action, 1988)

Worthern, Frank. *A Step Further: Love in Action Newsletters, 1986-1987* vol. 1 (San Rafael, CA: Love in Action, 1989

Worthen, Frank. *Establishing Groups Meetings* (San Rafael, CA: Love in Action, 1990)

Yamamoto, J. Isamu, ed. *The Crisis of Homosexuality* (Wheaton, IL: Victor Books, 1990)

Yarhouse, Mark A. *Homosexuality and the Christian: A Guide for Parenst, Pastor and Friends* (Minneapolis: Bethany House, 2010)

York, Frank V., and Robert H. Knight. *Homosexual Activists Work to Lower the Age of Sexual Consent* (Washington, DC: Family Research Council, 1999)

About the Author

Pastor Hill was educated at Occidental College (1963-1965), UCLA (1965-1969), with a BA in 1967, and an MA in East Asian History in 1968, both from UCLA; also at School of Theology at Claremont (1981-1982) and Fuller Theological Seminary (1982-1985), with an M. Div in 1985, from Fuller.

He was the Director of Evangelism (1981-1984) and then the Minister of Evangelism (1984-1985) at the First United Methodist Church of Pasadena, in Pasadena California. He was the Pastor of Highland United Methodist Church, in Highland, California (1985-1991), and has been Senior Pastor at Clairemont Christian Fellowship: A Spirit-filled United Methodist Church, in San Diego California (1991 to the present). He was ordained a Deacon in The United Methodist Church in 1984, and an Elder in 1988.

His books include *The Drinks Are on The Kingdom: A Study of the Wedding at Cana* and *To Be Made Whole: A Handbook for Inner Healing.* He also has articles and chapters in *The Journal of American Pastoral Psychology, Pastoral Care and Counseling in Sexual Diversity,* edited by H. Newton Malony, and *The Faithful Support: Affirming the Church's Position on Homosexuality,* edited by H. Newton Malony and Maxie Dunam.

Pastor Hill was the President of the Board of Transforming Congregations, a ministry to present information from a transformational perspective, primarily among United Methodists, from its founding in 1993 to 2000. He has spoken on the subject matter of this book at Fuller Theological Seminary's School of Psychology and at various churches and conferences.